REFLECTIONS OF A REPENTANT HEART

A JOURNEY THROUGH REPENTANCE AND RESTORATION

LAURETTE LASTER

REFLECTIONS OF A REPENTANT HEART
Author: Laurette Laster
© 2020 Library of Congress 1-8024539721

ISBN 13: 978-0-578-75535-9 (Paperback edition)

ISBN 13: 978-0-578-75535-9 (eBook edition)

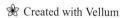 Created with Vellum

To my sons and grandchildren and all those to come.
My prayer is for healing and restoration of all things promised by God.

ACKNOWLEDGMENTS

I never considered myself a poet, an author or a writer. To my remembrance I had written only two poems, one around 1990 and another in 2007. When this gift of writing broke forth I was the most amazed, and continue to be.

Feeling I was to incorporate the poetry in a book I prayed asking God, is this simply a desire or is it a calling? Only my husband knew my desire to return to the corporate world and rejoin the ranks of employment outside the home and our business. I positioned myself to hear from The Lord and pray concerning this issue. Was this writing simply a pipe dream or was this from Him? I had to know!

A short time after this decision a friend from church said to me, "I believe I am supposed to give you a scripture." As we walked to the main service I said to him, "Well give it to me. If you have a word for me from The Lord give it to me." He said I want to write it down, I'll bring it next week. The last thought on my mind was my prayer.

The next Sunday Henry handed me a slip of paper. I was excited and rushed to my seat to open and read it. Never expecting what was about to happen… when I opened the slip of paper I saw what he jotted down, Rev. 21:4-5. I opened my bible to read these words-

"And God will wipe away every tear from their eyes; there shall be no more death, nor sorrow, nor crying. There shall be no more pain, for the former things have passed away." Then He who sat on the throne said, Behold, I make all things new. And He said to me, Write for these words are true and faithful."

The scripture describes the promise of repentance, I knew I had my answer. Now I know so I began my transition. Bringing forth a dream The Lord placed in my heart of becoming a writer and a published author; and Reflections of a Repentant Heart is born. A book about a biblical journey into being made new. I still have that slip of paper tucked in my study Bible.

First and foremost to my Lord and Savior, Jesus Christ, He loved me into a wonderful wholeness that I never dreamed possible. Oh how blessed I am to be redeemed, forgiven and made new.

And next to my mom. So much more than my mom, my mentor and challenger, she knew me best and believed in me, and with me, even when she thought I had lost my mind; after seeing and recognizing the call of God on my life she called me Reverend Lollipop. No mama, Dorothy is not in Kansas anymore.

To my husband and best friend Greg, your love and devotion shines forth, exemplified by your hard work and fervent prayers. You encourage me to believe, passionately push me to reach onward to pursue and fulfill the call of God for my life and to write. For all the countless times I would say; may I read something to you? You so graciously said yes and listened intently. We couldn't see where God was leading but by faith we continue on to know. One of many ways your love equips me. How do I love thee…

Also to our very good friend, Irby who helped us build the sukkah (2017) the season the poetry burst forth. You listened and obeyed God.

Lastly to all who have helped shape my life I am forever grateful. Even to those who slammed doors in my face, I see now God used you to push me to this place. God meant it for good.

AUTHOR'S NOTE

A JOURNEY INTO REPENTANCE, forgiveness, restoration, and intimacy with The Father, His Son, and His Holy Spirit.

Assured of one thing seasons come and seasons change, my prayer and purpose for sharing this book of my experiences and reflections along with a few of my poems is to encourage you. As you continue in your Christian walk, my hope is to offer you support.

I pray that as you repent you also reflect. May you develop an even stronger relationship with our Lord Jesus Christ. I pray your relationship with our Lord becomes deeper and more meaningful as you journey through all your seasons, especially the greatest season—total surrender through repentance.

I also pray this book of reflections will touch your heart, ushering you into His Holy Presence, into the Presence of the Almighty. If you are not already madly in love with The Lord Jesus, the Redeemer of your soul, I pray as you turn each page, your love will blossom and grow as you understand His heart for repentance. If you have had a relationship with Him for years, this is a set time to steal away and renew your vows, deepening your love with Him throughout this journey. If you are deeply in love with our Lord Jesus, I pray that through reflections you will come to love Him more.

If you find yourself with this book in your hand, I believe it has been placed here. Is it possible that Jesus is leading, luring, and loving, you into this very time and place, for such a time as this? Has The Lord placed this book into your hands, inviting you into a special meeting time and encounter with Him? You…His beloved!

Is it hard for you to comprehend that Jesus desires to have an appointment with you? I believe you are in His appointment book. Today is your time and the beginning of one of the most amazing times of your life.

"No man (mankind, man or woman) can come to Me, except the Father which hath sent me draw him (or her): and I will raise him or her up at the last day." (John 6:44, Paraphrased)

Maybe you have found yourself thinking, why am I thinking this thought? Or why am I thinking about _____ (you fill in the blank), it happened so long ago? Have you considered that The Father is wooing you? Have you felt a deep longing to know what is going on? Can you picture for a moment a loving father soothing his child, with sweet words and hushing tones? The Father is summoning you, whispering your name; saying, "Come unto Me, all ye that are weary and heavy laden, and I will give you rest." (Matthew 11:28, New International Version)

The purpose for repentance is for refreshing. Repentance is necessary in order to have an intimate relationship with our Heavenly Father. Repentance breaks off heavy burdens, looses ungodly yokes, and sets the captive, you, free—free to be exactly what The Father has created you to be.

Often, I hear people say I sense revival coming, or saying what we need is a good old-fashioned revival. I do not disagree with either of those statements, but do we know what revival is? If I were to ask you the following questions could you answer?

- What is a revival?
- What hinders revival?
- What starts a revival?
- Why do we need revival?

The answer is simple; revival starts, continues, and builds momentum in a born again repentant heart. Revival is a grace encounter. It is the manifest evidence of a sinful heart having had a life changing encounter with the unmerited favor of God, through the grace of our Lord Jesus Christ's finished work on the Cross, His burial, and His resurrection. Revival is evidence that a heart has been thoroughly cleansed and made new by the grace of The Almighty. Knowing we are forgiven and loved by God is the key to revival. Forgiveness begins with repentance. It is "Amazing Grace."

Websters Dictionary defines Revival as:

re·viv·al. [rə'vīvəl]

NOUN

an improvement in the condition or strength of something.

synonyms:

Improvement · rallying · picking up · betterment · amelioration · turn for the better · advance · rally · upturn · upswing · comeback · resurgence · renewal

an instance of something becoming popular, active, or important again.

comeback · bringing back · re-establishment · reintroduction · restoration · reappearance · resurrection · resuscitation · re-launch · reinstallation · regeneration ·

[more]

•a new production of an old play or similar work

•a reawakening of religious fervor, especially by means of a series of evangelistic meetings: "the revivals of the nineteenth century"; "a wave of religious revival"

•a restoration to bodily or mental vigor, to life or consciousness

Do you sense The Father calling you? He is calling for you to come into an intimate relationship, or more intimate relationship with Him through our Lord and Savior Jesus Christ. Jesus Christ, who died for you and me that ALL of our sins may be forgiven and our guilt and debt cancelled once and for all. According to Hebrews 9:14-15, only the Blood of Jesus Christ can cleanse our conscience.

Restoration, a comeback, regeneration, resuscitation—doesn't this describe being made new? Yes! Absolutely yes, this describes what happens in our mortal bodies, when we encounter the Breath of The Almighty. The Bible describes this encounter as a quickening of our mortal body, when Holy Spirit breathes new life into our bodies and we become spiritually alive. We are alive and born again. Our spirit is born from above and alive to God. "God has delivered us from the power of darkness, and has translated us into the kingdom of His dear Son" (Colossians 1:13 King James Version).

When we are born into the earth if all goes according to plan we take our first breaths, often with a cry to clear our lungs so they will operate at full capacity. In years past the doctor held the newborn upside down and smacked them on the bottom to initiate crying and breathing. This may seem a little harsh but, in reality, it was necessary for clearing the airways. The doctor knew in order for the baby to live it had to breathe, and it was the custom of the time. There was a reason for the doctor's actions.

If a newborn is not breathing or their breathing were to stop, they would be rushed for emergency care. What would make us believe our encounter with Holy Spirit, The All-Powerful Living Spirit of God would be a onetime encounter? Once we take our first breaths we breathe in and out involuntarily for the remainder of our lives. The life-giving breath we breathe is given by God. We do not have to be reminded to breathe; however, our life depends on the air we breathe. Our new life depends solely upon Holy Spirit and His guidance and help, which is the Life-Giving Spirit of God.

"For it is in closest union with Him that we live and move and have our being; as in fact some of the poets in repute among yourselves have said, 'For we are also His offspring." (Acts 17:28, Weymoth New Testament)

So our new life is like breathing, only now we are breathing in this new life with Christ Jesus. I cannot allow anything to block my airways and live. I also cannot allow sin to block the Holy Spirit from flowing into my life or I will surely die. It is in Him that we live and move and have our being.

The first enemy of our heart is guilt. Guilt comes as a result of having done something we perceive as wrong or bad. Then comes the nagging notion of I owe. The message from a guilt-ridden heart is *I owe, and I must somehow repay this wrong.*

Nothing less than the perceived wrong being paid for can relieve or bring release to a guilty heart. We cannot serve it away, do enough good deeds, no amount of charitable service can pay the debt. We cannot pray it away nor does God expect this. However, we have a need to pay because we know we owe. Sin is called debt in the Bible. Guilt must be paid or canceled in order for the human soul to find rest and relief and come out from under the bondage of sin and guilt.

Can the debt, brought about by our sin that causes this guilt, be cancelled? The answer to this question is found in 1 John 1:9 which reads, "If we confess our sins, He is faithful and just to forgive our sins, and to cleanse us from all unrighteousness." (KJV)

With these thoughts in mind, I invite you along as we encounter a fresh new life, a refreshing of our spirit through the work of repentance. I pray you remain tender-hearted toward The Lord, knowing what pleases our Father, and shunning all evil.

INTRODUCTION

When I was a general manager of a busy corporate casual dining chain, I returned home after a long, hard shift. Walking into my house, I discovered a stench beyond belief. The smell was nauseating, nearly knocking me over.

Having worked an open/volume 14-hour shift on this busy Friday night, I was looking forward to getting into my nice clean house and out of my work clothes into something more comfortable and relaxing for a few minutes before going to bed. As I entered the kitchen through the garage door, there it was—pungent, sickening, stifling—the smell of a dead mouse. It is the worst smell you can imagine. Picture walking into this at 10:00 PM at night, already physically, mentally, emotionally, and spiritually exhausted from a work day. This was not part of my evening plans!

This was in the summer when the midday temperatures would reach into the 90's. Being a single woman at this time and very frugal, I looked for ways to save money and decrease my utility bills. *Waste not, want not,* isn't that the saying?

If I were going to be gone for several hours or all day, before leaving my house I would adjust the thermostat. I didn't think it was necessary for my air conditioner to run all day when there wasn't anyone home. I would sometimes set my thermostat to 88 before leaving for work. With this said, entering my kitchen, dog tired, all I had on my mind was some down time before going to bed.

I had to be up at 5:30 AM the next morning to prepare for my Saturday morning shift. As you can imagine, a dead stinking mouse was not on my list of things to end my day with. Another problem to solve, another issue to deal with, one more opportunity requiring a solution, something else to clean up, and one more thing to be righted before E.O.D. (End Of Day in the corporate world). Just one more thing that had to be done and one more task to complete before ending this work day. The discovery was overwhelming, to an already over-taxed day. I knew I had to find and dispose of this dead intruder that upset my plans filling the air with a sickening stench. I prayed; I silently prayed. "Dear Lord, please don't let this mouse be in a wall."

After adjusting my thermostat to 78 degrees, I began to tear my kitchen apart. How I wanted to cry! Going to my limited supplies of tools, I took out a screwdriver and began the job. I decided to delve right in, so I took the bottom cover off of my dishwasher—no, not there. Next, I removed the bottom broiler drawer from my stove and searched the entire area, no, not there either. I looked behind the fridge, no, not there. I was praying, "Oh Lord help me find this dead mouse. Please Lord, do not let it be in the wall or in a place I can't get to it." I complained. Oh! I mean I explained to the Lord, that He knew I couldn't sleep with this ripening smell permeating my entire house.

The feeling of knowing I could not possibly sleep or even stay in the house with this pungent odor became overwhelmingly obvious as I continued to work.

I was tired, now feeling utterly hopeless, I prayed, "Oh Lord, I need Your help!"

I checked under and behind my washer and dryer. I did not have a prayer for moving my washer or dryer; they were in a very tight space that required lifting to get them out. I needed to get on the top of them to look behind and to the sides of them. I kept a laundry basket in front of the washer and dryer area which was to the side of the refrigerator.

I moved the basket to make some room and lo and behold there he was (we'll call this mouse "him" for the sake of this story). There, almost in plain sight laid this very small, very dead mouse. Oh, that smell! You know that smell, right? How can something so little and almost insignificant smell so bad?

He was right in front of me in a very accessible spot. He was in an easy to get to place. Why had I assumed he was under or behind something?

I'm guessing about an hour had passed with me taking things apart, having to put them back together in this hot smelly atmosphere before discovering him. There he was, between the fridge and the laundry basket. I grabbed the broom and dust pan to dispose of this disgusting intruder who had ruined my evening when I heard The Lord say in my spirit, "This is what sin smells like to Me!"

I was shocked and stunned all at the same time. This shook me to my core and still does to this day.

As I disposed of the mouse taking him outside and then cleansing the area, my heart ached. I thought about God having to leave His earth dwelling, I thought about Him no longer able to visit and walk with Adam in the cool of the day. How that because of sin and the sickening, nauseating aroma of sin leading to death, Our Father and Creator in His Holiness could not dwell or rest (get it?) with sin until this problem was solved and thoroughly cleansed. I thought about how our Father God couldn't dwell in the house with the death that sin had brought. I thought about how God had to take everything apart and begin the redemption process of cleansing every crack and crevice of our lives. As the Apostle Paul tells us, a little leaven leavens the whole lump. One small dead mouse stinks up the whole house.

Then my heart broke.

This event still comes to mind today. I realize if The Lord had said to me in my spirit, "Hey Laurette guess what? Sin smells like a dead mouse to Me," it would not have had the same effect or impact on me. Maybe I would have thought, "Oh yea! I know that smell, right God, its pretty yucky huh?" Then having had that thought, and after a trite answer, I may have moved right on with my day and my week not taking the time to understand what God meant.

I realized that by living out this disgusting event, The Father gave me insight and allowed me an opportunity to "get understanding," as Proverbs 4:7 says. This event required action on my part. I was responsible for cleaning this mess up because it was in my house.

In a sense, I was ushered into a partnership of reconciliation. I learned an invaluable lesson. That in the searching, and finding, and then removing this dead putrefying mouse, this situation was going to have profound meaning to me. Having gone through this event and hearing what The Lord told me, changed how I think about sin and what I believe about the little sins that we turn a blind eye to. I understood what The Lord was sharing with me.

I pray you learn to hear what The Lord is teaching you through life's events. Pay attention to the small seemingly uneventful disruptions and details of your day. He is speaking and He longs for you to have understanding. He longs to be understood, just as you and I long to be understood by those we love. How can we learn of His ways if we don't spend time with Him in His word and have ears that hear? How can two walk together unless they agree? We have an appointment to learn of Him and His ways.

"Do two men walk together unless they have made an appointment." (Amos 3:3, New American Standard)

DAY 1

"THE TAX COLLECTOR stood off alone in the corner, away from the Holy Place, and covered his face in his hands, feeling that he was unworthy to even look up to God. Beating his breast, he sobbed with brokenness and tears saying, 'God, please in your mercy and because of the blood sacrifice forgive me, for I am nothing but the most miserable of all sinners" (Luke 18:13, The Passion Translation).

This is a perfect description of the posture and birthing position of repentance. We are told to bear or bring forth fruits worthy of repentance. Birthing is to bring forth something by pushing out or expelling something from inside us. Would you agree that this is a picture of repentance?

And I said: My God, I am ashamed and embarrassed to lift my face toward You, my God, because our iniquities are higher than our heads and our guilt is as high as the heavens (Ezra 9:6, Study Bible).

What better place to start than with The Lord Jesus Christ's description of true repentance. Jesus is teaching and describing true repentance to those in attendance and now to us, the readers. Jesus explains what godly justifiable repentance should look like. Jesus is speaking to Pharisees, those who go to the synagogue because they think they are justified by keeping the law; rather, a real believer is one who goes because they know they are in need of a savior. Pharisees believed they could do good works by simply obeying the law, thereby erasing or overriding their bad deeds. They believed they were superior to other sinners based on their knowledge and study of the law and works performed.

Yet our Lord and Savior will define the outward sign of an inward work of repentance. This is what true heartfelt repentance should look like. Repentance that justifies us with God the Father looks like a deep heart-changing birth, one from death to life. Here we have a didactic description of purging or pushing out (a birthing), an expulsion of guilt from our soul in action. Repentance is deep heartfelt work, an emptying of ourselves of the world to create an emptiness to be filled by His Spirit. What better way to learn than to follow the One who paid our debt and ransomed our souls from Hell. What Jesus desires to see is a repentant heart, a heart willing to do the deep work, like Jacob, that said I won't let go until You (God) bless me. Read Genesis 32:24-30.

Think for a minute about being charged with a crime that you are guilty of. Instinctively, you probably pray for and cry out for mercy. If, on the other hand, you are innocent, you may tend to ask for and demand justice. In the book of Romans, the apostle Paul assures us that, "All have all sinned and fall short of the glory of God" (Romans 3:23, KJV).

With this being said, we are all sinners and all are guilty. If all are guilty, all are in need of God's mercy. In order to have a deep and intimate relationship with another, transparency is required; we must be open and honest with each other. It is impossible to feel safe and to be vulnerable with someone who is dishonest or keeping secrets. God desires a deep transparent relationship with each of us.

If you have been in a relationship where trust has been violated, you know exactly what I am saying. If we as mere mortals know when trust has been broken, it is certain our Father in heaven is aware of any sins you and I have committed.

So what about The Holy Spirit? In order to have a deeper walk with our Lord Jesus Christ, through His Holy Spirit, this will require us to have some tough conversations. It may bring up some difficult topics, conversations that you wish to avoid. We may pretend not to sense His touch but say, "Let's not talk about '*that*'." Many years ago, while doing the deep work of repentance and grieving over my absolute ignorance and awful sins, there was one place I didn't want to go, my brother's death. I knew The Lord was saying I wouldn't have complete healing without visiting this place, but I didn't want to. I had prayed for God to make me whole and wholly His. I had a decision to make. I thought facing *all* my awful sins would be enough without having to visit the one last stronghold. You know what I mean, right?

The decision to be whole meant I would have to lay aside my fear and reluctance and say yes to Him, or say no—the decision was mine. I had learned by now that God would not strike me dead. In years past, I had been so afraid of life and God. I saw God as a harsh, punitive God who couldn't wait to catch me doing wrong. I knew God was out there somewhere but didn't know Him as a loving Father.

I believe if I had chosen to avoid the gut-wrenching pain of dealing with my brother's death, I wouldn't have the freedom I have today. I also believe if I had not dealt with his death, I wouldn't be writing this book now. You see, I was dreading this fear and pain; there was some deep-seated gnawing guilt—that I somehow should have been able to save my brother from his tragedy, God knows I wanted to. Had I done enough? Had I let God down? Was I in big trouble with God? Did my brother die remembering all the places he believed I had failed him? Had I failed him? Had I failed God? Was it my fault?

I challenge you to invite the Holy Spirit into (all) the recesses of your heart. Ask Him to make you aware of anything that is blocking you from having all God desires for you. Covert (hidden) or overt (explicit) sin is still sin that must be repented of. Have you, like me, been afraid of God or afraid of what He might require you to sacrifice?

Any sin, whether it is our sin or a sin committed against us by another, not forgiven and not confessed is a hindrance to our becoming whole. What is a hindrance? A hindrance is a roadblock or blessing blocker to our human soul. God has orchestrated one way for our souls to be healed and made whole and that is through repentance, followed by His indwelling Spirit.

Unconfessed sin will block God from indwelling you. Unconfessed sin or sin that you are carrying the pain of is a blessing blocker. When we confess our sins, great or small we are un-conned. We cannot be conned into believing we are not loved if we are fessed-up. Then we have no secrets with God.

Do you remember or have you heard the statement, "He or she needs to fess up?" When I was a little girl, old westerns were popular and I heard this often. As long as you or I hold sin in our heart, we are bound up, conned into separation from The Father. Sin takes up space and robs us. Can you imagine your child or a loved one locking you out of their room or their house or refusing to unlock the door and fellowship with you? What a heartbreaking thought. What if your son/daughter or a loved one were locked in a vault and terrified by fear, tormented by the thought of never getting out? Now imagine if you were attempting to communicate with them that the key to unlock this vault were within their reach but they refused to hear you. I believe you get the picture. Jesus is saying I have left you a key to the lock.

Ask yourself if now is the time to have those conversations where we say things like, "God I'm really, really mad at You, because You let that happen. How could You? I feel like I'm not important to You God because You didn't save me from _____. I have pushed You away, because I thought I had to have that other relationship…or, I sensed it was You, but I was scared to commit. Help me trust You." The Father knows everything about you and me, nothing is hidden from Him.

When I finally quit running, I found this so comforting; He already knew. Wow! He already knew all the SINS I had committed against Him. He knew all the ugly, dishonest, fear based compromises, and yes, He even knew *that* sin (you know, the big one); but yet, He was wooing me, longing to have a relationship with messed up, "tore up from the floor up," me!

And He desires that same deep relationship with you, no matter what you have done. He has already prepared the way through the Cross of Jesus Christ. Your sins are paid in full, if you receive His work and love He poured out for you at the Cross. Our sin debt is cancelled by being laid on Him at The Cross.

Heaven's hope, according to Colossians 2:9-14 (The Passion Translation) is:

That we understand and realize that through our union with Him we have experienced circumcision of heart. All of the guilt and power of sin have been cut away and is now extinct because of what Christ, The Anointed One, has accomplished for us. For we've been buried with Him into His death. Our baptism into death also means we were raised with Him when we believe in God's resurrection power, the power that raised Him from 'death's realm'. This realm of death describes our former state, for we were held in sin's grasp. But now, we've been resurrected out of 'that realm of death' never to return, for we are forever alive and forgiven of our sins! He cancelled out every legal violation we had on our record and the old arrest warrant that stood to indict us. He erased it all--our sins, our stained soul--He deleted it all and they cannot be retrieved! Everything we once were in Adam has been placed on His Cross and nailed permanently there as a public display of cancellation.

The Cross is our key into wholeness. This is what repentance gains us, access into life in Christ.

If you have made the decision, pray this prayer:

"Lord, I invite You into every area of my life. Speak boldly to my heart during the next forty days. I am preparing and setting aside this time to spend with You. I want to clear out anything that hinders Your Holy Spirit from speaking to me and abiding in me. I give You complete permission to break open my heart and show me anything that breaks Your heart. I ask that You do it with Your tender mercy and the grace, that grace I've heard about but not sure I've experienced. I am ready and I am willing. I am willing to become willing. I no longer want to keep You locked out. Amen."

Reflection:

What do you believe about repentance and doing the work of

repentance? What is true repentance? What does The Cross mean
to you?

_____

_____

_____

POETRY:ABOUT THE FATHER'S BUSINESS

You separated
    Darkness from the light
    Called one day
    And the other night

You placed the waters
    Oceans deep
    Setting the shores
    Boundaries you keep

You spoke forth life
    In seas and on land
    Some would swim
    Others to stand

You set barriers
    Marking and making
    Establishing boundaries
    Each one breathtaking

Oh why do we push
    Why do we shove
    Attempting to change
    What is fashioned with love

If we could grasp
    Seek to understand,
    Each one was fashioned
    Made by Your right hand

Boundaries for protection
    Barriers secure
    Working within,
    Would be mature

You set the seasons
    And set into orbit
    Sun moon and stars
    Painted the portrait

You said count
    See If you can
    Stars which were tossed
    Out of My hand

Foolish man
    Why disobey
    Haven't I said
    I Am The Way

Stop all this nonsense
    Stand still and see
    The salvation of The Lord
    Only offered by Me

White unto harvest
> The fields do gleam
> We have work to do
> I need a strong team

With head bowed down
> Repent, ask for My forgiveness
> Don't you know it is time to be
> About The Father's business?

© laurette laster

"Why did you seek Me? Did you not know that I must be about My Father's business?" (Luke 2:49 NKJV).

DAY 2

"THEREFORE SAID HE UNTO THEM, the harvest truly is great, but the laborers are few: pray ye therefore the Lord of the harvest, that He would send forth laborers into His harvest" (Luke 10:2, KJV).

"Therefore bear fruits worthy of repentance, and do not think to say to yourselves, we have Abraham as our father, for I say to you that God is able to raise up children to Abraham from these stones" (Matthew 3:8, NKJV).

What are fruits worthy of repentance? How about,

"Oh, taste and see that The LORD is good" (Psalm 34:8 NKJV).

Have you known that you needed to apologize to someone? You had a strong urge and unction that you should do this. An urge and an unction that overrode your common sense seemed to be propelling you. Then you did it. And just like that, the nagging regret vanished and was gone. The barb in your soul was loosed being removed by the obedience you heeded. You just knew that you needed to go make it right and you didn't care what it cost. This is the sweet taste of repentance that is worthy fruit to God. God isn't asking us to feel it, but rather that we become obedient doers of His word.

"So always let His word become like poetry written and fulfilled by your life!" (James 1:22, TPT). It may have been an extremely difficult task, one you really didn't want to do, but you did and it just felt right. Like poetry it had rhythm that made sense. And so it is getting things right between us and The Lord. A repentant heart being drawn by God desires to make it right no matter the cost. We are called to bear fruit, "being fruitful," is a command from the beginning of creation. This command was first given to Adam and Eve in the Garden of Eden. God has not changed His mind concerning being fruitful.

The Greek word for fruit is karpos Strong's Concordance #2590 (figuratively) everything done in true partnership with Christ, i.e., a believer (a branch) lives in union with Christ (the Vine) by definition growth resulting from two life streams—the Lord living His life through ours—to yield what is eternal.

Read Galatians 5:22-26

Prayer:

Oh Lord, teach me how to be one with You. I have tried time and time again, trying to be good enough, thinking I would be acceptable while attempting to make up for my sins with good works or deeds. Show me how to abide in You. I don't want to hide anymore; I am tired of pretending. I ask that my life flow with Your Spirit like poetry. I want a productive life, a more productive life, exactly what You had in mind when You created me.

Forgive me for thinking I knew better or had to figure it out. Reveal Yourself to me, cleanse me of all rebellion, all reactions and the urge to have my own way. I do not want any works of rebellion to linger in me from this time on. I want to be found abiding in You. I want to be pleasing to You Lord. Show me how to bear fruit.

Dear Lord Jesus, I must confess I never realized You wanted me to abide with You, and You with me. I desire a real and lasting friendship with You. I want, like Abraham, for You to call me Your friend. I desire for my life to flow from Your eternal truths, to have true eternal lasting value. Forgive me for believing I was waiting on You. I ask that You forgive me for keeping You waiting. I do not want to wait any longer. I say today that I am Yours and You are mine. I want to be Your friend. Amen!

Meditate on Song of Songs 6:3 (The Passion Translations):

"He is within me. I am His garden of delight, I have Him fully and now He fully has me!"

Reflection:

Look for ways that The Lord is bringing this to life before you today. Write down what The Lord is showing you and thank Him for drawing you and continuing with you as you proceed on this journey. Is your heart hungry for more of God? As you pray, tell Him. Tell The Lord what you are hungry for. Lift your answers up as a prayer and praise!

Oh Lord I am hungry for:

_____

_____

_____

POETRY: FROM BUD TO BLOSSOM

From bud to blossom
 Did you witness the change
 In the heat of day
 Structure rearranged

From bud to bloom
 To show the way
 Never doubt;
 Look what happened in just one day

Closed off and guarded
 When suddenly appears
 Soft petals and color
 Bursting with zeal

Soft and tender
 How do you grow
 From morning to night
 I didn't know

Changes were happening
    All around
    From bud to blossom
    Now Flowers abound

Keep to the faith
    And never give up
    You can go from a berry
    To a plentiful cup

Of fragrant petals
    Soft pleasant texture
    While no one is looking
    Not mere conjecture

God's perfect design
    First patented then sealed
    He created it all
    With beauty He filled

So much to learn
    So much to achieve
    From a bud to blossom
    Only believe

laurette laster
    © 2018 June

DAY 3

LET the wicked forsake his way and the unrighteous man his thoughts; let him return (turn around and go the other way, (Teshuvah) to the Lord, that He may have compassion on him, and to our God, for He will abundantly pardon (Isaiah 55:7 Paraphrased).

When constructing a tall building, it is necessary to dig deep for piers that support the foundation. The pier may require piles to help support the structure also. The larger the building, the deeper the piers and piles must go. It is the same with repentance. You may have met or know some, can we say, "Shallow Christians." I am convinced this is because they were not instructed and taught according to the word, or possibly they have been taught and believe grace does all the work for repentance. Yes, grace is amazing but that is God's part. Grace is God's work and His free gift to us. Grace is God's gift to us despite our guilt. Repentance is acknowledging that we have been rebellious and have gone our own way, thereby shunning and hurting the heart of our Father and Creator.

Rebellion can be due to ignorance, fear, or pain, etc., but these actions will need to be repented of. Doing the deep work of repentance will usher you into a more intimate and glorious (weighty) relationship with Jesus. As you long to know Him more in order to fulfill His will for your life, the deeper your repentance must go. What kind of tree do you desire to grow spiritually? How high do want to go? Exactly how fruitful can you dream to be?

Did you know and are you aware in order for a tree to grow taller the roots must grow deeper? I have heard it said that the tree above ground is a replica of what is below ground. There is work going on underground that often we are oblivious to. The underground work not seen makes what is visible possible. Now that's a mouthful isn't it? When you see a mature Christian, one who is stable, this Christian has dug deep into the things of God and gone through many root seasons. This man or woman has learned and become aware of God and His kingdom, His ways, and what He requires. It does not happen overnight. As a matter of fact, just like planting and growing a fruit tree, it cannot happen overnight. We must go through root seasons, climate changes, be well watered, and get plenty of "Son-shine" in order to grow and become healthy and bear fruit.

If you are able, I encourage you to go and see an orchard. Go and look at the trees and get close to some fruit trees. You can also go learn about fruit trees at a garden center, or a tree farm or maybe a weekend trip to the country. When God is asking us to do something, He gives us metaphorical or figurative illustrations to help us understand what He is literally asking or describing to us. We see these examples throughout His word. He speaks through naturally occurring events. If you are unable to go to a garden center, pull up a YouTube video, and enjoy some short videos— how to care for an apple tree or what apple tree grows best in your area. If you are really serious, plant a tree or plant some seeds and begin to care for them. You can tend and watch them grow.

Have you been trying to grow fruit (works) that is not native to your new (heart) soil? Not all fruit is edible nor does it all taste good. Read Galatians 5:16-21. Here we see examples of rotten (worldly fruit), works that we do not want to produce. If these works (fruit) are growing in your heart, ask The Father to forgive you. Then ask Him to send the Holy Spirit, The Helper, to come and help you uproot these. You must have a deep desire to uproot anything that is not native to God's garden. If God doesn't want it neither should we.

Repentance is asking forgiveness for being callous or distant from the heart of God, and what He loves and desires. We cannot tolerate even a hint of sin and believe to be completely set free. A half truth is a whole lie. This isn't saying we can or will achieve perfection, we are telling our flesh we are cleaning house to get the sin out. Our desire must be for a clean heart, not works of whitewashing or hoping while pretending. God is not looking for perfection; He is looking for faith and a pure heart. We put our faith into action, believing if He said it, He will do it.

Prayer:

Lord Jesus, I want to partner with You to do a thorough work of repentance and become a mature fruitful Christian. I want to stand tall knowing Jesus is my sure foundation. As I come before you today, my prayer is that I will not be a shallow immature believer that is unable to bear fruit. I do not want to be touchy, irritable, or unable to nourish and reach others with Your love. I want to boldly confess You before men. I want to do Your will. Lord I am ready to dig deep and uproot anything not of You while growing deeper in Your truths. I know I have work to do. Show me, teach me, lead me, and shelter me through the upcoming days. I want to purge the self out, doing a complete work of repentance. Amen

Reflection:

Is The Lord showing you something He desires you let go of and up-root? What do you need to dig up or plow under? Picture in your mind a hearty fruit tree and see it covered and flocked with delicious fruit.

_____

_____

_____

POETRY: NEW SEASON

Plowed and turned, ready anew
    My field is prepared, new season in view
    Those who seek now shall find
    The law of love on hearts will bind

At Your command, meditate and grow
    Studying Your word, so I may know
    No more side roads or detours
    It is only with Your word, I confer

Receive my orders and assignment
    My steps are planned, now in alignment
    Not only Your acts, for Your ways I long
    Heart get ready to sing a new song

There is a place You God, created
    How long oh Lord, I have waited
    To hear you say and call for me
    Speak my name and off I'll be

At your instructions, joyously obey
    Yes I'll observe to follow in Your way.
    © laurette laster 2017

"This Book of the Law shall not depart from your mouth, but you shall meditate in it day and night, that you may observe to do according to all that is written in it" (*Joshua 1:8 NKJV*).

DAY 4

"THE TIMES of ignorance God overlooked, but now He commands all people everywhere to repent" (Acts 17:30 English Standard Version).

When my oldest son was six or seven, he decided he could bathe himself and shampoo his hair, without any assistance. You know when they reach that age of "I can do it myself." A good caring mom takes care of their kids and their hygiene, right? I seriously doubted his ability to do a thorough or 'good enough' job. I didn't want to say, "You can't do a thorough job," so I told him, "You need my help." He insisted he could do it on his own. So we had to give it a try.

I said, "Okay, go take your bath." Before the water was run, it seemed he was finished and back, almost immediately. I asked, "Did you bathe?" He replied, "Yes, I did." His little face still had dirt on one of his cheeks and I went to the tub to see the soap bar bone dry. I asked again, "Are you sure you bathed with soap?"

Then he knew I knew, and the answer was no, he did not bathe. He took a little dip but didn't think it was necessary to go through all the motions I put him through during bath time. All the so-called formalities of bathing and shampooing his hair didn't have much meaning to a child. Why? Because he didn't understand that each function had significance to the overall success of hygiene.

When they were young, my sons loved to play in the tub during bath time; on this particular evening, there was something going on and he wanted to hurry. He didn't notice the dirt under his fingernails or my real fear. I didn't want others to think, "What kind of mom doesn't keep their kids clean?" But a dirty kid wasn't my biggest fear. My biggest fear was he would get head lice. Yes, head lice. I am so thankful to say my sons made it through school never having been infected with head lice. In our small, rural school it seemed there was an outbreak at least two or three times a year. When I shampooed their hair, did I ever scrub their head? You bet I did! I didn't want to give one little nit a chance to stay nor reproduce and infect the whole house.

It is the same with us as adults when we do not see the harmful effects of allowing a little sin to remain on us. We may even be unaware of it. My son didn't notice the dirt under his fingernails, but I sure did. Think how much more The Father sees the sin on our hearts or the effects of our sinful nature and actions toward others. There are germs everywhere we go on this planet. Our immune system protects us from germs, but there are more serious contaminants that we would not dare want on us. So what about spiritual germs and debris?

A strong healthy immune system will find, isolate, and destroy most harmful germs and bacteria. Often, we are unaware of the danger that exists. If we can ward off deadly diseases and infections with the physical armor God has supplied (our physical bodies), how much more with the spiritual? He created our bodies to withstand less than perfect conditions but has supplied us with protection.

If our immune system becomes weakened, it is unable to fight off deadly diseases. Vice versa, when we allow sin to hide in our heart it weakens our spiritual condition and spiritual immune system. Our spiritual immune system is where our faith toward God resides. Faith equips us so we have confidence toward God.

Scripture states "Without faith, it is impossible to please God. If our hearts do not condemn us we have peace with God" (1 John 3:20-

22 NKJV). Suffering from conviction (not condemnation) is like allowing a nit to get comfortable and hatch. Then before you know it, it will reproduce; infecting others, contaminating anything it comes in contact with, and it will look for a host. Thus, we would be pretending and suffering due to ignorance of the infestation.

God cannot hear our prayers if we hold un-confessed sin in our hearts. He knows.

Trying to feel clean with un-confessed sin or hurts would be like taking a shower and never washing our face, shampooing our hair, or bathing our body. We appear to have showered, but the dirt and the smell are still there. Going to church or being a good person isn't the work of repentance, even though a repentant soul does attend church desiring to be a person of good works. After we repent, we desire to be with people of like faith and go to church to learn. Hungry souls must be fed, but attendance while refusing to change is like taking a quick dip. The dirt is still there.

A shower should leave us clean, refreshed, and invigorated. Rinsing off is inadequate. James tells us when we become doers of the word this heartfelt change (shower) brings about a deep desire to be obedient. In order to feel invigorated, all the dirt and smell must be gone. It's not a quick dip.

Showering is being outwardly cleansed from all the filth that has been accumulated. The filth or dung we have allowed to be smeared on us or the filth others have hurled at us, either by abuse or by hurtful actions, needs to be cleansed and washed out spiritually. Like head lice we may have gotten close to someone we did not know was infected; putting ourselves at risk. This work of repentance isn't something we say I can do this myself. We can't say, "I'll bathe this filth off of me" (See Proverbs 20:9-10).

Sin is spiritual filth that leads to death and is only cleansed supernaturally by the shed blood of Jesus Christ. This work requires His Holy Spirit. We remember repentance is initiated by God Himself. It is the grace, the extreme love and very goodness of God that leads us into repentance: (Romans 2:4). If we find ourselves examining or revisiting past situations that are resurfacing, we might say it is by invitation only. We cannot have the relationship we desire with His dear Son, unless we do our part of the work of repentance and do the work His way. Repentance opens the door to faith and trust. Faith and trust are evidenced by obedience brought about as a result of a soul washing encounter with God, known as repentance.

As Romans 6:23 says, "For the wages of sin is death, but the gift of God is eternal life through Christ Jesus our Lord."

We are assured God's word will wash us clean. If we read and obey, we are allowing His word to help cleanse the filth from our minds by being renewed to His ways. We are saying no to old ways of the world while allowing God's word to work in our lives. Yes, "we are in the world, but we are not of the world" (John 17:15-21).

The dirt and filth, the bacteria, and the lice may get near us but at salvation we are sealed with His Holy Spirit. If we are sealed, we can no longer be comfortable sinning.

Seeing sin through the eyes of Jesus will create in us a sincere desire to pray and help others who are trapped as we once were. We allow Holy Spirit to lead us into repentance just as Jesus describes. Having confessed being cleansed of "certain" sins, we never want to be guilty (infected) of that again. "For godly sorrow worketh repentance to salvation not to be repented of: but the sorrow of the world worketh death" (2 Corinthians 7:10 KJV). Godly sorrow cleanses our souls.

Commit to reading your Bible daily or listening to the Bible on CD or audio. With today's technology you can listen to the Bible on your phone or tablet. Some, like me, may be auditory learners. Think about what the apostle Paul tells us in Romans 10:17. Faith comes by hearing, and hearing by the word of God (KJV). Soul (mind, will, and emotions) transformation begins by hearing the *living* word of God.

God has created us as auditory learners when it comes to building faith; "For, faith comes by hearing and hearing by the word of God" (Romans 10:10 NKJV). His Spirit ministers to us as we wash our mind with pure water, His *living* word.

Prayer:

Heavenly Father, I ask You to open Your word to me. Open my mind and my inner ear to understand what I am hearing. As I listen to

Your word, speak to my heart. I want to be cleansed and refreshed like a long cool shower after a hard day's work in the hot sun. I want to stand under the outpouring of Your *living* word. I ask that the cleansing waterfall of Your word thoroughly cleanse and refresh my heart and mind, washing me from the inside out. Amen

Reflection:

Why is the word of God important in repentance? How can we be cleansed and refreshed? List two things to start and continue to help maintain a daily (spiritual hygiene) regimen, bathing and cleansing your heart, mind, and conscience.

_____

_____

_____

POETRY: AWAKE MY HEART

From Your heart comes streaming down
    Unending love beaming all around
    Loving kindness, like light of dawn
    By Your grace we are drawn
    From dusk to dawn and back You trace
    Faithful love, amazing grace
    Breath of God, Ancient of Day's
    Here I am, hungering for Your ways
    Awake my heart, awake behold
    "In the beginning," mysteries unfold
    Coming forth from Ancient of Days;
    Teach me Lord to know Your ways.
    laurette laster © 2017

"It is good to proclaim Your loving kindness in the morning, Your faithfulness in the evening" (Psalm 92:NLT).

of sinful actions is pride focusing on self. Remember guilt is the first enemy of the heart.

Repentance on the other hand is seeing with spiritual eyes. We see how our sins, transgressions, and our willful disobedience is ignorance. We acknowledge missing the mark God Himself has set. Missing the mark hinders the good work God has prepared in advance for us. Think about it; God prepared a work for us to be a part of for the furtherance of His kingdom, during our time on the earth...

"For, we are his workmanship, created in Christ Jesus unto good works, which God hath before ordained that we should walk in them" (Ephesians 2:10 KJV).

As God opens our eyes, we see in part or dimly (lest we be destroyed). Now we see only an indistinct image as in a mirror, but then we will be face to face. "Now what I know is incomplete, but then I will know fully, even as I have been fully known" (1 Corinthians 13:12, ISV). God allows us to see through the eyes of love. God's love is purer than we can imagine. God reveals how sin hinders the plans prepared for us and others. Sin can and will destroy our future. In the Old Testament, the report of the ten wicked spies caused an entire generation to die off in the wilderness, not entering the Promised Land. Our sin and doubt can cause others to doubt God's ability to do what He has promised. Repentance is acknowledging our wrong and asking God for forgiveness. God is faithful! He will forgive us and allow us another chance to obey Him. We should not want to play with or take advantage of God's long suffering and kindness. We do not want to insult the grace of God.

It is the breaking of the heart that opens the dark recesses of the mind. The Apostle Paul describes this as having our hearts circumcised. Circumcision is a cutting away of the outer covering. Before repentance, our thinking is likened and described as futile. It is called futility of mind several times in scripture. King James Version uses the word "vanity."

What does it mean to be futile or vain? The definition of futile is to serve no useful purpose. What a sobering thought, of no useful purpose or being without eternal value. "Where there is no vision people cast off restraint thus being rendered useless." (Proverbs 29:18, Para-phrased)

So we understand this phrase in the depth the apostle Paul is describing: What we have been doing, though it may be good, it is not serving The Lord's purpose, therefore having no useful purpose in His kingdom. Wow, pretty deep huh? We have become His poetry, a recre-ated people that will fulfill the destiny he has given each of us, for we are joined to Jesus, the Anointed One (Ephesians 2:10, TPT).

Strong's Concordance:

#4161 poiema - The Greek word for workmanship or masterpiece is Poiema. This is where we get the English word *poem*.

4856 sumphoneo - pronounced soom-fo-neh-o meaning to agree together or be in harmony. To come into agreement; this is where we get the English word *symphony*.

In bringing forth fruits worthy of repentance we are in agreement with the word, the will, and the work of God. We are set apart, sancti-fied for His use, His workmanship, His masterpiece or His poem, His chorus. We are becoming part of God's symphony, His writings, His poetry, His very own work of art. Wow!

Coming clean before The Lord is beautiful and it is beautifully designed by God, this is a picture of repentance. As difficult as it may be to go through the deep work of repentance; we never regret this work. We are being written into His kingdom legacy as a poem. We are bringing forth music. We are instruments in His symphony; His very own work of art, on Heaven's canvas, created in Christ Jesus anew. We are a new creation. Isn't this beautiful? Yes! It is amazing and beautiful.

Prayer:

Oh Lord Jesus, I desire to be clean and free to do Your will, unhin-dered by all worthless futile thoughts and ideas I and others have had. I could not bear hearing that my life had no useful purpose for Your Kingdom. I desire Your help to become all You have created me to be. "Create in me a clean heart, O God, and renew a steadfast spirit within me" (Psalm 51:10 NKJV). Show me Lord anything that displeases You. I long to be Your very own workmanship. Amen

Reflection:

Ask the Lord what is taking up your time that may be good works, but it is not God works. List what He shows you. Ask Holy Spirit to reveal any futile or vain workings in your life, possible dead works such as a people pleasing (trying to impress others, even your pastor or coworkers, etc.) rather than God. Desire to be a God pleaser. Write down your dead, futile, works and lift them up before Him asking for wisdom.

_____

_____

_____

POETRY: SING THAT SONG, WRITE THAT RHYME

Go ahead and sing that song
 Just remember to whom the notes belong
 Continue to write and pen those rhymes
 He pours them out each and every time

There are photos yet to snap,
 Before its time to call it a wrap
 And furniture still yet to design
 Yes, there is still plenty of time

There are pictures left to paint
 No time to grow weary or become faint
 Be sure to go ahead and dance
 Always remember to take that chance

Share your time, gifts, and talents
 Always keeping record to stay in balance
 For we should ne'er, no never forget
 From whom these gifts we do beget

He freely gave from up above
   His Perfect Son, His perfect love
   So do not get proud or even puffed up,
   Every good gift can sure dry up

The gifts we are given, we'll be sharing
   Are given with special love and caring
   For in each and every "Due Season,"
   Jesus Christ will always be the reason

He resists the proud gives grace to the humble
   Remembering this we shall never stumble
   Then when at last we finish our race
   And meet The Lord face to face

These words could ring true in our ears
   Never puffed up nor shrinking back in fear
   You gave it your all and you were fervent
   Well done thy good and faithful servant
   © laurette laster

"For every good and perfect gift come down from above, from the Father of light" (James 1:17).

DAY 6

READ LUKE 15:1-10 and focus on the following:

"'Just so I tell you, there will be more joy in heaven over one sinner who repents than over ninety-nine righteous persons who need no repentance'" (Luke 15:7 Berean Study Bible).

T he Lord Jesus Christ wants to eat and fellowship with you. When we come into agreement with the work of repentance, heaven is aware of our actions. Don't you like the ratio of one to ninety-nine? Perhaps you have been ashamed of an action or a sin or someone has shamed you for what you have done. When you read this scripture what does it say to you? Does it say to you, "You sorry low-down, no good useless piece of work?" No it does not say that. Do you feel that way? If yes, this is condemnation and is in the psychological realm.

Repentance is a change of mind, it is not a feeling. Yes our feelings and emotions are vital but they cannot have the place of the wisdom of

God's word. Repentance is a verb and requires action. You make the decision for a permanent change.

Strong's Concordance:

#3341 Metanoia to change one's mind or purpose.

#3340 metanoeo from 3326 meta-changed to have another mind

3539 noieo, "think" properly, think differently after- to "think differently after a change of mind" to repent (literally, "think differently afterwards").

The word metanoia is defined as repentance, but as you can see above has much deeper implications. The full meaning is more than to suffer or experience guilt, regret, or shame; it implies hating the sin, making a decision to turn around and away from sin by going a new direction. Repentance is a work of Holy Spirit that occurs in the inward man, cardia—the inmost being of the heart, creating deep desire to change; thus, it begins to reprove or retrain the mind. If we are in a car or other modes of transportation and turn around the scenery will be different.

Repentance is much deeper than feelings, but we definitely feel the stirring deep within. You can decide to do something without feeling like you want to. If you rely on feelings it is like allowing your flesh to decide to only eat sweets and dislike vegetables. If we eat only junk food, we will not grow into healthy adults with healthy bodies.

If we live on feelings and emotions contrary to the word of God, it will be impossible to have a healthy mind. Junk food may seem to do the job but it is proven that refined sugar is linked to many cancers and causes behavioral issues with children. With this being said, to give in to flesh or carnal desires is detrimental to your mental health and to the kingdom of God.

Have you ever acquired a taste for a food or drink? At first it may not actually taste good but you continue to partake in it until you actually like the taste. Many years ago when I began to 'practice' smoking cigarettes, it was in complete rebellion and ignorance. Smoking was definitely stupid to my lungs, taste buds, and my health. But I was young and stupid and lacked proper self-respect. I wanted to be cool. I continued practicing smoking until not only did I acquire a taste for cigarettes, I became addicted. I am not proud of my years of smoking I am simply using this as an example. Why do we work so hard to acquire a taste for the things of the world, but think we shouldn't work to acquire a taste for the things of His kingdom?

When we begin the work of repentance and studying the Word of God, it may not be easy or seem palatable in the beginning to take up your cross, crucify your flesh, die to self, etc. But trust me; you were born for this walk. You will see in time that it is a perfect fit and custom designed for you and your calling.

The teachings and messages you begin to hear will be spot on. You will realize the messages bring correction or wisdom into your life. When these truths come alive in our life, we immediately begin working to retrain our beliefs. It is so rewarding to remove the lies replacing them with ever enduring truth. God's word is truth. "For we overthrow arrogant 'reckonings,' and every stronghold that towers high in defiance of the knowledge of God, and we carry off every thought as if into slavery--into subjection to Christ." (2 Corinthians 10:5, Paraphrased)

Our eyes and our ears are gates. God's word unfolds and opens up dark places in our mind. God's word translation says, "Your word is a doorway that lets in light, and it helps gullible people understand." "The entrance of your words gives light; it gives understanding unto the simple" (Psalm 119:130 KJV).

We should expect to see correction through revelation thus becoming instructions and directions for us to follow. We do not have to understand or have a taste for the correction in order to begin putting the instructions into practice. The word of God and the correction brought about by His word is very pleasing to our spirits; we gain an inner peace from obedience. Our souls and spirit are actually starving for this fresh cool (living) water. It is living water to our parched souls.

When we make the decision to put these actions into effect, we are nourishing our spirit. Our spirit will help our fleshly body acquire a taste for what pleases The Lord. We are bringing our thoughts into subjection to every word. When we continue to put these principles into practice and see life-changing results we become quickened in our mortal bodies and build momentum. The realization that we are pleasing to God is overwhelming peace. We become addicted to God. This is a good addiction, a life-changing addiction. What exciting news! We are putting off the old man and being made new in our souls: our mind, will, and emotions.

When we walk according to the word of God, not according to our fleshly desires we have made a turn, and are headed in the right direction. Let's be reminded that repentance (metanoia) is to *turn* around and walk according to the will of our Creator...

Read Isaiah 55:7-8

Prayer:

Lord Jesus, show me what You would have me change my mind about. I don't want to be gullible or naïve or ignorant. I want to learn Your ways and walk in Your wisdom. I know Your thoughts are not my thoughts and Your ways are not my ways (Isaiah 55:8).

Let the wicked forsake his way, and the unrighteous man his thoughts: and let him return unto the LORD, and he will have mercy upon him; and to our God, for he will abundantly pardon. For my thoughts are not your thoughts, neither are your ways my ways, says the LORD. Amen

Reflection:

What are some ways you realize your behaviors and thinking are not pleasing to God? Have you felt you know you need to turn around and change direction? Write down what The Lord shows you. Lift these areas up to God and then lay them on the altar of sacrifice. Ask God to help you turn away from them.

"For the things in the world--the cravings of the earthly nature, the cravings of the eyes, the show and pride of life--they all come, not from the Father, but from the world. And the world, with its cravings, is passing away, but he who does God's will continue forever" (1 John 2:16-17 Weymouth New Testament).

_____

_____

_____

POETRY: HERE I AM

From Your heart
    Comes streaming down
    Unending love
    Is all around

Your Loving kindness
    Is sure as dawn
    By Your grace
    I am drawn

From dusk to dawn
    And back You trace
    Faithful love
    Amazing grace

Breath of God
    Ancient of Day's
    Here I am I
    Teach me more of Your ways
    © laurette laster

DAY 7

"Let the wicked forsake his way, and the unrighteous man his thoughts;
let him or her return to the LORD, that He may have compassion on
him, and to our God, for He will abundantly pardon" (Isaiah 55:7
English Standard Version)
"Let us examine and test our ways and return to the LORD!"
(Lamentations 3:40, ESV).
"Therefore say to them, thus declares the LORD of hosts; "'Return to
Me, says the LORD of hosts, and I will return to you, says the LORD
of hosts'" (Zechariah 1:3 ESV).

ACCORDING TO STRONG'S CONCORDANCE, #7725 shub is to turn back,
return, answer, this expresses a radical change of mind toward sin, and
implies a conscious moral separation from sin. This is changing your
mind and making the decision to hate and forsake sin and agree with
God. Also, to shub to turn and go the other way. We no longer serve
self; we desire to serve God and His purpose for our lives.

The LORD, when speaking through the prophet Isaiah, defines to
us what He has planned when we turn or turn back to His righteous

ways of thinking and acting. God's plan is to abundantly pardon. We often have this picture of an angry, punishing God who is begrudging and withholding good from us; we think He sadistically enjoys punishing us. This warped sense of perception is generally attached to God from wrong thinking that God is like a parent, or perhaps a caretaker, who acted with cruelty. Furthermore, we may believe God is waiting or hiding in the brush, to catch us doing something wrong and before He jumps out saying, "Ah ha! Now you've had it.!"

Let's think about this for a moment. When Adam and Eve sinned, God came looking to meet with them in the cool of the day. God wasn't hiding; Adam and Eve were hiding from God, and that is the result of sin (hiding). When sinning, we feel the need to hide from God, the One who always wants what is best for us.

God is our loving Father. He says in Isaiah 1:18, "Come now, and let us reason together," Says the LORD, "Though your sins are as scarlet, They will be as white as snow; Though they are red like crimson, They will be like wool.'" We have a concerned Father. He says, "Look, you are covered with sin, and I am going to clean you up." What a promise! The stain that our sin has caused cannot be cleansed with any earthly works or doings.

When we quit running from God and His truth, and instead turn (return) to Him, we become the grateful, undeserving recipients of His amazing grace. We see the picture of redemption and restoration at work in our lives. Part of restoration is to restore us to our right mind and way of thinking.

"Let the wicked forsake his way, and the unrighteous man his thoughts: and let him return unto the LORD, and he will have mercy upon him; and to our God, for he will abundantly pardon. For my thoughts are not your thoughts, neither are your ways my ways, saith The LORD. For as the heavens are higher than the Earth, so are my ways higher than your ways, and my thoughts than your thoughts" (Isaiah 55:7-9, KJV).

Prayer:

Lord Jesus, show me what I need to turn away from. You are calling me back to You. I'm sorry I ever left. I want to come back into a fully committed relationship with You; so, today and this week, make me pliable, teachable, and tender to Your yearnings. Amen.

Reflection:

What is The Lord asking you to turn away from? What are two ways you can turn back and turn your attention to what pleases The Lord? What are you able to change now in your life that you know will please the Father? What do you need to quit doing that you have felt conviction about? Write them down and then lift them up in prayer asking Your Heavenly Father to shower you with living water that replaces these dirty waters.

_____

_____

_____

POETRY: HIS PLAN

Because I know
    You beckon me
    I will come away
    Return to see

Fear on the inside
    Muffles a scream
    What if I can't
    Is this just a dream?

Then I remember
    Straighten to steady myself
    It is in You alone scripture says
    My soul finds rest

If I don't follow
    How will I grow
    I'll push in and continue
    And study to show

Lord, order my steps
    Delightful way
    I'll let go and trust
    Yes, simply believe today

By faith I go
    By faith I can
    Yes I will
    I'll follow Your plan

© laurette laster 2017

"Let all that I am wait quietly before God, for my hope is in Him" (Psalm 62:5 New Living Translation).

"The Lord directs the steps of the godly. He delights in every detail of their lives" (Psalm 37:23 NLT).

DAY 8

"In those days came John the Baptist preaching in the wilderness of Judaea. And saying, "'Repent ye for the kingdom of heaven is at hand'" (Matthew 3:1-2, KJV).

"From that time Jesus began to preach saying, "'Repent, for the kingdom of heaven is at hand'" (Matthew 4:17, ESV)

THE MESSAGE throughout the Old Testament shows God forgiving the sins of Israel, then Israel being led away, again and again, following false gods and worshipping idols. God sends hardships against them (to us also) to bring about understanding to help them see the error of their ways so they would understand their need of repentance.

Today we read our Bible and clearly see and understand God's covenant fulfillment by the death, burial, and resurrection of Jesus Christ. We are blessed to look into what the angels longed to look into, God's divine purpose. We understand God the Father was attempting to get and keep the attention of His children by teaching, training, and disciplining them, hoping they would turn back and repent. God's reasons were to help His people see that with Him, their lives would be blessed. Yet by going astray and committing adultery or acts of whoredom, their lives would lead to death and destruction.

The highest form of love is discipline; think about this. Discipline takes effort. It is much easier to ignore a problem (for a time) than to deal with the actions of wrong doers. Discipline is time consuming, often costly, and requires time and effort to be lovingly applied. I am not referring to cruel punishment; I am asserting that discipline, as in training, brings about changed behavior.

The people of God had been praying for a word from the prophets. Can you imagine the fear? The people had not received any word from God for over four hundred years? Do you think they were praying and seeking the LORD? I believe they surely were. I believe they were lamenting and crying out to God, asking for God to give them a word. With earnest desire and prayer they would posture themselves to hear. When we are desperate, we take on a whole new stance or, better yet, we bow. God never ignores a desperate prayer, never. When we are desperate, we get real, God loves real!

There had been no word from the prophets spoken, but after four hundred years of silence, the long silence now has come to an end. (Malachi to Matthew is known as "The Silent Years")

We enter the book of Matthew to learn of the genealogy and birth of Jesus. In the book of Luke, we are taken straight into the scene of John the Baptist prophesying and preaching, "Repent and be baptized for the remission of your sins for the kingdom of heaven is near." God was ushering in the next scene. The stage has been set for The Fulfillment. The fulfillment promised and prophesied from the mouths of the prophets throughout the first 39 books of the Old Testament.

What is Jesus describing when He came preaching to repent? He is saying the time has come for the kingdom of God to be made manifest and we need to clear our land, prepare for the new life hidden in Christ. Get our land plowed and ready to plant. Get our house cleaned up and expect The Lord to make His abode with us. The work of repentance is purging our souls from sin and dead works. It is preparing our hearts to be a place for our Lord to dwell according to what God requires, accepting the rules and the plans He has for our lives.

"Give your minds to the things that are above, not to the things that are on the earth. For you have died, and your life is hidden with Christ in God" (Colossians 3:2-3 WNT).

Many years ago, I was hired to be a manager for Applebee's by Concord Hospitality. I remember vividly my first day on the job, at my home store. I had trained at another location for the position, three states away.

When the time come for me to begin my duties at my home store, the General Manager handed me a card, several keys on a ring, and some written information with instructions; among this was the combination to the safe. Handing them to me he said, "I confer to you the keys and the information of the kingdom." Being a born again, on fire Christian in love with Jesus, I thought at first this statement mocked the word and the message of Christ. I learned later, God was going to use Applebee's to teach me about His kingdom, preparation, and learning how to live according to God's counsel and teachings. This was going to be training in leadership and authority, and yes, a huge responsibility.

With kingdom advancement comes accountability and responsibility. This responsibility was different than I had known. I had always been overly responsible. I had taken on the cares of the world and tried to fix things I hadn't broken. I didn't even know how they got broke. I just knew and recognized they were broke and thought I should fix them. This was different, very different. What was different?

I was coached on how to measure and perform. The proof was in the numbers. Everything I was responsible for was measurable: labor; food cost; profit and loss; repair and maintenance; employee retention; employee turnover; and guest complaints.

The wisdom of God is not inherent. We must understand, as Proverbs 4:7 tells us, "that wisdom is the principle thing" and in all our getting, we need to get under-standing. Understanding comes by standing under the authority of His word, and simply obeying His word.

"Do you not know that the wicked will not inherit the kingdom of God? Do not be deceived: Neither the sexually immoral, nor idolaters, nor adulterers, nor men who submit to or perform homosexual acts, nor thieves, nor the greedy, nor the drunkards, nor verbal abusers, nor swindlers, will inherit the kingdom of God. And that is what some of you were. But you were washed, you were sanctified, you were justified, in the name of the Lord Jesus Christ and by the Spirit of our God" (1 Corinthians 6:9-11 BSB).

I love the scriptures above. Paul says and that is what some of (us) you once were. So sin is what must be dealt with and repented of so that we can be washed and sanctified.

Repentance is necessary if you are to be able to stand up to the enemy and enter into the kingdom. If we do not confess our sins, and truly turn away from sin we are deceiving our own self. 1 John 3:21 says if our heart does not condemn us, we have confidence toward God. As long as we know we are trying to hide something, we cannot be a bold Christian. Satan whispers, "I know what you did." But if we confess our sins, God is faithful and just to forgive us our sins and to cleanse us from ALL unrighteousness. Some translations say He purifies us. Isn't that good news? Do you need and desire to be purified from all unrighteousness? This is not only sins we have committed but sins committed against us as well. Those things that have left us feeling dirty and ashamed, not good enough, or not loved.

(1 John 1:9) ...those things!

"I am now standing at the door and am knocking. If anyone listens to My voice and opens the door, I will go in to be with him and will feast with him, and he shall feast with Me" (Rev 3:20, WNT).

In order to endure hardships, we need to realize there is a sure reward. We have numerous examples in the word pertaining to the Patriarchs and Matriarchs who believed God and saw their prayers answered. We cannot doubt but only believe. Read Hebrews chapter 11. This chapter is called the hall of faith. At the mountain of Sinai the people couldn't endure to hear the words God was speaking. Once we know the will of God, we are held accountable to His will.

I can remember a time when I was not living for The Lord, and I sure am glad He wasn't rewarding me according to my deeds. If you are honest, I bet it is the same for you. "But God desires that men and women everywhere repent. His desire to make His abode with us cannot be fulfilled unless we repent and turn away from sin." In this scripture, found in Revelation 3:20, Jesus is speaking to believers in church. How can a believer not have feasted with Jesus? How can someone be in church and not know the power of the Almighty? Maybe right now you are saying to yourself, "I've been in church for years, this doesn't apply to me." Just going to church on Sundays does not give us authority. I know many weak willed, very loving but weak willed Christians who are enabling others. Very good Christian people who are weak willed and unable to stand up for what is right or they are afraid to speak the truth for fear of offending others.

Throughout the Bible, we see ordinary men and women accomplishing extraordinary feats by trusting God. Faith believes God is able to do what He says He will do in His word. Remember, you are not here today with this book by mistake. God has an appointment with you and He is going to meet you in extraordinary ways. He is going to empower you and equip you for the good work He has planned for you before you were born.

Prayer:

Dear Heavenly Father, I am sorry, I have been like Thomas, I have been a doubter. I have said I don't believe I can do the things necessary until I see _____ or _____ in order to be all You are calling me to be. Forgive me Father, I repent right now for thinking I could ever do, or accomplish anything real or lasting for Your kingdom without You. I am here to sign up for the work of repentance because I want to know that I am a true kingdom citizen and fulfill my calling. I open the door of my heart and I say welcome Sir, please come in, I've longed to feast with You.

Lord Jesus, I want to be made new. I want to walk in what You have for me. I know that any and all sin, doubt, willful disobedience, soul sickness, soul ties, confusion, negativity, wrong thinking, unforgiveness and lack of training will nullify the work You have for me to do. Show me how to work the work of repentance so that I may be bold for You and for the kingdom of God. I truly desire to be set free from all bondages and strong holds and any wrong thinking that is holding me back. I commit today to a new start with You. I will not hold back or hide. Amen

But we are not people who shrink back and perish, but are among those who believe and gain possession of their souls (Hebrews 10:39 WNT).

"But where there is no faith it is impossible truly to please Him; for the man who draws near to God must believe that there is a God and that He proves Himself a rewarder of those who earnestly try to find Him" (Hebrews 11:6 WNT).

Reflection:

As we learn what pleases our Lord, we are going to put some things to death, take some off, and put some on. This is the very real part of changing our minds. Seeing as God sees requires time and effort at our own expense. What is God showing you that may be hindering your ability and the plans He has for your life? Do you feel disqualified? Do you doubt if God has a plan for your life? How can you feed your faith? Read Colossians chapter 3. What are the five things you need to put to death? What are the five things you need to put off? What are the five things we are told to put on? Write these down and highlight them in your Bible.

_____

_____

_____

_____

*If you are **not** planted in a local Jesus believing, Bible teaching, sin hating church, I encourage you to find one. Pray and ask The Lord where He would have you go. If you find that others are comfortable in their sin and justifying sinful behavior while attending church, run don't walk to the nearest exit. When the power of God dwells in the church body, along with conviction of sin and a deep desire to come clean in the presence of God is apparent, you may have found a home.

When you find the right church, ask to meet with the pastor. Find out what is available that you can become involved in, and then get *involved. In order to grow in wisdom and knowledge you need to become consistent. If this is an area of struggle for you, repent and ask The Lord to help you. I included pledges at the back (page 347) to use as contracts. When you see an area of struggle and repent before The Lord, commit and present it before Him, then sign and date the card. You may choose to cut out the card and place it in an area where you will be reminded daily of the commitment you have made. Placing a reminder where you see it daily is a great way to jump start your new life, the life that is now hidden in Christ. The only way to grow is to become enmeshed in the things of God. Find a safe Bible study, where you are taught about Jesus and the word, not just church doctrine. Small cell groups are a wonderful place to learn and grow. Ask questions and pray about everything.*

POETRY: IN YOUR IMAGE AND LIKENESS

Like the ocean knows the shore
    It goes thus far but never more
    You've set limits for our security
    Teach me Lord, hearts keeping purity
    In detail and design with perfect precision
    Not by happenstance or chaotic derision
    A Masters Plan in Your mind that day
    You molded us from a handful of clay

Pour out Your wisdom and give us insight
    Oh Lord what is our purpose show us the light
    We are children of the day not of the night
    Born with a measure of faith to fight the good fight
    That you have planned before You began
    Creating in Your likeness Your woman and man
    Then we shall know and answer the call
    We are servant to You the One who gave it all
    © laurette laster 2017

DAY 9

"Do not fear (phobeo or phobos) little flock it is the Fathers good pleasure to give you the kingdom" (Luke 12:32, NKJV).

"Whoever conceals his transgressions will not prosper, but he who confesses and forsakes them finds mercy" (Proverbs 28:13, ESV).

"Good and upright is The Lord; therefore He teaches sinners in the way. The humble He guides in justice, and the humble He teaches His way. All the paths of The Lord are mercy and truth, to such as keep His covenant and His testimonies. For Your name's sake O Lord, pardon my iniquity, for it is great. Who is the man that fears the Lord? The secret of the Lord is with those who fear Him" (Psalm 25:8-12, 14, NKJV).

Strong's Concordance #5401, phobeo or phobos the Greek word used here is defined as "to have fear or be alarmed." This is where we get our English word phobia. Take notice that Jesus refers to His followers as "little flock" meaning a group or a literal flock, and I'm sure most of us immediately see the image of innocent sheep, right? This is because we (believers in Messiah) are called the sheep of His pasture. This is a term of endearment. This is a loving term describing the Father as The Shepherd and His desire for His people. But Jesus assures us it is the Fathers good pleasure to give us, you and me and all His followers, His flock or His group the kingdom. God is actually attempting to restore to you what He had in mind when He created you. He teaches sinners in the way they should go.

As we talked about previously, Jesus came teaching and preaching, "Repent for the kingdom of God is nigh." Jesus makes reference again that preaching repentance and remission of sins should be in His name to all nations beginning at Jerusalem. This occurred while talking with His disciples walking with the two on the road to Emmaus (Luke 24:17-48).

The greatest sin is unbelief. Not believing Jesus is God's only begotten Son that He came to pay a debt we owed, is what sends a person to Hell. We are deceived by Satan when we do not clearly see nor believe in the work Jesus has done for us on the Cross. This may cause us to live in shame and confusion, or lack, and fear.

I used to believe sins or bad actions kept us out of heaven and sent us to Hell. I had this crazy idea that we had to be able to be good enough to go to Heaven. The sin of unbelief is what keeps us out of heaven and sends unbelievers to Hell. That is why we are instructed and told to repent and believe in the finished work of Jesus Christ for the remission of our sins. Once we understand that Jesus died in our place we can appropriate His work on the Cross for our sin. We realize our debt was/is paid in full. We no longer have anything to fear.

No matter how unworthy you may feel, and no matter what you may have done, you can receive God's unmerited gift of grace. The gift of His forgiveness is for all who call on the name of The Lord. Literally, reach out accept the gift of God's unmerited favor toward you. Isn't it amazing?! Now we know why it is called *Amazing Grace.*

What is the kingdom, and why must you and I repent? What is God attempting to place in our hands or within our reach? What is Jesus telling us about the kingdom of God? Jesus is telling us, ready or not, the kingdom is coming. For, Jesus was talking to His followers not just the disciples when he said, "Repent for the kingdom of God is nigh." To His people or flock this is a commandment not a suggestion. The Greek word for kingdom, Strong's Concordance # G932 is basileia; this word is best defined as dominion, royalty, realm, or stewardship.

Whose kingdom is reigning? Unconfessed sin allows the enemy room in our hearts and in our heads (thoughts) to torment us. Guilt is an awful torment, but so is revenge and holding on to hurts. Resentment can turn into revenge by holding onto a wrong and willingly refusing to forgive. By refusing to forgive, we actually allow sin to grow and have dominion. If this continues, we no longer have dominion, sin does.

To be unforgiving is equally wrong. Holding un-forgiveness toward another is a sin before God. Even if we believe we have every right to withhold forgiveness, God says He cannot forgive us as long as we hold un-forgiveness in our hearts toward another. Forgiving someone who has wronged us "DOES NOT" make what they did okay. What they did is a sin and when we forgive we are allowing God to deal with them His way. We can trust that our Father, The Great Shepherd, doesn't take delight in anyone abusing His sheep, the sheep of His pasture.

Jesus tells us "For if you forgive men their trespasses, your Heavenly Father will also forgive you." (Matthew 6:14, NKJV). If you are having trouble praying for those who have wronged you pray the prayer our Lord taught His disciples to pray in Matthew 6:9-15, and focus on verse 12 until the words come. When asked by His disciples, "Lord, teach us to pray," the prayer Jesus taught included forgiving others. This is part of "…as it is in Heaven, so shall it be on earth." So we forgive others debt because we desire our debt to be forgiven.

God is faithful and will avenge His people, and you will begin to see this more clearly as you forgive, right now.

God wants to set you free from the enemy and his torment that is holding you hostage by that hurt or wound. If you have any un-forgiveness in your heart, I urge you to stop right now and confess this un-forgiveness to Jesus and pray for the person or persons you have resentment toward. Remember you do not have to feel like being obedient for the power of God to work. The power of God operates in an obedient and willing heart. It is by doing not by feeling that we give and honor God. Our obedience is powerful permission for God to work in our lives. If we are holding onto un-forgiveness, we can't take hold of kingdom promises. Obedience ushers in grace and mercy. Our attitude is vital; but being obedient to God's word and following His will is how our spirit trains and subdues our natural (carnal) man.

"Bless them who curse you, and pray for those who spitefully use you" (Luke 6: 28).

Years ago, I had a terrible thing happen to me. I would get on my knees and through a waterfall of tears I would say, "Oh God, bless _____ and _____. Let them be happy and have all the blessings they desire." I would cry and say, "Oh Lord, I don't want to be bitter." I would tell God while on my knees, "I don't mean this, but You said to do this. I don't want to lie to you, how can You want me to lie to a Holy God? Through all the confusion and in spite of my feelings something happened."

You see, I was confused but obedient. I didn't want them blessed; I wanted them annihilated. My flesh did not want to feel this pain and rejection. But when I look back at this today, I see a kingdom principle that was followed and I was set free. They didn't change but something inside of me did. I remember when I had the feeling everything was going to be okay. Jesus showed me the circumstances didn't have to change for me to see the situation through different eyes. I changed by praying for them. I believe with my whole heart this kept me from becoming bitter. It is a kingdom principle to pray for those who so spitefully use and abuse you, and I promise it works. I know. I offer this advice (get on your knees and pray for them daily) to others I am mentoring when they are struggling to forgive. It is not fun. It takes tenacity and humility, but it will stop the enemy dead in his tracks. I know this is why I did not become bitter. I also realize today I was allowing Holy Spirit to guide and lead me. I didn't even know about the scripture to pray for those who spitefully use and abuse you. Wow! Please understand that forgiveness is not restoration. The Bible does not tell us that we must put ourselves (heart) back into the hands of cruel people, Jesus does tell us to pray for them. I know today it isn't for them; it is for us to be set free. Read Luke 23:34. Jesus isn't instructing us only; He also lived and modeled it for us.

The enemy, Satan, wants to hold you back from reaching out to receive what the Father has for you. Often the sins committed against us make us feel like something is wrong with us. If the enemy cannot stop us with guilt, he will try to make us feel like we are not good enough.

But I know this is your time and this is your personal invitation from The Lord Jesus Christ. I'm sure you know what I am saying. That feeling of "Who do you think you are?" or that old nagging feeling of "What if they knew what I have done?" … It has probably been playing in your mind for years. It is time to realize that is the voice of the enemy. He is the accuser of the brethren. God will correct us because of His great love; He will chasten us, but He will not ever tell us we are not good enough, unlovable, or that we are unworthy. Jesus died for you and me, and we are God's own workmanship created in Christ Jesus for good works. We must learn to recognize Satan's voice and the lies Satan uses against us; then, we must say what God says.

Hebrews 10:17 helps us see God's assurance. He assures us that He will not allow sin to be used against us. Once it has been confessed and forgiven, we do not have to be afraid (phobeo). His removal process, called repentance, cleanses all sin away.

Meditate:

God removes all evidence that there was sin when we truly repent, confess, and change our mind. God longs to redeem the time the enemy has stolen. He has a plan and a purpose for your life. If you are willing to believe, repent, offer forgiveness for wrongs done to you, and forgive the wrongs of others, The Lord will forgive you; it is His promise.

Prayer:

Heavenly Father, I want to manage my life and not walk in fear or regret. I do not want to be or become bitter. Show me how to forgive those who have hurt me, even though what they did was horribly wrong. Help me to understand forgiving them removes the power of the pain and resentment and takes away the right of this hurt to remain in my heart.

I acknowledge that forgiveness does not mean restoration. I do not have to have a relationship with them or become vulnerable to their hurtful actions again. I am willing to become willing, and I need Your help with this. I understand this does not mean relationship restoration at this time, but it may in the future. This is my willingness to forgive those who have hurt or wronged me so that I can be free. Show me who I need to forgive. I trust you and I want to inherit all You have for me. You said in Your word that if I forgive those who have sinned against me, You will forgive me for the sins I have committed against You. I accept Your forgiveness because today, I choose to forgive_____ totally. Amen

Reflection:

How can you begin to walk in forgiveness? What are some decisions you can make that are evidence you have made the decision to forgive? What is one wrong thought (stronghold) you can tear down today? Make a list of the persons you need to forgive and pray over the list. If you want to get radical (and punch Satan in the face) get on your knees as you pray over these names.

_____

_____

_____

POETRY: A POEM OF REPENTANCE

Weep no more
    My soul longs for solution
    The time of returning
    New start revolution

Not a trite wish
    Nor halfhearted command
    But studied and sought
    From Your very own hand

Engraved impressed
    Upon my heart
    Repentance cleanses
    Now a new start

Broken heart, contrite spirit
    Weep and confess
    Heavy laden, and torn
    Finding no rest

You bid to me and say
　　Your yoke easy, burden light
　　Help Me Oh Lord
　　To understand my plight

Until at last
　　I bow at Your request
　　Accepted in The beloved,
　　It is for me You did invest

Under Your wings I find
　　Protection peace and calm
　　Your Spirit my comfort
　　My deliverance and healing balm

My name is recorded
　　Written in Your book
　　Part of Your heavenly plan
　　Repentance is all it took

Meditate on your word
　　Both night and day
　　I'll read, I'll study
　　I'll hearken and obey

Then I can know
　　And have true success
　　Thank you, Lord Jesus,
　　For Your righteousness!

© laurette laster 2017 September

"The sacrifice you desire is a broken spirit. You will not reject a broken and repentant heart, O God" (Psalm 51:17 NLT).

DAY 10

"I will give them a heart to know that I am the Lord, and they shall be
my people and I will be their God; for they shall return
(metanoia/repent) to me with their whole heart" (Jeremiah 24:7).

EARLY ONE MORNING, and early in my born again walk several years
ago, I (freshly baptized in His Holy Spirit newness) was in prayer
when I heard a whispered voice. The Lord asked me a question. I was
completely amazed by His grace and still am today!

Today I have a better understanding of His amazing grace, and I am
able to grasp the meaning and gift of grace. Having completely turned
to the Lord, with a live or die vow, I thought surely He would punish
me for my sins. After all, I deserved to be punished for my sins, right?
An eye for an eye, isn't that what God says? I had such a harsh understanding of God. I believed that to follow God and His will, meant
deprivation and misery. Too often I had heard about starving preachers
and seen weird people portraying the will of God. What sad imagery
and beliefs.

I was sure God would send me to Africa requiring me to become a starving missionary. Isn't this another sad belief? I was so afraid He was going to make me do something I didn't want to do or even more force me into a mold that wasn't designed for me. *There is an image He desires to see in each of us, but it is The Reflection of His Dear Son, a reflection of love for others.*

In Psalms 37:4, we are told He gives us the desires of our heart. "Delight yourself in the Lord and He will give you the desires of your heart" (Psalm 37:4 NIV). Notice it doesn't say, He makes us do what we dread, making us miserable all the days of our lives, paying us back for wrongs we've done, and what we are sure to fail at. *No.* The very thing God is leading us to and developing us to be is exactly what we were born to do!

After letting this reality sink in, I fell madly in love with Jesus. His love and tenderness over and for me had blown my mind, so I decided whatever He asked of me I was going to do it. I no longer had that terrible fear of committing to His will. I would do anything He wanted me to do.

I had never known such safety and compassion. Yes my development was very difficult, but knowing He was working something out in me, caused me to love what He was doing. "A satisfied soul loathes the honeycomb, but to a hungry soul every bitter thing *is* sweet" (Proverbs 27:7).

In prayer one morning in a whispered voice He asked, "Why do people eat out of dumpsters?" Catching me completely off guard I whispered back, "I don't know. Why do people eat out of dumpsters?" He whispered in that precious voice, "Because they are starving." Wow! Now I'm completely undone. Pretty simple, huh? Only someone who is suffering from malnourishment and starving eats from dirty dumpsters.

In my attempt to understand grace and forgiveness and how He views sin, this allowed Him to ask a simple question and answer me. His simple question, and very simple answer, spoke volumes and opened my understanding to a deeper level. I knew what He wanted me to understand in a broader sense. Sin is sin, and all sin is wrong, and it is in violation of His love.

Sin ensnares us with a lie and can be caused by soul starvation. In order not to starve to death, or so I thought, I had indeed eaten out of many dumpsters of the worlds system in my life. I had compromised my soul for acceptance and a counterfeit love. Fear of rejection caused me to compromise and do some serious dumpster diving. Like Proverbs 27:7 says…

"A person who is full refuses honey, but even bitter food tastes sweet to the hungry"

Does this make sense? Of course it does. It makes perfect sense. That is exactly why someone would eat out of a dumpster. Someone who is well nourished and accustomed to eating at a table of prepared goodness would never resort to eating rotting dirty food out of a dumpster. Who in their right mind does this? No one in their right mind would eat from dumpsters. Someone who didn't know about, nor tasted the goodness of the Lord, never realizing it was available to them, or available for them, that is who eats out of dumpsters. Then I realized I had been eating from dumpsters due to my own soul starvation.

I was beginning to see Him and experience His great love. I was beginning to understand His forgiveness of sins, and I was beginning to learn about His great love for His people, including me. Knowing God's precious people, outside of covenant, are starving helps us to understand why someone who seems to have it all (worldly wealth) can be hopeless and commit suicide. I understood more the love of a loving, caring, concerned, and nurturing, Father. I saw the heart of our Heavenly Father helping me understand.

This is our Father's view of His children caught in sin, eating out of the dumpsters of circumstances and wrong choices causing us to live according to the worlds system. All the while He is saying, "Come unto Me all who are weary and I will give you rest" (Matthew 11:28).

I was beginning to believe and trust that I could reach out and receive taking hold of all that Jesus died to give me. In order to take hold of this I would learn to let go of a bunch of guilt and condemnation, no longer dragging these around with me.

Wow, our Lord is so tender and so merciful. He doesn't want His children homeless, cold, and alone, or starving and eating from dumpsters.

If we went in search of our lost child or loved one realizing he or she had fallen on hard times and discovered they were eating from a dumpster... Well, we would immediately render aid! Bidding him or her to come and allow us to help him or her get back on their feet? Isn't this the Good Samaritan Jesus describes in the gospel of Luke 10:25-37, that shows mercy to one along the road? We would get busy setting a table before them.

How does this look through the eyes of our Father and His pure love for His people? Pure love looking into this depravity of a starving soul, made a way.

Psalm 23:5 Good News Translation says it like this; "You prepare a banquet for me, where all my enemies can see me; you welcome me as an honored guest and fill my cup to the brim."

That is what a Loving Heavenly Father does for His children. He doesn't want us to continue to eat from the dumpsters of life.

Contrary to some beliefs God is not in heaven reviewing the tapes of our sins/sinful lifestyle thinking or saying, well that's good enough for you, seeing what you've done. Look how terrible you are, you'll never learn will you? What I just described is called retaliation. Our Father bids us to repent and 'return' home. He has set a place for us at His banquet. Love trains, and disciplines, and yes if needed will punish, but love never retaliates.

"My ears had heard of You but now my eyes have seen You. Therefore, I despise myself and repent in dust and ashes" (Job 42:4-5).

Prayer:

Heavenly Father, I want to say thank You for Your amazing grace and unmerited favor. Your hand of forgiveness is extended to all who repent and ask for forgiveness and help. Your hand extended as One ushering us to our place at Your table. I know today that Your hand of grace is fully extended to me and I have a personal invitation to join You at Your table through Jesus Christ who died for my pardon. I am accepted by You, today, right where I am. I repent for feeding out of the dumpsters of life and compromising myself. Thank You for my invitation to Your banquet of love, and for reserving my seat at Your table. Oh Jesus thank You, thank You, thank You, a million times over, THANK YOU. Amen

Reflection:

What are some things you have settled for that you now know are like eating from the dumpster of life? What do you need to turn away from? What is keeping you from realizing The Lord has prepared a table for you? Ask The Lord to show you to the table. His hand is fully extended toward you. Your seat is waiting. (Read Luke 15:14-24)

_____

_____

_____

POETRY: MY SOUL CRIES OUT

My soul cries out
    I must be free
    Your voice cries back
    Come unto Me.

My soul screams out
    I can't see the road
    Your voice answers back
    I'll remove that heavy load

My soul is begging
    Pleading for pardon
    Your voice comes closer
    Follow Me to the garden

Your voice calls out
    Seek My affection
    My soul is weeping
    Searching for direction

My soul does wonder
    Why all this derision
    Your voice answers back
    Valley of decision

My soul is listening
    I know the sound
    It is Your voice
    To my knees I fall to the ground

My soul is rejoicing
    In Uncontrollable moans
    Your voice I've heard
    I'm coming home!

© laurette laster

"To turn them from darkness to light, and from the power of Satan to God, that they may receive forgiveness of sins and an inheritance among those who are sanctified by faith in Me" (Acts 26:18 NKJV).

DAY 11

"I TELL YOU, No! But unless you repent you too will all perish" (Luke 13:3,5).

K airos is an ancient Greek word meaning the right, critical, or opportune moment. Ancient Greek has two words for time—Chrono and Kairos. Kairos is defined as a moment for a decision or an action. It is the right or appropriate time to say or do the right or appropriate thing. Chronos is the word we use for chronological time, such as a day or an hour. Kairos is a moment or a season or a time set by God. Due season, or harvest time is Kairos (Read Luke 13:1-8).

"I tell you, No! But unless you repent you too will all perish" (Luke 13:3,5).

God is all about timing. Everything in the Bible is strategically laid out and planned. God is a God of divine order. Everything He does is perfect therefore He is not a man that must repent. God cannot lie (Read Numbers chapters 22-23).

You will see someone who has a grievance against God's people with the desire to drive them out by cursing them. In fact, Balak hired

Balaam to curse the children of Israel. In this narrative found in Numbers 23:19 we find out some very key truths. These truths do not change:

1. God is not a man that He should lie
2. What God says is what God does
3. What God speaks is a covenant promise

If you have made Jesus the Lord of your life you are blessed and no one can curse you. [Balaam was an evil prophet not a false prophet]. The only way we can be cursed is to be seduced and believe a false prophet and participate with the devil and his lies, disobey God and believe the lie thus cursing ourselves. Now do not misunderstand, words have power. Proverbs tell us life and death is in the power of the tongue.

James 3:6 tells us that the tongue is the smallest member but can set the course of hell in motion. What I am saying is that if someone has called you harsh vulgar names, used profanity when addressing you and otherwise spoken lies and curses over you, realize that is exactly what they are, they are lies you may be holding them in your heart as truth. These may have been spoken by someone who should have loved you but didn't know how.

We are instructed to tear down strongholds and to take every thought captive to the obedience of God's word. Lies spoken by evil prophets can become strong holds in our minds.

We believe what God believes and what God has spoken about us. With this being said, you will have some additional work to do concerning forgiving others and denouncing the harsh cruel words spoken over you and to you and about you.

We are told to forgive and offer forgiveness to the persons who have abused and spitefully used us. Yes this means even those who have verbally, mentally and emotionally abused you. You also need to denounce the authority of the lie. The person who did this spoke out of a spirit of anger, resentment, or possibly rage but certainly not from God's view of you. As difficult as this will be you need to make a list of the names of the persons who did this to you. Make another list of the character assaults and insults that have been spoken over you. This will take more time but after you renounce each of them one by one you will be so glad you took the time to work this spiritual principle. This is how you break soul ties also.

We must do some hard work but oh how sweet it is to get our fields ready to plant. We cannot have a harvest if we do not plant, and we cannot plant if our ground is full of hard stony places, poisonous weeds, briers, and thorn bushes.

Thorn bushes rip and tear our clothing and our flesh if we get too close. If there are memories or words that are still tearing at you causing you to bleed, these must be uprooted. We may try to ignore or cover up, denying they are dangerous. Thorns and briers will tear into us unless they are uprooted and burned. If ignored they will continue to come back: over and over, time and time again.

You are not cursed. God is not against you and He is not pleased these things have happened to you. God is not plotting or using awful situations to punish you. You are blessed by God. As a child of God you are to live a life that is pleasing to The Father. The true desires of your heart lie in the very center of His will for your life. Maybe you haven't given much thought to this idea.

Have you considered that God in heaven has a plan for your life? Is that surprising to you? Do you feel like the least likely person for such an assignment? Oh trust me I certainly did. I even tried to convince God He was making a mistake, listing for Him each reason (sins) I wasn't qualified.

Perhaps you're thinking, "I *have* believed there was more, but now look what I have done and look how I've ruined my life. Look what has been done to me. Because of my sin (s) I am disqualified." If you believe you are disqualified, you have agreed with Satan and bought the lie. God is calling you, through Christ' finished work on the Cross, to repent and then receive your forgiveness.

No matter what you have done and no matter what has been done to you, God can and will redeem you. If there were some tough times allowed, they were only allowed to get your attention with the intent to cause you to repent. His desire is for you to turn. No matter what sins you have committed God will forgive you, if you repent out of a sincere and broken heart and ask Him too. God made provision for us to be forgiven and to come into right standing with Him. God redeems the time. It is a mystery and it is amazing but it is real and it is true. He wants to justify you through the shed blood of Jesus Christ. Justify (just as if I), as if I never sinned.

That is why God requires we repent. We turn from going our own way. Return to The Lord, discover and follow the plan He has set for our life. We acknowledge Christ' atoning work on the Cross as done for us.

You confess with your mouth and believe with your heart unto salvation (Romans 10:9). Then and only then will you know just how loved by God you are. When we appropriate Jesus's work and His death and His sacrifice as a gift to us that paid for our sins, we are saved and forgiven. Even before we understand all that this means it is credited to our account. It is gifted to us.

You are loved. You are chosen. You are chosen for this very time, to come to God with a repentant heart. It is an invitation to come away with Him, for refreshing and cleansing. He has designed and has set aside this very Kairos time with you in mind. He desires to save you out of sin for communion with Him.

Perhaps He is attempting to get your attention. God has a plan to take you out (of Egypt or sin), to take you in (into the Promised Land or into the calling on your life, His call). Perhaps you find yourself in a situation that seems unbearable. If so, maybe it is Jehovah Sneaky Himself, who landed you here. God knows and sees just where you are. As a matter of fact He is right there with you. Even if you are in a jail, a rehab, a hospital, in a divorce dispute, or facing a kid going to prison, the death of a parent or spouse and even a child, or sitting in your living room about to give up, He is there. Never give up, He is with you.

Often when we find ourselves in difficult circumstances we discover maybe for the first time in our lives, God is real. God doesn't cause bad things to happen to teach us a lesson, but because we have allowed ourselves to go where we shouldn't, often God will use the very hardships to get our attention. Let's face it, God could have killed you any number of times. I bet if you look back you can name at least one time (or more) when you know God spared your life. I can think and list several times He spared my life. And now I understand why. I didn't know my value, He sure did. Because "He is long suffering not wanting any to perish" (2 Peter 3:9).

Why did God spare your life? Have you ever wondered this? I can tell you why; it is because He is protecting your life and has a plan for you to be in your rightful place with Him. He has ordained this time, this Kairos for you to repent so that you do not perish.

Many years ago, I read a story about a business owner who called all his managers to his cabin for an outing. The owner owned a million-dollar company and was going to promote from within. He was looking for a new CEO for his company and he needed a CEO he could trust. The managers were not aware of why they had been invited. When the managers arrived, they had on the best suits they could afford. Groomed and ready, they each looked their best, hoping to gain favor from the owner. They wanted to impress the business owner.

The owner greeted and shook each one's hand. Looking them in the eye, he thanked each one for accepting his invitation to come. He said, "I'm sure you are all wondering what this is about." Excited to have been invited each one just stood there beaming. He then handed each manager a shovel, giving them instructions to go outside and to dig a 2X2 trench around the entire perimeter of the cabin. He opened the door and held it as they exited the cabin going outside.

The owner had raised a window and now sat down to listen as the managers talked among themselves. Some griped, some complained, some said exactly what they really thought of him, and so forth. They were discussing how they should handle this. Some were insulted and, feeling dishonored, even threatened to leave and not return to their job. Looking around one to another, they noticed one manager had remained silent while hearing their complaints. One of the managers addressed him as he was standing there with his shovel. Saying to him, "what do think about this?" He answered and said, "Well he told us to dig a trench so why don't we just do what he asks?"

At that very moment, the owner stood up from his chair went and opened the cabin door and said, "ladies and gentlemen may I introduce to you the new CEO of the company."

"If ye be willing and obedient, ye shall eat the good of the land" (Isaiah 1:19)—The promise of temporal blessings as the reward of a true repentance.

The prophet Isaiah is talking to a selfish people who are not interested in the governing by God. Isaiah in an effort to wake the people up and make them aware of their spiritual condition says to them there is a blessing in repentance. Willingness sometimes comes after the act of obedience. Repentance is a change of mind, the submission of our wills to the obedience of His word.

God is looking for those who are willing and obedient. Never doubt the insignificance of what God is asking you to do. We must believe God is a rewarder (Hebrews 11:6).

"The Lord is not slack concerning His promise, as some men count slackness; but is long-suffering to us-ward, not willing that any should perish, but that all should come to repentance" (2nd Peter 3:9 KJV).

My husband, Greg and I, call these WOO moments. These are Windows Of Opportunity. Opportunities we are given, that convict us or convince us to repent and get back in right standing with God. The door is not open forever, these are opportune times or windows of opportunity. Remember what you read?

Jesus told this parable Luke 13:6-9. "A man had a fig tree planted in his vineyard, and he went to look for fruit on it, but did not find any. So he said to the man who took care of the vineyard. For three years now I've been coming to look for fruit on this fig tree and haven't found any. Cut it down! Why should it use up the soil? Sir the man replied, leave it alone for one more year and I'll dig around it and fertilize it. If it bears fruit next year, fine! If not, then cut it down."

Do not overlook your appointed time, or day of visitation.

Prayer:

Oh Father I have been foolish in understanding You and conviction. I repent of my foolish thinking. I do not want to miss any WOO moments. I am turning back to you with my whole heart. I believe this is my time of opportunity to become fruitful and not just exist or use up the soil, like Jesus said. Show me why you saved me? What did You have in mind when You created me?

Reflection:

Name a time God has spared or saved your life. Why do you feel like God spared you? This would be a perfect time to praise your Father in heaven for His great mercy. Begin asking God what your destiny is? This took me years to discover with several frustrating events. I believe it was that way so that at the discovery I was sure.

_____

_____

_____

POETRY: A SEASON IN TIME

A time of reflection
    A time to assess
    What is working well
    What is causing duress

    A time of reflection
    Take time to inspect
    Is my life bearing fruit
    The kind He expects

    I'm not to compare
    Or look at another
    Not to be jealous
    Nor envy a brother

    I am only measured
    By His perfect design
    So I must assess this heart
    Never allow for decline

Oh my soul listen
 Align with His word
 Become a doer
 Of what ears have heard

 A season in time
 Set aside for reflection
 This is my heart check up
 And I have no objection

 © laurette laster 2018
"But be doers of the word not hearers only, deceiving yourselves" (James 1:22).

"BUT THIS IS how God fulfilled what He had foretold through all the prophets, saying that His Messiah would suffer. Repent then, and turn to God so that your sins may be wiped out, and that times of refreshing may come from The Lord" (Acts 3:18-19).

We see by the above scriptures that salvation through repentance has its origin from the beginning. Reading Acts chapter 3 we see, healing by believing on the name of Jesus and faith in Him. We see many marveling at what has happened. We also hear Peter saying 'Repent' and turn to God so that your sins may be forgiven, and times of refreshing may come from The Lord. In Gods plan of repentance we are made whole through confession of, then turning [away] from our sins. This isn't a trite suggestion or offer, or maybe you should repent if you have time, no it is an appointed time that God opens to the person He is welcoming in.

Apart from the mercies of God we cannot and are not ushered into this time and place.

Mo'edim- appointed time, purpose, plans and provision. The word Mo'edim literally means appointment time. Mo'eds are rehearsals. The

Most High has set apart precious times to meet with His people. Jesus Christ, Yeshua Hamashiach, the Messiah of Israel, came and gave us a full understanding of the springtime appointments and He has promised to come again and will fulfill the fall appointments. Read the Feasts (appointed times), of The Lord in Leviticus, chapter 23.

"The Lord said to Moses, "Speak to the Israelites and say to them: These are My appointed feasts, the appointed feasts of the Lord, which you are to proclaim as sacred assemblies. Some translations call them holy convocations" (Leviticus 23:1-2).

In the book of Leviticus, we see seven feasts of The Lord. You may not know about them or you may have read about them and think they are Jewish feasts. If you read Leviticus 23 you will see for yourself these feast are The Lords feasts. God Himself calls them, "My Holy Feast or My Holy Convocations."

God has worked His plan from the beginning. After the fall of mankind we see that God repented that He had made man.

And it repented the Lord that He had made man on the earth (Genesis 6:6).

God began to work His work of redemption. Redemption is only made possible through the sacrifice of Jesus Christ on the Cross at Calvary. Jesus became our perfect sacrificial Lamb to take away our sins.

The message of repentance didn't end at His death, it began. His death [suffering] made the way for repentance to be preached for remission of sins. Jesus doesn't neglect to leave us with the same truth He began His ministry with. Repent for the kingdom of God is at hand. We have an appointment with Him speaking to His disciples after His resurrection, before His ascension to The Father in Luke 24:47. Jesus departing instructions, "repentance and remission of sins should be preached in His name to all nations, beginning in Jerusalem" (NKJV).

As you continue with the work of repentance you have probably began to understand how far you are from Gods original plan. Have you ever asked yourself what might have been if _____ hadn't happened? Or what could have been in your life if things were different. I know I did. Perhaps you are sorry for the things you've done and can't figure out why you did those things. My heart broke for what could have been if the right protection had been available to me and around me. I wondered what could have been if I had been protected during my childhood from the harsh reality of poverty, peoples poor choices, family dysfunction, insecurity, alcoholism, an absentee father who abandoned our family, and me, before my birth, sexual abuse, an orphan spirit, the list goes on and on, but God.

Of the things I've listed and more in my adult life, I continued on in the dysfunction, pregnant in high school, deciding I could fix it by staying in a dysfunctional marriage, continuing on with my dysfunctional normal, I believe are the exact reasons I have the intimate relationship with our Heavenly Father today. I believe the very things the enemy sent to destroy me, chased me down a broken trail, that eventually overtook and broke me. Once I realized I couldn't do it on my own any longer I cried out to God. I was beyond broken and didn't know what to do. I so desired to get it right and be good enough. I wanted to be different. My mom and my siblings thought for sure I had a chance to make it. My brother used to say you can make it. I knew what he meant. I could be different; they even said, because you are different. He tried to protect me, as best a messed up big brother could.

I was sorry for the awful choices I had made. My heart was so sad when my eyes were opened seeing my choices through kingdom truths.

It isn't as if I didn't know what I had done wrong. I knew when I made poor choices. I had just been so busy, being busy, trying to do good that I didn't have time to stop and look at them. I didn't stop and do the work of repentance. I thought I needed to pay God back, how stupid of me. You know the white elephant in the room. It was as if I had lived from reaction to reaction. Today I see it like trying to live in a field full of land mines. Never knowing what your next step might uncover.

And apart from this wreckage and carnage, God had an appointment with me and Jesus was coming to rescue me out of the miry pit, it was more than I could wrap my head around. When I realized Jesus gave His life and willingly paid for my sin that I could be forgiven, well to use Isaiah's words, I was "undone;" this completely wrecked me.

When God repented for having made mankind, He didn't change His original blueprint of the plan He had in mind. He now offers restoration through redemption and forgiveness by the blood of His only begotten Son, Jesus. He found a righteous man in Noah and with he and his family God began over to work His plan.

Repentance erases the sin data and can be likened to resetting an iPhone back to the original factory settings. This may seem like a strange analogy but go with me here. Have you erased your saved data, settings, apps, and contact information from a cell phone before? Right before you are about to finish the process of erasing you receive a warning message. The message states if you erase this information you will be unable to retrieve it. Wow, how about this.

God says I will remember your sins no more for My namesake. He chooses (when we repent) to reset us. He sets us back to factory settings, sending His Only Begotten, Dear Son to die that we may be forgiven and give us His Holy Spirit who teaches us all things that pertain to life and godliness. This is the work of repentance. Would you allow and ask The Lord to reset you back to the original work of His hands? Is it your desire to allow Him to make you into His own work-manship, one who pleases our Father? Are you ready to have His commandments written on your heart and in your mind? Are you ready to have God blot out your transgressions?

Isaiah 43:25 "I, *even* I, *am* He that blotteth out thy transgressions for Mine own sake, and will not remember thy sins" (KJV).

Micah 7:18-19 "There is no other God like you, O LORD; You forgive the sins of Your people who have survived. You do not stay angry forever, but You take pleasure in showing us Your constant love" (GNT).

Hebrews 10:16-17 "This is the covenant I will make with them after that time, says the Lord. I will put My laws in their hearts, and I will write them on their minds." Then he adds: "Their sins and lawless acts I will remember no more" (NIV).

Don't miss your appointed time nor cut it short. God has you in His day planner.

Prayer:

Dear Jesus, I believe You paid my sin debt by Your death on the Cross. Reset me to the factory settings, I am returning to You. I place myself in Your hands. Reset me to the original design, to The Manufacturer's specified settings. Help me erase the data of the world that I have been listening to. I want to know You, to read Your word. I purpose in my heart to record Your sayings in my heart. I need a new software upgrade. Amen

Reflection:

To reset to factory settings, what would that look like to you? To have the years restored to you that were eaten by locust? In Joel 2:12-32, we are told of God's plans. If we read this scripture in context of the chapter and the book we see that God sent these hardships against them to cause them to repent. God says that "I sent against you"; God is offering restoration a redeeming of the time or Kairos in return for their repenting. If you could look at the years of sins as apps, what apps do you want The Lord to erase or wipe out? Write them down and lift them up to The Lord and ask Him to show you how to rewrite on the software of your new heart and mind His sayings. Remember you must agree to have the old settings erased (removed) in order to receive your new heart. Only then will God send His Holy Spirit to you.

_____

_____

_____

POETRY: I WILL RESTORE THE YEARS

When I walk In The Spirit
    Things of life make perfect sense
    More than when I went against Your will
    Looking back seeing past tense

Now I see what happens
    When I willingly repent
    The obstacles sent against me
    You do stop and they relent

Hardship sent to break me
    Put an end to this old flesh
    So You can restore
    And serve to me Your best

All the years consumed
    And devoured as You looked
    Only record now I see
    Restoration in Your book

When You said You would restore
    And pay back all they stole;
    It was because You waited patiently
    For me to reach toward the goal

Of Your mark and the prize
    Of Your will and high calling
    Now I see how all have sinned
    And from whence we all have fallen

So I stop and bow my knee
    Oh Lord how did I get here
    Restore to me the years
    When I didn't lend my ear

To listen or to hear
    All that You have planned,
    Now my only desire is truth
    I humble myself under Your mighty hand.

© laurette laster 2018 August

"I have blotted out, like a thick cloud, your transgressions, and like a cloud, your sins. Return to Me, for I have redeemed you" (Isaiah 44:22, NKJV).

DAY 13

"THE TIME IS FULFILLED, and the kingdom of God is at hand; repent and believe in the gospel" (Mark 1:15 ESV)

"Therefore, just as sin entered the world through one man, and death through sin, and in this way death came to all men because all sinned" (Romans 5:12 KJV).

"And you hath He quickened, who were dead in trespasses and sins; in times past ye walked according to the course of this world, according to the prince of the power of the air, of the spirit that is now working in the sons of disobedience" (Ephesians 2:2-3 KJV).

S tudying and reading the above scriptures we can determine this truth: we were dead in our sins and trespasses before our new life in Christ Jesus. But now hath He quickened you and me. Jesus makes us alive in Him and now we are dead to sin. Does this sound too good to be true? I know it did to me many years ago.

If we are dead to sin, why do we sin? The answer is simple; we have a flesh and a [self]-ish carnal nature. Our flesh is where sin nature lives, and has to be retrained. Our carnal self, the flesh, our earthly suit doesn't get saved; our spirit gets saved, renewed and reconnected to our source. Once our spirit is saved we no longer spiritually desire the things that are not pleasing to God. However, we do not go through divine osmosis, losing all appetite to sin. Sin is spiritually appalling and we must retrain our carnal nature to despise sin. The Holy Spirit is helping us through conviction. Why would Jesus say if anyone desires to be My disciple, he/she must take up their cross daily? (Luke 9:23).

Jesus says this as a reminder, telling us we choose by our volition and free will, to lay down our earthly desires. We place our fleshly appetite and desire on the altar of God to be burned up. We lose, crucify, or give up, by lying down, our old life in order to gain real eternal life through Christ. This is how we are born again or born anew. If it were easy everyone would do it, right?

We do the work of repentance, by changing and renewing our mind deciding we want to think like Jesus thinks. Learning to think like Jesus is a lifetime assignment, and we won't arrive while on this earth. I certainly haven't obtained it, I don't know any who have. According to the apostle Paul, he didn't either, so we can give ourselves some growing room. We must read and study our Bible. When we become a new creature or a new creation we are given a new life and a do over. We write on the tablets of our mind what God has written in our heart and in our mind. These are the things that are pleasing to God.

We are in the world but not of the world. Years ago I would get a secular song stuck in my head. At my job there was always music playing. Don't get me wrong, I like soft rock, classical, and other genres, but we get it that some of the lyrics aren't exactly right for a born-again Christian. If I felt the song was not pleasing to The Lord I would choose to sing another song that was pleasing to Him. Remember we don't fight thoughts with thoughts; we fight thoughts with words, The Word.

So now we have the task and responsibility to reprove our old way of thinking, allowing and inviting Holy Spirit to convict us. We might say He is going to convince us to desire the new way of life. God will change our desires when we sell out to Jesus. Holy Spirits job is to convince us that God's ways are higher than our ways and that what He says in His word He will do, He will definitely do.

Repentance is a legal and official transaction. Once the work of repentance is done it is recorded in the courts of heaven, and on file. So when the accuser shows up to accuse us, Jesus goes to that file cabinet and pulls out the book of life and there it is—our name, written and covered by His blood. The repented sins are no more, they no longer exist.

This record shows that our sin debt has been cancelled, being laid to His account, stamped paid in full (Colossians 2:13-15). Repentance and remission of our sin is official and binding. It is a legal transaction upheld by God Himself.

The work or redemption does not free us from consequences of sin. However, I want to add that I have been a recipient of this grace and I have seen this happen for others also. It is part of the amazing grace and work of God. Nothing is too hard for God. We pray and put all our trust in The One who has called and chosen us.

Sin leaves us with a debt that has to be paid. The plan of redemption is His work on the Cross, from the foundations of the world. Jesus shed His pure innocent blood for the remission of our sins. His blood covers and atones for our sins, blotting out our transgressions, once and for all. Now the law has been fulfilled in Christ. We are redeemed from the curse of the law of sin and death. The law of God is perfect; we are redeemed from the law of sin and death. These are separate and are not the same. We are not set free to use or abuse God's grace.

Scriptures tells us that God is not a man that He would lie nor the son of man that He should repent. The kingdom of God is legal, binding, strategic, and eternally official. The laws governing God's kingdom are perfect. These laws are permanent, perfect, lacking nothing, therefore His law cannot be added to. Kingdom laws are binding and eternal.

Another way to explain this giving us a visual is to say these laws are set in stone. Get it? On Mount Sinai, God carved out, and wrote on two stone tablets, with His finger, the Ten Commandments. The first set of commandments Moses threw down and broke when he descended from the mountain seeing the children of Israel in sin, worshipping the golden calf.

After dealing with the sin of the golden calf (Exodus 32), Moses returned up Mount Sinai, meeting again with God, saying to the children of Israel, perhaps I can make atonement for your sin. At this return, God required Moses to carve two tablets, God wrote the Ten Commandments, again, on stone with His finger. I find it very interesting and telling that God required Moses to chisel out the tablets the second time. When returning to meet God, God required Moses to chisel out the second set of tablets. He brought Moses into an even deeper relationship of accountability and responsibility. Think about this for a minute—Moses is told to bring two tablets when he returns. I believe there is a message in a message here. God will not do the work for us again. He does it once and it is perfect and complete!

After Adam and Eve's disobedience they were expelled from the garden. Had they been allowed to remain [after sinning and introducing sin to our nature] and eaten from the tree of life in their fallen condition there would be no redemption from sin. We would have lived eternally in death. So by expelling them and sending them out of the garden, God was protecting us. Boundaries are very important to God and His protection is perfect. And we know that Adam and Eve played the blame game. They did not truly repent however Eve did confess.

The law didn't come until it was given to Moses on Mount Sinai. The covenant came by Abraham. After receiving the promise of Isaac, Abraham was willing to offer him. But grace and truth came through Jesus Christ (John 1:17)

Now we get busy doing the work of repentance in order to be reprogrammed. Once we hear the gospel and believe there is (or should be) evidence by our changed behavior. This is fruits worthy of repentance also said to be the work of repentance. Our new creation must be reproved in order to appropriate the works of Jesus Christ and His fulfillment on the Cross. Jesus said repent for the kingdom of heaven is nigh. He didn't say repent because I said so. He didn't say repent because this is the right thing to do and you are a sorry no good dog, and you have wearied Me to the breaking point, you have let Us down and Holy Spirit is pretty sick of you too. Look what I had to do for you, can't you show some appreciation…

No, Jesus said repent because the kingdom of God is at hand. The kingdom of God was being reinstated and placed back into the hands of God's chosen people, His body, His called out ones. The Ecclesia, the called-out ones, His rightful heirs, and heirs to the promise. Now if you are children of God you are heirs and heirs of the kingdom of God. (Romans 8:17)

You are born again by believing with your heart that God raised Jesus from the dead and confessing with your mouth, you can appropriate the finished complete work of Jesus Christ on the cross. Baptism is an outward sign to the public that we are choosing to die to sin and desire to live a new resurrected life being raised with Christ. When we confess and believe that Jesus was crucified, dead, and buried, and that God raised Him from the dead after three days, and that we are sinners in need of a Savior, Jesus work on the Cross is transferred to our account. His perfect work is credited to our powerless, empty, and insufficient account.

"Having canceled the charge of our legal indebtedness, which stood against us and condemned us; He has taken it away, nailing it to the cross" (Colossians 2:14 NIV).

We cannot pay the price required for the remission of sin. The only payment God will accept is Jesus work, apart from accepting the work done by Jesus, no matter what we do, no matter how good we are. No matter how much good we do, no matter what works we add to our resume, no matter what, we cannot come close to paying the penalty for the debt we owe. Living in the right neighborhood, wearing expensive clothes, driving the newest limited edition… None of these things matter when sin is ignored. Only repentance clears the way.

The apostle Paul likened his work to dung and he wrote over half of the New Testament. Paul was at the top of the who's who in Rome. He knew and had memorized the entire writings' the five books of the Torah and sat at the feet of Gamaliel. The apostle Paul knew every word of the law, and likens his righteousness to dung or rubbish, probably quoting from the book of Isaiah. Isaiah prophesying says we all have become as an unclean thing, and all our righteousness is as filthy rags. His use of the word 'rags' needs to be understood, having profound meaning. What was the apostle Paul talking about when he referenced Isaiah and "filthy rags?" The Hebrew word is, (ukabeged ehdim, literally and like as rags of menstruation). He is referencing strips of cloth "rags" women used during their menstrual cycle. Women were considered unclean during their cycle. So he is really driving this point home. Our righteousness is as filthy rags compared to Gods requirement and Jesus finished work.

This is why we need a Savior. Only Jesus and His spotless blood, taken into heaven and placed on the mercy seat, and His stripes are the atoning work that is acceptable to our Father in Heaven. Only believe.

Jesus lives to make intercession to God, on behalf of all believers. This is a courtroom setting more legal, than anything on earth that we can compare it to (Hebrews 7:25).

Repentance and Jesus atonement makes all of our old nature and any residual evidence inadmissible in His court. We are forgiven. The charge is wiped from our record. All evidence is expunged from our account. Our sin is justified, just as if it never happened. Our willful disobedience and sin is wiped clean and cleansed by His perfect blood. We are reset back to factory settings. We have work that must be done to reprove our hearts and minds to His truths or rewrite the software. But now His Holy Spirit makes everything eternal come alive. We can see the gospel preached by watching the sun rise.

We have received remission of our sins through Jesus blood and His atoning work on the Cross. Praise God!

With these legal terms and transactions taking place in the courtroom of heaven, Satan no longer has any jurisdiction over you, none, nada, zilch, and zero. His evidence is erased. Praise God, It is not only inadmissible, it is forgiven, expunged, and we are justified and we can plead not guilty, being placed under the blood of Jesus the Messiah. God's grace teaches us to say no to ungodliness (Titus 2:11-12).

Now this is the kind of replacement theology we can talk about to others. Our old life is put to death and now we receive a new life in Christ Jesus. We are alive to God and dead to sin. We replace Satan's lies with God's immutable truth.

"Heaven and earth may pass away but the word of God endures forever. And we are born again by this word" (Mark 13:31).

Insurance companies offer different options when purchasing insurance. We can purchase replacement cost insurance or cost plus depreciation, or simple liability insurance. As Christians having done the work of repentance we have replacement cost, meaning that when the old (house, roof, siding, whatever was damaged) and needed replaced there isn't depreciation added. The insurance is based on replacement or construction value. We are guaranteed a new life in Christ Jesus. Hallelujah! This is something to rejoice about for the rest of our life. If we have been in a funk or feeling down this alone can bring us out of stinkin thinkin.

The hardest for me to forgive was myself first, and a few others that enjoyed the pain they inflicted on me. I didn't realize that by not completely forgiving them or myself, I was in essence telling God His plan was insufficient, that what Jesus did wasn't quite enough. I was saying that His eternal work of redemption was lacking on my part and not harsh enough to punish my sins and the sins of my so-called offenders. What arrogance and pride. I had no idea I was being self-righteous and prideful but I was. I believed I was helping God punish me while being sure we didn't let the others off the hook. I couldn't imagine being forgiven.

If you are struggling with forgiving yourself, I assure Jesus has paid for your sin(s) with His atoning work and if you confess from a broken heart and ask for His forgiveness, you will be and you are forgiven, no matter how many times it takes. If we think it isn't enough, well that my friend is self-righteous.

That is something you need to repent of, right now. We are going to take a minute and clarify again that repentance and asking Jesus into our heart to be our Savior is all He asks us to do We no longer have to eat from the dumpster when the table is set before our enemies. We have a place at our Master's table. Stop and close your eyes and picture the table of forgiveness before you.

"Blessed, He says, "are those whose iniquities have been forgiven, and whose sins have been covered over. Blessed is the man of whose sin the Lord will not take account" (Romans 4:7-8).

Maybe like me you have thought you deserved to be punished for what you have done and have been self-punishing by participating in wrong behaviors and relationships or self-sabotage. Sin brings death to self-esteem and leaves us with a warped perception of how we believe God sees us. Perhaps you have thought not forgiving yourself, while self-punishing is somehow appeasing to God. If you have believed this, I want to assure you it is a lie from the pit of hell. Ask me how I know. I did this for a long time. I knew that what I had done was awful and, in my terms, unforgivable. So with my limited ability to forgive myself, I expected God to hold my sins against me. I'm not sure what I thought about the Cross. I did not have any concept of the crucifixion of Jesus and why it had to be that way. God has done a perfect work for the price of sin through His only begotten Son, Jesus Christ. We cannot add, nor take away from His perfect work. The work is complete, it is perfect, and it is finished (John 19:30).

If you have been struggling to forgive someone who has hurt you, I assure you God saw and Jesus knows what they did. Jesus does not take kindly to His sheep being abused and He will recompense you.

Forgiving them does not let them off the hook. What it does is remove your hands from around their neck and allows God to vindicate you from all the wrong. Letting go and forgiving allows our Healer opportunity to work on our heart, setting us free from the damage done and the pain we carry from the memories. When holding on to old injuries and wounds we are attempting to extract payment for the wrong, this is revenge. God tells us, vengeance is His. It is like trying over and over to choke the life out of them while strangling and suffocating on the very thoughts.

"Don't take revenge, dear friends. Instead, let God's anger take care of it. After all, Scripture says, "I alone have the right to take revenge. I will pay back, says the Lord" (Romans 12:19 GWT).

God has purchased you (paying the price) and redeemed you so that you can be free to live for Him. What does it mean to live for God? What is God expecting of you? God knows that when you have a true born again experience you will be changed, you will have a deep desire to help others become free. You will worship Him and tell others of the wonderful works of God. That is why God will not put new wine in old wine skins; you will be bursting at the seams to tell of the marvelous works of God. Only new wine skins can expand with this gospel and revelation.

God redeems us for His service, and God calls us into a ministry. What ministry you may ask? Well brothers and sisters, we are called into the ministry of reconciliation. We must be completely free from guilt, condemnation, and all un-forgiveness, in order to operate effectively and powerfully with pure motives in this ministry and to help lead others out of Satan's trap.

So if anyone is in Christ, he is a new creature: the old state of things has passed away; a new state of things has come into existence. And all this is from God, who has reconciled us to Himself through Christ, and has appointed us to serve in the ministry of reconciliation. We are to tell how God was in Christ reconciling the world to Himself, not charging men's transgressions to their account (if they repent), and that He has entrusted to us the Message of this reconciliation. "On Christ's behalf therefore we come as ambassadors, God, as it were, making entreaty through our lips: we, on Christ's behalf, beseech men to be reconciled to God" (2 Corinthians 5:17-20 WNT).

The reason we must learn to appropriate Jesus' finished work on the Cross to our account and confess all our sins is to make it personal. A personal encounter is yours and no one can take it from you. We then become effective ministers of freedom to others. Those whom The Son sets free are free indeed.

Hebrew 6:1 says it this way: A BETER SACRIFICE: "Therefore, leaving the discussion of the elementary principles of Christ, let us go on to perfection not laying again the foundation of repentance from dead works and of faith toward God."

There is nothing more we can add to the work that Jesus did on the Cross. We must do a once and for all work of repentance to move into the things God has destined for us to do. You cannot think you need to repay God by doing works; no, we do good works because we love Him.

You realize and accept, then appropriate the work that Jesus did so that you can be free from guilt and condemnation. Once free you have no desire to repeat the evil deeds done in your flesh while in unbelief. Will you grieve? Yes of course you will. Will you wonder how God can be such a merciful Father (I certainly hope so) by forgiving your iniquity? Oh I pray you do. I encourage you to ask Him how He is so merciful. I believe He has a specific (very personal and intimate) way to let you know that you will understand. It is one of the ways He loves to make it personal, something just for you, from Him. It is your gift from Jesus that you reach out and receive. Maybe you've always been one that is there for others and do not know how to receive. If so pray and ask Jesus to teach you. You do not want to leave your gift or gifts unclaimed. You don't want Jesus to think His gift isn't wanted. Do not let it remain in an unclaimed merchandise bin.

Prayer:

Dear Heavenly Father, You are my redeemer and the God of my salvation, I need Your help in receiving my forgiveness. Help me understand Your love and how to appropriate the works of Your dear Son Jesus Christ in my life and allow me to see me through Your eyes..

Lord Jesus You are my Savior and I am saved by You and for You. How do I become a new creation, how do I walk this out? Help me read and understand Your atoning work for me. I want to take this work personally because You died for me that I may be free. I proclaim I will read Your word. I will study to show myself approved by God, a workman not ashamed rightly dividing the word of God (2 TIMOTHY 2:15). I will not be held in bondage to religious dead works any longer. I do not want one gift you have for me to remain in the unclaimed merchandise bin. (*See pledge on page 347*).

Reflection:

What has Satan had you believe that God would not wipe away and that you could never be forgiven for? Read Hebrews 8:12 out loud.

What does God word say in 2 Corinthians 5:17?

I want to add here that there is a deep work of repentance that you will never repent of again. God has something He desires for us. To be changed our eyes have to be opened, yes, we should sorrow and grieve deeply over our sinful actions. His word describes to us that there is a sorrow produced with repentance that is a once and for all, or never to be repented of again.

For the kind of sorrow God wants us to experience leads us away from sin and results in salvation. There's no regret for that kind of sorrow. But worldly sorrow, which lacks repentance, results in spiritual death (2 Corinthians 7:10 NLT).

We can become buried with guilt and depression and this is not pleasing to God. He has offered us grace and forgiveness through repentance. Grief and gratitude can both be working simultaneously. We can grieve for our sins while being grateful for His amazing grace at the same time.

The willful act of sin is what we are turning away from and changing our mind about sinful living. I don't know what that sin is for you; it is between you and our Father, but He knows and He is faithful to forgive you and cleanse you from all unrighteousness if you confess.

However, we should desire to live a repentant life and be sensitive to The Spirit. As I prayed and sought the Lord about this, I believe He gave me this illustration, and I share with you, what He showed me.

Often when others do not understand repentance, they think I am suggesting bondage and groveling forever attempting to place them under the law . No there is a onetime work, but we must remain sensitive to Holy Spirit and be willing to apologize (change course) for short sightedness and other sins. We realize we are going to mess up, of course we realize this. His grace covers our sins but do not devalue His grace and think we don't have to see and acknowledge our wrongs. Anything less would be foolish but we do not think it's chalked up to grace. We need to recognize we missed the mark and adjust our thinking to agree with the word.

The illustration The Lord gave me was as follows: It is like in a marriage covenant messing up doesn't nullify the covenant. We do not dissolve the union; we have a vow with the other person. We do not nullify or throw the marriage out and say okay it's over and then go through the whole ceremony process, time and time again.

There are growing stages and learning times required while growing up into the Head which is Christ. Just as we grow physically so we grow spiritually, seedtime and harvest. Being insensitive or messing up doesn't mean the marriage or a family relationship is null and void. But it does require that you bring a sacrifice. Sacrificing our pride on the altar of obedience can be very humbling and extremely difficult, especially when we believe we are right. But when we retrain and turn to His ways, our lives become so peaceful. We desire and value the relationship over self and peace over pride and take the sacrifice of sincerity and deliver an apology to the other party. We own our part and become willing to work through the damage to restore intimacy to the union. This is repentance. This is how we live a repentant lifestyle.

Becoming a Christian does not insure we will not sin but once we have received salvation we have the promise He will neither leave nor forsake us. 1 John 1:8-9. If we say we have no sin we deceive ourselves, and the truth is not in us.

"I will make an everlasting covenant with them: I will never turn away from doing good to them, and I will put My fear in their hearts so that they will never turn away from Me" (Jeremiah 32:40).

This sounds like the marriage vow to me, does it to you? For better or worse, sickness and health and until death do we part? And doesn't it sound like we are going to have to work this out to have peace in the house?

The good news for believers and those who have received the salvation of the Lord is that for us death means to be face to face with our Lord and share with Him for eternity. Nothing can separate us from the Love God has for us, we are his beloved. Read all of Romans chapter 8.

When you go through deep waters, I will be with you. When you go through rivers of difficulty, you will not drown. When you walk through the fire of oppression, you will not be burned up; the flames will not consume you (Isaiah 43:2 NLT).

Oh trust me, we will mess up, you can count on it. But like a marriage we want to immediately apologize and set the record straight. God doesn't throw the covenant with us away when we sin. He has made a way for us to be restored back to our right standing simply by saying; I have sinned against You and others and I desire to make it right.

This I say therefore, and testify in the Lord, that you should no longer walk as the rest of the Gentiles, in the futility of their mind. Having their understanding darkened, being alienated from the life of God, because of the blindness of their heart; who being past feeling, have given themselves over to lewdness to work all uncleanness with greediness. But you have not so learned Christ (Ephesians 4:17-19).

If indeed you have heard Him and have been taught by Him, put away lying, "Let each one of you speak truth with his neighbor," for we are members of one another. Be angry and do not sin, do not let the sun go down on your wrath, nor give place to the devil, let him who stole steal no longer, but rather let him labor working with his hands what is good, that he may have something to give him who has need. Let no corrupt word proceed out of your mouth but what is good for necessary edification, that it may impart grace to the hearers.

And do not grieve the Holy Spirit of God, by whom you were sealed for the day of redemption. Let all bitterness wrath and anger, clamor, and evil speaking be put away from you with all malice. And be kind to one another, tenderhearted, forgiving one another, even as God in Christ forgave you (Ephesians' 4:17-32).

Prayer:

Oh Father I am so sorry for _____. I ask that You accept my apology for _____. I understand that my pride must be laid on the altar. You are the all consuming fire, burn away anything that is not pleasing to You. Show me how to remain sensitive to Your Holy Spirit and like King David become a master repenter or Baal Teshuvah. Amen.

Reflection:

When we sin who and what are you truly sinning against? Read
Psalm 51. Tell the Lord what you want to confess to Him.

_____

_____

_____

OH TASTE AND SEE

Oh taste and see that The Lord is good
    His love endures forever
    Look and see the great things He has done for you
    Our Lord, Most High from heaven

When in reflection
    Take time to trace
    The mercies the favor
    Unmerited grace

Making Yourself known
    Right before our eyes
    You are The Lord Almighty
    Trusting in You we can rely

Showing up each time
    We do grumble and groan
    Thinking of Your favor
    Likening it to a loan

Willingly receiving, while
    In dread of the interest rate
    Thinking to borrow
    While bartering our fate

How many times did we dare say
    If You will do this, I'll do that
    Like a Dr Seuss book
    The Cat in the Hat Comes Back

You are our Rewarder
    Desiring only to be found
    Leaving many signs
    Blessings softly sprinkled around

If we continue on
    Seeking earnestly we find
    Yes, diligently seek You
    You were there all the time

We thought it a transaction
    Like a business deal
    You require covenant
    A relationship seal

Believe in our heart
    Confess with our tongue
    The Lord Jesus Christ
    He is the Only One

The Way and The Truth
    His Life our reward
    Eternity in heaven
    What a day to look toward

So we will not be afraid
  Or wonder if You care
  Our stock is riches in heaven
  This is the believers share

© laurette laster 2018 April

"In my desperation I prayed, and the Lord listened; He saved me from all my troubles. For the angel of the Lord is a guard; He surrounds and defends all who fear him Taste and see that the Lord is good. Oh, the joys of those who take refuge in Him! Fear the Lord, you His godly people, for those who fear Him will have all they need.

The Lord hears His people when they call to Him for help. He rescues them from all their troubles" (Psalm 34:6-9,17 NLT).

"Now without faith it is impossible to please God, for the one who draws near to Him must believe that He exists and rewards those who seek Him" (Hebrews 11:6 Holman Christian Bible).

DAY 14

"THOSE WHOM I LOVE, I reprove and discipline, so be zealous and repent" (Revelation 3:19).

This is the message given to John the revelator, for the churches, during his vision, unveiling and disclosure, of the revelation of Jesus Christ. The Bible is clear that to those who do not receive chastisement from the Father's Spirit, they are illegitimate or to put it another way they are counterfeits. We shouldn't say they are counterfeit Christians though. In order to call yourself or someone else a Christian, you would need to see by their actions they are working the works of Christ. James, the half-brother of Jesus tells us to be doers of the word, not hearers only (James 1:22).

Ephesians 5:1-5 verses tell us "therefore be imitators of God as dear children." To be called a Christian you must be a child of God. These verses explain what it is to imitate God and the behavior or fruit we should look for in someone we call a Christian. The behavior is likened to fruit visible on a tree by which you can know what kind of tree you have.

The term Christian was first used in the books of Acts. The Pharisees began calling those that followed Jesus Christ, Christians. The meaning was they were acting like Jesus. This term is like saying you act like your parents and using the terminology "oh they are a little ____." So a Christian is someone who believes and lives out the principles doctrines of the kingdom: exhibiting to the best of their ability the works that have been paid for by Christ Jesus. A believer becomes a child of God realizing the price of Jesus life, and His obedience on the Cross. This is how we become Heirs of salvation and heirs of the promise.

Hebrews 12:6 in The Contemporary English Version says it like this. "The Lord corrects the people He loves and disciplines those He calls His own." So with this scripture, we realize that if God loves us and if we are His children, like a loving earthly father, He will discipline and correct us.

Why does a father discipline his children? There are many reasons. To keep them safe, to help them mature, to teach them wisdom and guidance, to help them become a responsible member of society, and the list goes on and on. With this being said, why would our Heavenly Father discipline us or chastise us?

Why would Jesus tell those in the church that they needed to repent, then explain, "Those I love I discipline or chastise?" In this scripture Jesus is not addressing unbelievers but those who are missing their calling.

If you haven't asked Jesus into your heart yet, what are you waiting for? If you are ready, say and read this prayer out loud. If you have already made Jesus your Lord and Savior offer this prayer as a petition for a loved one who needs salvation, and pray it forward. We cannot receive salvation for someone but we can pray and petition heaven to move on their behalf. When you pray this prayer Holy Spirit immediately translates you into Jesus Christ. This is an immediate transfer and you become a new creation. (*See salvation vow on page 347*).

Pray this out loud.

Dear Lord Jesus, I am a sinner. I believe you came to die for my sins and to be my savior. I believe. I ask You to be my Redeemer and the Savior of my soul. I believe You went to the Cross, that You died for my sins. I believe God raised You from the dead and that You are alive. Jesus, I am a sinner and I want to receive Your forgiveness and spend eternity with You in heaven when I die. I believe in my heart You are The Risen Lord, and now I have believed and have confessed with my mouth that I want you to forgive me for my sins. I ask You Lord Jesus to be my Savior and my Lord, forever Amen. (Read Romans 10:8-11 and Romans 8:12-16).

Remember, repent means to change your mind, the Greek word, *metanoia,* is to change what you think. So is it possible someone could be doing good works but missing the mark? I think the answer to this question is absolutely YES.

I believe the reason God chastises us has a deeper purpose and plan. If God wanted to punish us for being wrong or make us suffer for what we have done He could leave us where we are. According to the apostle Paul this is a kingdom principle that should be instituted by the church, the believers. In his letters to the Corinthians he tells them to put such a one out for the crucifying of the flesh. He also describes how he turned one over to Satan for the crucifying of the flesh and perhaps the salvation of their soul.

I believe God allows us to remain in some situations so that we get sick and tired of living in the pig pen (Luke 15:11-32).

Before being saved, we are dead in our sins and trespasses and without hope. I was doing a great job punishing myself how about you? The guilt I was dragging around made me a door mat.

The discipline God uses requires changes in our thinking and will alter our direction. Why do we need to change? Because the change God is working in our life, is aligning us with His purpose for His "good" pleasure. And I can promise you this, it is and will be exceedingly abundantly more than you can think or ask. But it will require hard work, changing your mind, and being developed because now our spirit desires change, so we hunger and thirst as Christ describes in Matthew 5. It requires effort and determination and hard work. The good news is heaven is backing us and cheering us on. You may feel all alone in the earth but there is a grandstand counting on you to run and win your leg of the race by keeping your eyes on Jesus the 'Author and Perfecter' of our faith, as they did.

"Therefore, since we are surrounded by such a huge crowd of witnesses to the life of faith, let us strip off every weight that slows us down, especially the sin that so easily trips us up. And let us run with endurance the race God has set before us" (Hebrews 12:1 NLT).

It does not bring God pleasure to see the wicked suffer. Isn't that an interesting thought? Perhaps you have been waiting for judgment and sentencing for your own transgressions and inequity. God longs to redeem mankind and bring us back to right standing with Him. Only through confession of sins and repentance, is there hope for right standing with God. This is only attained by receiving Jesus as our Lord and Savior. The work He did at Calvary and the price He paid at the Cross and His crucifixion is the only payment God will accept. There is no other way by which a person can be saved, except the work of His only beloved Son by which He wrought salvation.

Acts 4:12 "Neither is there salvation in any other: for there is none other name under heaven given among men, whereby we must be saved" (KJV).

Prayer:

Dear Heavenly Father, Father of our Lord Jesus Christ I repent for not understanding Your ways. Help me to align with Your purposes. Father I ask for eyes that see and perceive. Give me the perception to understand what I hear. As I read Your word, teach me. My heart cries out to hear from You. I am listening. Thank You for my salvation, my redemption, and my forgiveness by the blood of Jesus. In Jesus precious name, Amen

Reflection:

Where will you spend your quiet time with The Lord? (Turn to the back of the book and sign and remove your commitment card to read the Bible and have quiet time with God daily. Date it and use it as a book-marker and a reminder).

Write down the plans for reading and meditation and prayer.

_____

_____

_____

POETRY: THE SHARPENING

Painful as it may seem
   But necessary it is
   A ripping may be felt
   To uncover the part that is His

So if we feel a shredding
   Don't fear or be dismayed
   It's only the sharpening process
   He wants to work in us today

He is going to peel back that hard cover
   And reveal a special message
   In the sharpener we will see
   The shredding revealed the lesson

So take some time to write it down
    For in the process of time
    Looking back we'll understand
    The sharpening is His perfect design

For we are His own workmanship
    Written upon His heart
    Don't give up or worry
    He is faithful to complete what He did start.

© laurette laster 2018

Without sharpening the lead, the pencils designed purpose would never be revealed. We cannot understand what He has placed inside of us without being sharpened [shredded] and allowing God to break off the hard outer self.

"Being confident of this very thing, that He who has begun a good work in you will complete it until the day of Jesus Christ" (Philippians 1:6 NKJV).

    "He who calls you is faithful, who also will do it" (1 Thessalonians 5:24 NIV).

DAY 15

"But if a wicked person turns away from all his or her sins that he or she has committed and keeps all My statutes and does what is just and right, he or she shall surely live; he or she shall not die. None of the transgressions that he or she has committed shall be remembered against him or her; for the righteousness that he or she does shall live. Have I any pleasure in the death of the wicked, declares the Lord God, and not rather that he or she should turn from his way and live?" (Ezekiel 18:21-23 ESV).

We are born with potential and purpose. God has given us an assignment for the advancement of His kingdom and for His "Good" pleasure. I am not suggesting nor am I teaching predestination or that there is a blue print for your life, with a playbook that you must find or forever be lost and in sin, but there is a purpose for your existence. God requires that we be fruitful; this is to help further His kingdom. I also believe that when we align with our assignment, we have peace and tenacity to endure hardship.

That ye might walk worthy of the Lord unto all pleasing, being fruitful in every good work, and increasing in the knowledge of God (Colossians 1:10).

What are your passions and what do you love to do? I believe we find our purpose connected to what we are passionate about. We find that what the enemy is using against us and what he uses to ensnare us will hinder us from fulfilling that very purpose. Remaining in sin and ignorance of God's ways is like driving in a fog. This lack of knowledge and limited vision is holding you back.

If you could do anything in the world and not have to worry about failing or the financing, or what other's thought, what would you want to do? What do you desire to be? Keep it simple. What is a desire in your heart? Maybe get sober, or be more devoted to your family, or hold down a job and be a trusted employee. Maybe you would return to the Lord with your whole heart and start over. Maybe you would get that GED or finish that college degree or do your part to repair a broken relationship etc. Never stop dreaming. God has placed a desire in your heart that is from Him and Him alone. Only when we give God permission to remove our heart of stone is the desire manifested and recognized in our new heart of flesh.

God's correction is always done with love never humiliation. If we do not humble ourselves under the mighty hand of God, we can be certain Satan will humiliate us with our sin.

Perhaps you had a harsh earthly father or mother or role model. Often in this case, condemnation, humiliation, harsh punishment, and otherwise demeaning correction can become normal to us. If this is the case, you may have learned to dislike or hate yourself. You may be overly critical and over examine your mistakes or shortcomings. Our self-talk begins to be negative and demeaning. Sounding more like the accuser of the brethren than what God thinks of us.

Harsh punishment that is demeaning damages our soul. We cannot love others if we do not have a balanced love of our selves. Not love of self but love for self and what God had in mind when He created us. Jeremiah 29:11

When we dislike ourselves and over exaggerate our shortcomings it is possible to become hopeless. If you did not receive right discipline and/or explanations about why you were being punished, or what you did wrong accompanied with fair expectations of what was expected, you may think harsh punishment is warranted and deserving and become self-punishing. Or worse yet, hate all discipline and become bitter. Either is very dangerous. Balance is the key to godly living and what The Father expects from us.

We had family members that were super (spooky) spiritual. Everything was a sign or of the devil. Then we had family members that were pretty rough with almost no godly behavior evident. The funny thing was both thought they were right or okay, and all were believers to one extent or the other.

One morning during prayer, The Lord showed me a bowling alley lane. Looking to the left side, He said, what is that? I said it's a gutter. Then showing me the right side, He said, what is that? I said it is a gutter too. Then I got it. I had been praying for His wisdom concerning this and this was His perfect answer. To The Lord, either extreme is a gutter ball. If we act so spiritual that others cannot relate and always fear stepping over the line, or act like heathens, repelling others, neither pleases our Father.

Thank goodness God helps us understand. Understanding and balance are key issues in the work of repentance. There is a why, there is a how, there is a what, and then there is a now, that the work is done. Jesus has done the work that paid for our salvation. His death and resurrection paid a debt He didn't owe and covers our debt we couldn't pay.

So now that we are saved and the work is done, have you wondered why did God save me?

"Because of the LORD's great love we are not consumed, for his compassions never fail" (Lamentations (3:22 NIV)

God longs for His children to have wisdom and understanding. Proverbs chapter one tells us wisdom calls out. "Have you heard that fear of the Lord is the beginning of knowledge or wisdom?" (Proverbs 1:7).

"Wisdom calls aloud outside; she raises her voice in the open squares. She cries out in the chief concourses, at the opening of the gates of the city" (Proverbs 1:20-21 NKJV).

Gates what gates? What are our gates? Where are our gates? What and where is our city? We are not talking about a physical location or a town or city limit markings. We are talking about gaining wisdom. The Bible uses metaphors to get us to think and to be able to relate. When you were young, I bet you at one time or another did, connect the dots paper. Connect the dots is an activity using numbers. When the numbers are followed you draw a line from number to number and you create a picture or a design by following the numbers in sequence. At first it may look like a jumbled mess. It appears to be a bunch of numbers scattered randomly on a page, but about halfway through you begin to see a design coming into view. That is how God works.

You get your first number and have to search for the next number. While scanning the page you become a little more familiar with the page and then remember, oh I saw that number. Then you can locate the next number easily. Our gates are our eyes, our ears, and our mouth. Our heart and our mind is our city, we need to learn to protect them and guard them. When doing the work of repentance, we must repent for what has been coming into our gates and replace our swept and cleansed heart and mind with the word and knowledge of The Father. I used to say when reaching for my Bible, "Father knows best." Some of you may be old enough to remember this show. Some of you may not be but you have Google. Go check it out. I was determined whatever the Bible said I was going to do it. And I was going to learn to love it no matter what.

Prayer:

Dear Heavenly Father, help me to do the work of cleansing and purifying my gates with Your word. Like Nehemiah my city walls were torn down by the enemy. I want to do my part of rebuilding the walls of safety and closing my gates to anything that displeases You. I want to be a worker in the repairing of the walls and not be distracted.

Like Nehemiah I will build with one hand and be war ready with the sword of Spirit which is Your word in the other. I realize You have a plan for my life. I have been so wrong about You and Your ways.

Teach me. Chastise me; teach me to become teachable so I can connect the dots. Cleanse me, wash me and I will be pure. Amen

Reflection:

Do you feel the conviction from The Lord concerning a behavior? What has defiled your gates? List the areas that have defiled your gates and then repent and ask for God to forgive each one. Do not forget you have done good things also. When you list ways your gates have been used for immoral lusts, list one good thing you have done also. Keep it balanced. Remember the key is balance in repentance, not self loathing.

_____

_____

_____

POETRY: THE WAYS OF GOD

Your words are wonderful and full of glory
    Written and heard all throughout Your story
    A book given and written by inspiration
    To tell of Your works to the generations

The children of Israel knew Your acts
    But with Moses Your ways became facts
    Following Your voice, He did lead
    For forty years a friend to You indeed

Face to face You were in tent of meeting
    Your glory would come down, cover sheeting
    His eyes and mind from people and distraction
    Keeping his focus on hearing commands for action.

Teach us the "Ways" that we should go
    So into Your image and likeness we may grow.
    Show us how to be Face to Face friends
    With You mighty Father from beginning to end

Revelation—interpretation—edification
    Calling out to me for my sanctification
    Found in right place, time for aligning
    During this time, this season of assigning

© laurette laster 2017

"Lord, listen to my prayer. It's like a sacrifice I bring to You: I must have more revelation of Your word!" (Psalms 119:169, TPT).

DAY 16

"I HAVE BLOTTED out like a thick cloud, your transgressions, and like a cloud your sins. Return to Me, for I have redeemed you" (Isaiah 44:22 NKJV).

Without an understanding of God's chastisements, you may think He is angry at you. In order that God may delight in us, there must change. First and foremost, our thinking is what has to change. When how we think changes, what we believe changes, then our desires change. When our desires change our actions change. Make no mistake, God hates sin but He deeply loves us, the sinner.

His desire and the purpose of Jesus death on the cross is that we may be reconciled and forgiven. We might think of it as being in right standing or put back in our right mind.

If you believe you deserve punishment, the enemy will deceive you. The enemy can wreak havoc in the life of someone burdened down with guilt and shame when we do not understand the ways of God. Without proper understanding you may believe God is withholding good from you. The enemy duped me for many years. God is love; He is the redeemer of our souls. God desires to redeem our lives from destruction, not into destruction. However God has stipulations, He requires all us, not a fraction, He doesn't want us playing church on Sunday morning. He has redeemed us from the hand of the enemy. He paid the purchase price. He wants to Shepherd His sheep (Read Luke 15:1-10).

Have you ever purchased something in need of repair? You know it needed a little TLC or tender loving care. If you have you probably had something in mind when you purchased it. Maybe you know what it was originally intended for. Or perhaps you had a plan for the item and knew just what it needed.

God knows the heart and mind of His creation. The Bible tells us who can know the heart, it is deceitful above all else. We are born in a broken world and sin messed up the programming. We have been programmed to believe wrong and think we are born a certain way. Sin is sin. Wrong is wrong. All rebellion is against the heart of love for The Father.

Matthew 12:30 and Luke 11:23 Jesus says; "you are with Me or against Me." Jesus explains if we do not gather with Him, we are scattering. Your actions show and decide which side you're on. You must be for Him and if you are not for Jesus, well, you know.

Gates and locked doors are very important in the safety of our valued possessions. The lack of gates or unguarded gates allow for scattering. Think of your thoughts like sheep. You shepherd your sheep. You keep the gates secured to keep them safe. You are the watchman or keeper of your thoughts.

When Satan comes to bombard your thoughts, and he will, you have to fight thoughts with words. Beware that you do not attempt to think through these times. The word of God is alive and powerful. Satan hates when believers know and believe the word. Satan knows the word of God, so how much more we must believe and know the word. Satan deceived Eve by twisting God's commandment given to Adam. His questioning what God said caused Eve to enter in conversation with him and entertain the thought of doubting God also. Satan attempted to deceive Jesus in the same way in the wilderness but Jesus knew the word and believed the word, and spoke, "it is written" then Jesus recited the scripture out loud to Satan. Jesus is the word. Jesus told Satan, it is written. In quoting the verses, Jesus tore down the temptations and the lies while saying out loud, "IT IS WRITTEN." When fighting the lies of Satan, you should have scriptures that you can say, "it is written." Remember when He, The Spirit of Truth comes He will guide you into all truth. Thy word is truth. God will cause scripture to jump off the page and bring it back to your mind when you are in a spiritual fight.

The work of repentance requires that you understand God's love for you. Jesus died so that you and I can be redeemed. Redeemed is buying back or taking back possession of property. Redeemed is to be brought back into right relationship. You are redeemed.

It is time to put this principle into practice. Say it out loud.

It is written, Ephesians 1:7 *"In You Jesus I have redemption through Your blood, the forgiveness of sins, in accordance with the riches of God's grace."*

It is written, 1 John 1:9 *"If I confess my sins, You are faithful and just and will forgive my sins and purify me from all unrighteousness."*

It is written, Jeremiah 31:34 *"You have forgiven my wickedness and remember my sins no more."*

Prayer:

Dear Heavenly Father, I repent for not believing You. Open my mind to study Your word. Make the word come alive in me as I read and pray. Open my ears to hear what You are saying to me. Thank You for loving me and redeeming me from the hand of the enemy. Thank You for forgiving my wicked ways and not remembering my sins. I want to know more about Your forgiveness for me and how to forgive others. Dear Jesus, thank You for dying for my sins, I can be forgiven. You died for me, help me to live for You. Amen

Reflection:

What is something you can think of that has been stolen from you. Maybe your trust, what about your innocence? Maybe you have been abandoned and your ability to understand the security of love has been stolen. Think about it and write down some things you believe the enemy has to repay you sevenfold for. God says He will restore to us. Ask The Lord to lead you into understanding how to pray concerning this.

"Instead of shame and dishonor, you will enjoy a double share of honor. You will possess a double portion of prosperity in your land, and everlasting joy will be yours" (Isaiah 61:7 NLT).

"The enemy must repay sevenfold. But if he is found, he shall restore sevenfold; he shall give up all the goods of his house" (Proverbs 6:31KJV)

What has the enemy stolen from you? As you list these you are bringing a legal accusation and making a list of what must be restored to you.

_____

_____

_____

POETRY: CHILD OF GOD

Child of God
    How you grow
    Child of God
    Do you know

Child of God
    Stay the course
    Until the day
    You find The Force

Young man of God
    My how you've grown
    Young man of God
    Coming into your own

Young man of God
    He has invested in you
    Warrior on the inside
    Coming into view

Young woman of God
 My how you've bloomed
 Young warrior of God
 Always make room

Young woman of God
 The Lord has gifted you
 Young princess warrior
 Do you recognize it too

Mighty man of valor
 God loves a return
 On His investment
 Continue to yearn

Mighty gentleman of God
 With you well pleased is He
 You've lived your life
 To see others set free

Mentoring and helping
 Being strong safe arms
 For those young men
 Who've dealt with harm

Mighty woman of God
 Oh look at the fruit
 For His investment
 He can compute

Mighty woman of God
 My how you've sown
 The kingdom of God
 Many others call home

Men and women of God
> Don't you dare give in
> No matter the battle
> It is for God we win!

The fields indeed are bright
> White now unto harvest
> The work looked futile
> When it was the farthest

Man and woman of God
> Look around what do you see
> Return on the Fathers investment
> For eternal equity

© laurette laster

"Blessed is the man who listens to Me, Watching daily at My gates, Waiting at the posts of My doors. For whoever finds Me finds life, and obtains favor from The Lord!" (Proverbs 8: 34-35, NKJV).

"If you wait at wisdom's doorway, longing to hear a word for every day, joy will break forth within in you as you listen for what I'll say. For the fountain of life pours into you every time that you find Me, and this is the secret of growing in the delight and the favor of The Lord" (Proverbs 8:34-35, TPT).

DAY 17

"And Jesus answered them, "Those who are well have no need of a physician, but those who are sick. I have not come to call the righteous but sinners to repentance" (Luke 5:31-32).

"Therefore if anyone is in Christ, he is a new creation. The old has passed away; behold, the new has come" (2 Corinthians 5:17).

If by keeping the law, you or I or anyone could do the works required to make us righteous Jesus would not have gone to the cross and had to die the awful death of crucifixion to pay our debt. When you realize you need a Savior, new life and repentance will have eternal value and meaning to you.

I love watching craftsmen at work. Men and women who have been given gifts to build and create are amazing to watch. They see in their minds eye the finished project, often before we have any idea what they are crafting. We can't tell them what they are doing because we don't know what they have in mind. They have a vision that they are looking at while working and building.

Is it the same with God? For us to be telling God what should and shouldn't be happening would be foolish. When Holy Spirit begins to show us all that The Lord has in mind for our life it should blow our mind. We should be amazed and shocked more than others, but yet by faith we believe knowing it is right on.

It is exciting and mind blowing. When this happens, you will say I can't do that. Just remember, if it isn't bigger than you, it isn't God. You don't know what He has in mind. While artist are working sometimes it is impossible to know what they are creating. Then when they are finished it is an amazing transformation. Well what about the great Creator? What about His work and transformations?

Romans 12:1-3 tell us to not be conformed to this world but to be transformed by the renewing of our minds. The word of God is where we begin to see the masterpiece God is intending to design.

God had something special in mind when He created you. You have purpose, if you are willing and if you repent. Jesus said repent for the kingdom of God is at hand. What did Jesus mean by this statement?

Repentance is the key that unlocks the door into God's kingdom. This is His kingdom, and His rules apply. Until we confess and repent, Satan, can undermine any attempts at our future. If the enemy causes us to feel guilty, shamed, useless, or whatever other failure we believe, we will quit or give up, thinking we don't measure up. I can tell you right now, in the flesh we do not measure up, so we can put that thought to rest. We are redeemed, forgiven, restored, and we are loved by God Himself. We are a new creation, created in His image and likeness, as many as our led by God they are children of God. We have a new identity and in Jesus our Lord and Savior, we are more than conquerors. If God be for us who can be against us? This doesn't mean we won't struggle it means we reprove our old thinking and realize God loves us and we belong to Him and He is able to perfect what concerns us.

We must follow His rules if we are going to receive what He has for us. God is sovereign. Look at the sun, the moon, and the seasons. His work is perpetual, eternal (was, is and will be) and God is sovereign.

Prayer:

Oh my Heavenly Father, I have so much to learn. I have wasted so much time; I have lost time that I want redeemed.

Your word tells me in Joel 2:25-26 that you will restore to me what has been eaten up, and that You redeem the time. Teach me and help me as I learn to trust You. Show me who You are to me, Oh Sovereign God and concerned Father. I love You. Amen

Reflection:

What are some things you believe about God? Good or Bad. Lift these up to God and ask Him if your thoughts and beliefs are right. Listen in the coming days for the answers write down what He impresses upon your heart. Beware of the enemies lies that try to creep in.

_____

_____

_____

AS YOU GO

Poetry: As You Go

Pay attention to the signs
    Along the paths you walk
    Some are smooth and pleasing,
    Others hard as rock

Pay attention to the scenery
    While going along your way
    There are many, many signs
    Speaking, as if to say

Yes this is the way
    Or do not venture here
    Others seemingly shouting
    Run, take cover, danger is near

While we must be able
    To discern as we travel
    Wisdom first in the heart

Into the mind it goes to unravel

Thoughts locked down
    Unable to bend
    Will create a life
    That has to mend

Take to the highway
    Look for the sign
    Legal U Turn-
    It's been here all the time

Teach my heart
    Oh Lord to discern
    No more to hold on
    How to unlearn

The ways of man
    The road I followed
    Now seem barren, hard
    Empty, shallow, and hollow

Tutor my heart
    As I turn these pages
    Learning from The Law
    Prophets and Sages

Searching and listening
    Inspired word pouring in
    This is "The Way" and
    And how to begin

I'm following directions
    Looking for the signs
    "The Way" marked correction

Good for the heart changes the mind

Lord, You have patiently waited
    When I lagged sluggishly behind
    Loving me even when
    I was deaf, mute, and blind

Grant to me new vision,
    Light shining on my path
    Seeing clearly now, Jesus
    In Your love, no fear of wrath

© laurette laster 2018

"Every scripture has been inspired by the Holy Spirit, the breath of God. It will empower you by instruction and correction, giving you the strength to take the right direction and lead you deeper into the path of godliness. Then you will be God's servant, fully mature and perfectly prepared to fulfill any assignment God gives you" (2Timothy 3:16-17 TPT).

DAY 18

"IF WE CONFESS OUR SINS, He is faithful and just to forgive us our sins and to cleanse us from all unrighteousness" (1 John 1:9).

In 2003, I purchased my first home after going through a divorce. For many reasons I lived with my mom from March 2001 until moving into this home in June 2003. It was a quaint two-story house, nestled between two Christian couples. The neighborhood was calm and quiet and had the cozy feel of country charm, but it set right inside the city limits. I felt safe. I knew the house was supposed to be mine.

I learned more spiritual truths and kingdom principles while cosmetically restoring this property and doing repairs, more than I imagined possible. This house would be an assignment and an appointment of learning His ways, in ways I could never have learned otherwise. And now I am about to learn new and exciting things. Hmmmm

"And houses full of good things that you didn't put there. The LORD will give you wells that you didn't have to dig, and vineyards and olive orchards that you didn't have to plant. But when you have

eaten so much that you can't eat any more, beware that you do not forget the LORD who brought you out" (Deuteronomy 6:11 CEV).

My first home came with several opportunities. The previous occupants were angry at having to leave the home. The owner decided it best to sell the property that was a family inheritance. The occupants (family members also) were angry at the owner for selling the house which now required them to relocate. In their anger they took down light fixtures to take with them. They dug up plants including crepe myrtle trees when they left. So needless to say, there was work to do. New carpet, light fixtures, and painting made this home move in ready. This home was my refuge and place of healing and peace. I had so much peace in this house.

On one of my first times there while getting the home live in ready, I had put twin beds together in the middle bedroom. After putting sheets and the comforter on them I snuggled down in one of the beds and drifted off into a deep sleep. When I awoke, four hours later, I was totally surprised. I thought oh no I wasted time that I should have been putting things away but something supernatural had transpired during my sleep, I knew it was supernatural. You see, I couldn't remember ever resting like this. The peace in this home was also recognized and experienced by others.

Yes, I prayed over my home, and yes, I anointed every square inch with prayer and oil, but mostly I consecrated this home to my Lord, and asked Him to live there with me. I knew this was supposed to be my home.

I actually didn't win highest bid on this home, a young couple had. I had looked at many homes, most turnkey, or move in ready. One home even had a beautiful in ground pool and was in my price range. So why this home, what was different about this house and property? But there was something different about this home and I knew the day I pulled into the drive, something was different. This home called to me. I am still amazed how God is in every minute detail.

I loved the feeling that overtook me the moment I stepped on the property. I immediately grabbed my cell phone and called my realtor. She said, "Laurette I am looking at the MLS and there isn't a home for sale on Old Denton Road." I said, "I am standing in the yard looking at the for-sale sign." Yes, you guessed it; they had just put the sign in the yard thirty minutes prior to God pointing this property out to me. He led me to this property even before they had time to list it on the MLS.

Sitting on my mom's porch with my morning coffee, praying about house hunting, I told the Lord, "Lord I really thought that was the house but I am willing to keep searching." To be honest, as any of you that have been here before will understand, I was overwhelmed looking at houses. Home shopping can be stimulating and exhausting. Newly divorced in my mid-forties, starting over, and unaware of what my future held, at times was overwhelming. Do not get me wrong, it was super exciting but remember I've stepped out into Him by faith; and did I mention I'm between jobs; I didn't have a job when this house came. I remember the disappointment I felt the day I got the call hearing my bid wasn't the highest or the winning bid. I was certain it was my home. As I set praying my mom stepped outside the door and handed me the phone. She said it is Cheryl, who just happened to be my realtor. I thought she had found another prospective property for me to look at. But that isn't what she said. This is what she said, "The first buyers have backed out and no one knows why. Yours was the second highest bid, the house is yours if you still want it." Yes, I said yes to the address. Of course I wanted this house, so I said yes.

I would come to question my decision of purchasing this home over others during the different and extremely trying stages of repair. Why hadn't one of the other move-in-ready homes called to me? Because He had plans and I needed to learn. And He and I were going to become a team.

Jesus is my CEO and He and I became a real team, an unbreakable bond became even stronger in this home. It was my sanctuary and it was our home. The Lord and I lived here.

I signed the papers finalizing the sale on April 17th 2003. The next day, I read the words below from a devotional I had been reading for four years. I couldn't have possibly planned this, nor did I think about the meaning, having read this before, but now, wow oh wow!

[God Calling April 18- Oh what light and joy flow out of this

house! Don't feel as if you have to try and help them. Just love them with little acts of kindness and tokens of affection, and inevitably they will be helped.

Besides, you have no choice. You told Me it was My home. I shall use it. Remember this: there would be no dark winter days if love were in the hearts of all my children].

Six years later, I began having Bible studies in this home. Greg and I officially became the teachers and this is where I grew in love with him. I didn't fall in love with Greg Laster. I grew to love him. I would grow to love this man as we each strived and strained to serve and love God with all our hearts while being developed to fulfill God's purpose in our lives.

God had prepared and I believe ordained this home as a meeting place for He and I, The Lord needed me to learn of Him that His yoke was easy and His burden was light. Not that I understood this at all while I was learning and being developed. Going through extreme tests and trials was not easy nor did it feel light to me at the time. But later I would understand these tests. This would be our sanctuary and He would meet with me in many supernatural events. He loved me and I was accepted in the Beloved. And more often than not this was a very exciting adventure, extremely difficult but equally as exciting.

On the North side were Mr. and Mrs. Crawford. Mr. Crawford was like a father to me. He watched over me; telling me one day. "I listen for you to come home at night. When I hear your door shut, I close my window and go to sleep." By this time I worked out of town as a general manger for a very busy casual dining restaurant. Many nights I didn't get home until one or two A.M. or later from a closing shift. Mr. Crawford watched and waited for me. Waited for me… He waited until I was safe inside my house then shut his window and went to sleep. There are no words.

I believe Mr. and Mrs. Crawford were on assignment. *"The LORD shall preserve thy going out and they coming in from this forth, and even for evermore" (Psalm 121:8 KJV).*

Mr. Crawford kept his home and his yard immaculate. He was retired so his yard and garden kept him active and gave him something to look forward too. He told me one day while in conversation that he feared he was creating someone else's nightmare and tons of work for someone when he was gone.

In 2008, my good friend and mentor Mr. Crawford passed away from cancer. Shortly after their children abruptly moved Mrs. Crawford to an assisted living facility in another city and their house sold.

The home was purchased by a newly married couple; they were young and full of life and dreams and energy. But soon they would realize they were in over their heads. This young couple couldn't maintain the home or the yard. The property suffered much abuse and neglect. The owner received citation after citation for city code violations.

Citations were issued for cars on blocks (in the front and back yard) failure to keep the lawn mowed, and maintained, per city code. There were dogs, large dogs, litters of puppies, huge holes dug in the backyard, smell of dog dung in the hot steamy Texas summer temperatures. Oh no what has become of this picture-perfect scene and Better Homes and Gardens home? You get it. The place turned into a mess within a couple of years. The property was a mess. The dogs were allowed to stay in the house a lot of the time also, so you know.

The beautifully kept property once adorning and displaying a Better Homes and Gardens yard had changed owners and the condition of the home and yard was very noticeable. I was saddened by the soon deterioration and condition of the property because I really liked the now divorced couple and their little child.

I was sitting on my patio one day when I saw the owner pull into the back yard with a trailer attached to his vehicle.

Almost instantly" I knew I was going to buy the property." In the story of Mary, the mother of Jesus, while visiting Elizabeth, after her visitation from the angel Gabriel: the Bible says that at Mary's greeting or at the sound of her voice, the baby in Elizabeth's womb leaped for joy, and Elizabeth was filled with The Holy Spirit. Luke 2. In my purchase of both of houses I use the phrase my baby leaped for joy, knowing this was from The Lord. I just knew it. I knew I was supposed to buy my first house and now once again, I have that familiar leap in my spirit.

I said are you moving? He answered, "Yes I am behind on my mortgage, and they will not work with me."

So Lord, we are buying another property? How can this be? Let's do it, Lord, oh yes let's do it. We will purchase this property. And it will be an adventure. I couldn't imagine buying one home, but God has bigger and better in mind.

After many months and several obeyed promptings from The Lord to call about the property, I purchased Mr. and Mrs. Crawford's house for thousands less than I could have thought or wished.

This house was now mine also. God meant for me to purchase this house. My mom and I made plans and began to dream. She was going to lease her home, and move into this house, we were going to be next door neighbors. My best friend would be moving in next door to me. It sounds very exciting and it truly was. But please don't think I just whistled a tune, while running through the hills with my hair blowing in the breeze, The Lord rolling out my red carpet before me and I tiptoeing through the tulips with the lights of the paparazzi camera's flashing.

I was scared and at times downright overwhelmed. I knew it was from The Lord. Often when reading the Bible we have a tendency to romanticize the events with angelic chorus's singing while the heavens open over the men and women of God. But is that reality? No it isn't. They like you and I had to walk by faith and not by sight. They went through long periods of waiting and struggle just like we do. They were prompted to do things that were over their head and stretched their faith. We need to read the Bible with the knowledge of their struggles. If it isn't over our heads it will not require faith.

While the foreclosure was being completed and receiving promptings from The Lord I would call about the property. I was told numerous times they were working on it but it would take some time. One morning in my car, headed to the bank to make the store deposit from the night shift, I heard in my spirit, call about the house. I had the banks number in my phone so I called Chase Bank to check on the property. I had such a sense of excitement, but I was ready to hear that they were working on it. Only this time the message was quite different.

I was told the property was turned over to a realtor, Bill Williams, in my hometown. Was I ever excited? I immediately called information, (before Google) and got the number of Remax Realtors, calling right away. Mr. Williams was surprised and ask, "How did you know about this property, I just received it late last night." I didn't say God told me, even though He had, I simply said, "I have been following this property because I am going to buy it." I explained I lived next door to the property and I wanted to buy this home so my mom could live next door to me. He took my name and number saying he would let me know. I called a few times just to remind Mr. Williams that I was going to purchase the property. (Because God said so) You know in case he forgot.

The call came and Mr. Williams told me he was coming to look at the property and I was welcome to join him. He said, "I haven't seen the property so I don't know what condition it is in, but you are welcome to join me." It just so happened the day he chose would be my day off. Coincidence? I don't think so. Confirmation is God's red carpet.

I met Mr. Williams early that morning so excited but I tried hard to contain myself. As he was unlocking the door Mr. Williams again reminded me, "I haven't looked at the house." He didn't know the condition of the inside, but I was so excited and didn't care. As we walked through the house, it was a mess. Dogs, big dogs in the house, you know. Everywhere I looked pennies were scattered all around. All over this urine stained dirty carpet were pennies. I began to pick up the pennies. Soon, Mr. Williams was picking them up with me also. He said, "I've heard if you find a penny it means your mom is praying for you." We looked all through the house and I was so excited I could barely contain myself. I didn't know how I just knew God said so.

You see, it wasn't like I was sitting on a huge savings account or that I was rich. I was a hard worker and I had faith. Maybe only mustard seed faith, but I had faith and it was growing.

After looking at the house, I rushed home with two pockets full of pennies that together Mr. Williams and I collected. What does it mean Lord? I knew I was supposed to believe to purchase the house for the number of pennies X 1000, but I didn't even have a mustard seed of faith for this. It seemed too good to be true but I really believed God, and I believed this was the amount I was to by faith believe to purchase this property for. I didn't know how God would make this house sell for so cheap but I had faith in God. So I had to believe even though it was too good to be true!

It's too good to be true God, but I believe You. Even when we cannot believe with our head, our heart just knows things.

Oh Father, You said in 1 Samuel 15:22, that to obey is better than sacrifice. I don't understand exactly what You mean by this new kind of obedience. In my warped thinking obedience has meant doing without, or harsh punishment for not being obedient. Help me to quit self sabotaging due to old beliefs. Help me to see You and know You as a loving Father, One who longs to be gracious to Your children. Help me understand and learn to be the person you have created me to be. I want to be pleasing to You. I long to feel wanted and welcomed and safe in Your presence.

Jesus, You came that I may have life, and abundant life, help me to walk this out until my feelings catch up with my obedience. Even if I am afraid, help me do it afraid. Push me, Lord.

Jesus is this dream in my heart really from You? Can I really be more than others have said? Teach me what all this means.

If you could be anything in the world what would it be? If you said something like win the lottery, be given a million-dollar inheritance, that wouldn't be from God. God says wealth gained quickly destroys. God teaches us His ways in the scriptures. God gives us the ability to produce wealth (Read Deuteronomy 8:18). Wealth and prosperity are not necessarily money. Seed Time and Harvest is God's abundant blessing and the process of being made new. 3 John 1:2 says that we are to prosper as our soul prospers. Jesus is worried about the condition of our soul more than our material things (Read Matthew 6:22-33).

What's in our soul is what we create. It is a picture of what is in us, becoming evident around us. Harvest is how God grows us up and into our promises. We grow together and become intertwined with Him. We grow up together into our blessings. This is another picture of balance. Be reasonable and look inside your heart. Don't be afraid, go ahead and look there is a dream in there.

You may have been placed under wrong ownership and fallen into the wrong hands but your life and these dreams are waiting to be redeemed. Say out loud, "I know my Redeemer lives, and He redeems my life from destruction.

I want to add here that I could not have done these things without the help of men and women God placed me with and before me. Like my attorney who was the most feared in 20 counties, who kept saying "remember I work for you," Teaching me authority when I was a beat down very frightened woman. And then my very good friend Frank Morris who just happened to be the CEO of a local bank and who showed me great favor over and over. Mr. and Mrs. Crawford, and Bill Williams and the countless others, who had gone before me, were teaching me while believing in me. My mom, and my uncle, and aunts had trained this girl up right, but I had fallen into the wrong hands along the way. None of the events I have shared happened overnight or without great cost. The changes happened through tears, through fears, and extremely hard work, but isn't that faith? Yes, I believe faith is refined in the fire of tears, fears and hard work. At our own expense, is what Mr. Laster says! I just know Father Knows Best!

"These trials will show that your faith is genuine. It is being tested as fire, tests and purifies gold—though your faith is far more precious than mere gold. So when your faith remains strong through many trials, it will bring you much praise and glory and honor on the day when Jesus Christ is revealed to the whole world" (1 Peter 1:7 NLT).

Prayer:

Dear Heavenly Father, I commit all my ways to You. I repent, I confess, I want to be cleansed of all the dirt and shame of my past. I say wash all of me, cleanse me of all unrighteousness. I want to do what You have for me to do. Help me refine my faith in You that You may be glorified. I do not want to shrink back. Redeem me completely.

Praise The Lord, oh my soul, and never forget all the good He has done. He is the one who forgives and continues to forgive all your sins, the one who heals all your diseases, who redeems you and rescues your life from the pit, the one who crowns you with mercy, and loving kindness, tender mercies, and compassion (Psalm 103:2-4).

Reflection:

With thoughts of the scripture above, If you could do or be anything in this world, what would it be? Is your dream to be a teacher, a coach, a nurse, a doctor, a world renowned author, a father, a mother, a preacher or just a born again you? You can change the world and be a disciple with passion when you fulfill your dream. What is it? It is important to write it down. It becomes more real and binding when we write it. (*Fill in the promise on page 350*).

_____

_____

_____

POETRY: ON LOAN

Thank you for this gift
>   At morning prayer does start
>   Poetic truths do often flow
>   From Your Spirit into my heart

Then I am allowed the gift
>   Oh what opportunities You bring
>   To let these words come forth
>   Out of communion with You they sing

A word a note or a picture
>   A rhyme or simple phrase
>   All from time in prayer
>   To You all my praise

Thank You for Your love
>   When reminded daily now
>   That as the gift flows freely
>   I am amazed and I am wowed

How can I say thank You
>   How do I show appreciation
>   I humbly pen the words
>   And offer to You my adoration

This gift is all about You
>   And all that You freely gave
>   Because You went to the cross
>   But did Rise on the third day

What beauty and what majesty
>   The gifts are on loan to tell
>   About Your exceedingly great glory
>   Of salvation from eternal hell

You saved me and you bought me
>   With Your redeeming blood
>   And now I write to teach
>   It is all about pure love

For You so loved the world
>   You gave Your only Son
>   Jesus obedient unto death on the Cross
>   Penned the words Tetelestai—it is done

Thank You for The Gift
>   Thank You for Your love
>   Father I pray their eyes be opened
>   Receive salvation from above

Look unto Jesus and be ye saved
>   Unto all the ends of the earth
>   Because it is hell without Him
>   Eternal life with Him in new birth

Believe in your heart
    Confess using your words
    Say it over and over
    Until you believe what is heard

He loved you 'ere you knew Him
    With His redeeming blood
    He will plunge you into victory
    Beneath the cleansing flood

© laurette laster 2019 April

"He will rescue you from every hidden trap of the enemy and He will protect from false accusation and any deadly curse. His massive arms are wrapped around you protecting you. You can run under His covering of majesty and hide" (Psalm 91:3-4, TPT).

DAY 19

"I HAVE NOT COME to call the righteous but sinners to repentance" (Luke 5:32).

In the early morning hours before dawn, getting ready for work, The Lord asked me a question. As I was drying my hair, The Lord, asked, "Do you know why you are so excited about the house?" I was waiting on the sale to finalize and there was a so much work that needed to be done to the house, but I was giddy with an unexplainable excitement about the whole thing. There was an excitement in my soul that I didn't understand. I got so excited and started to open my mouth and answer The Lord, when I realized, I did not know why I was so excited, and not this unexplainable excitement I had. I could have come up with probably ten answers off the top of my head, but I knew that wasn't what He was asking me. I realized I did not know why I had such an excitement about the entire transaction, the events surrounding the sale, the purchase, the pursuit, the pennies, and yes, the promise that lay ahead.

I turned off my hair dryer, I turned to look up, and I said, "I don't, No I don't know why I am so excited about this house. "Why am I so excited?" I asked. He said these words that I will always remember, "because you know what it looked like when love had it." Oh wow, think about that. "Because you know what it looked like when love had It." And yes I did know what it looked like when love had it.

At that moment I had a deep and profound kingdom understanding and I knew, then I knew, and I really got it.

Remember the condition of the house I described in Day 18? Our lives may be like that property when He calls us. But God is our creator and He knows what the property is intended to be and more than that, He knows what it looks like when love has it.

I could see the previous condition of this home, so I had a picture, or a vision to restore it back too. Had I not seen the home in its previous condition and loved Mr. and Mrs. Crawford, things may have been different. I may have been so overwhelmed by the mess that I would have told myself it needed too much work and repair. I may have thought, like we tend to believe about ourselves that it was beyond help. I knew how the previous owners, Mr. and Mrs. Crawford, loved and cared for the property and I loved them and considered them friends.

Their care and concern were evidenced by the beauty of the house and the condition of the lawn and surrounding grounds, the garden and outbuildings. Starting with the manicured lawn, the well-tended garden, the always trimmed hedges, it was all beautiful and well-mani-cured and cared for. They were the ones who loved the property and it showed. So I had an image or a vision—a picture of what the future of this house and property were to look like. I wanted to restore it back to the beauty I knew it once had when it was in the hands of love.

You are made in His image and likeness if you repent and remain in Him, in the faith (read Colossians 1:12-22).

God is your creator. God is Love and in Him is no shadow of turn-ing. God doesn't change His mind. You have purpose. If God is placing it on your heart to repent, or if you know you need to repent it is from God. He would like to come along side you and redeem you. He is the God of restoration.

You are in a fallen broken world. Satan usurped Adam's authority in the garden. Satan deceived Eve and they together decided to disobey God's command. But what is worse is that they obeyed Satan's command or suggestion. In this world, Satan, loves to steal us at birth or early childhood. He loves to take away our authority and security and thus steals our identity. But God is rich in mercy, when you were dead in your sins and trespasses...

Have you heard stories about babies who were switched at birth? I bet you have. Think about this with your own life. Satan has done a bait and switch game on you. Perhaps you are thinking or have had the thought; God couldn't use me with what I've done. Or I don't have anything that God could see as useful. Well think again. Because I believe that very thought may be proof He is calling you.

God isn't surprised and like "Oh Wow, wait, you did what? Oh, I didn't realize you did "THAT." No, God knew you before you were formed in your mother's womb. He knows what is holding you back. He knows the root issues and the way Satan has stolen your purpose. Or perhaps God is waiting for you to thoroughly repent. Only you know that. But I know God is for you. Maybe it's time to come clean with Him, remember, He already knows.

I hear The Father saying, "Do you know why I am so excited they are reading this right now? Because I know what they look like when love had them."

God is love and He loves you. He loves you too much to leave you where you are. He has plans for you, and they are for Good. Read Jeremiah 29:11-12. Will you say yes? Read verse 13 because with your whole heart is how He is found.

Prayer:

Dear Heavenly Father, what good news this is. It really is too good to be true. But I know it is true. I am blown away that You love me so much that You have made a way for me to be forgiven and completely restored. You see the vision You have for my life. You redeem my life from the destruction and plans of the enemy. You have purchased me with the blood of Jesus, Your only begotten Son. I am loved by You, and valuable to You. I say yes, I will live boldly for You. Redeem this life Father. Show me what my life looks like in the hands of Your love. Amen

Reflection:

Pay special attention to dreams and conversations in the coming days and weeks. God is going to be speaking to you, don't trust these things to memory. Write them down. If you haven't started a notebook or journal by now, it is time. Date your entries. Later you will be so glad you did.

_____

_____

_____

POETRY: YOU WILL FIND ME WHEN

Oh to see God's power in the pulpit
 To crave deeper worship with the praise
 Oh to see hands being lifted to heaven
 Reaching for Jesus while they are raised

The need for joy and unexplainable peace
 A deep longing to become more reverent
 We need to see the manifestation
 Of our Lord's Holy benevolence

Oh this change I crave
 This groaning deep within my heart
 Could not be satisfied by
 By playing a spectators part

The stage has been set
 Revival has started
 It is reserved for participants only
 Not to be achieved by spectators or the half-hearted

What was His message
    Can you help me remember
    I'll find Him if I look
    Maybe it is in December

Should I look in January
    Wait, maybe it was June
    Oh can you help me remember
    Was it morning or around noon

This is the message told to Jeremiah
    Of this I have personal experience and proof
    We shall seek for Him and find Him
    With our whole heart longing for nothing but truth

God is not mocked nor does He lie
    And He will not ever be deceived
    For in His kingdom law it is measured
    He lives by, what we give is what we receive

He gave His All, His Only Begotten Son
    And nothing less from us will do
    So being made in His image and likeness
    He requires we give our whole heart and being too

© laurette laster 2018

"And you will seek Me and find Me, when you search for Me with your whole hear" (Jeremiah 29:13, NKJV).

DAY 20

"Go and learn what this means. "'I desire mercy, and not sacrifice. For I came not to call the righteous but sinners'" (Matthew 9:13).

By the time it was time to make my bid on the home Mr. Williams and I had become acquainted. It seemed to me that anything to do with this home was slathered with God's unfailing favor and love. When the bank finally put a price on the property and home it was several thousand less than the original amount I had thought to believe for. This is so like God, right? I was amazed, needing to borrow a few thousand dollars to finish the work on the house and guess what? The total cost of the house was exactly the total God told me to believe for. Yes, that original amount I thought to believe for. This two-bedroom brick home, with one bath, a covered patio and carport on a .4 acre fenced lot with a beautiful lawn and mature trees was purchased at a very low price. Now that is our God! Mr. Williams said, "Had I known it would go for this price, I would have tried to buy it myself."

Mr. Williams wanted me to have the home because of my pursuit and purpose for this home. He even wrote the bank a letter on my behalf that accompanied my bid and check. He told the bank that the others bidding on the property hoped to purchase it for rental or investment property, I on the other hand had plans to move my mother next door to me. Mr. Williams explained that I owned the property adjoining this property. So, I added a hundred dollars extra to my bid check, handed it to Mr. Williams and left his office and prayed. Then I waited and I prayed. I was hopeful yet still anxious; I just knew the house was ours. God said so; I just wanted to finalize the deal.

While praying and seeking The Lord concerning this property, one afternoon I had a vision. While standing at my kitchen sink washing dishes, I caught a glimpse in my mind's eye of a gate between the two properties. I knew this was confirmation of His will, and He would see me through.

I don't recall how long it took to get the answer about the purchase, but we got it. They accepted my bid. I called my mom while flying down I-35, I said, "Mama we got the house." God was on our side. Oh did we rejoice. But now there was a lot of work to do.

But first the gate, God showed me a gate between the properties in a vision and I wanted to get it installed first. So from my patio door to her patio door was about forty five foot with a gate leading the way.

Didn't He say He was the gate and that the sheep could come in and go out and find pasture? "Yes, I am the gate. Those who come in through Me will be saved. They will come and go freely and will find good pastures" (John 10:9 NLT).

Where was I going to begin? I decided pulling up the carpet was the reasonable place to start. It was dirty and nasty; it stank and needed to go.

I was teaching a Bible study with and had become very good friends with a man named Greg Laster. He called me on the day I decided to start taking up the carpet. He asked what I was doing. I said, "Pulling up carpet." Greg insisted I wait, so he could help. I said, "Well you better get here soon if you want to help because I'm pulling up this carpet today."

Greg did come by on his way home from work and together we were able to pull the carpet loose, get it rolled up, and drag it outside. I know I couldn't have done it without Greg's help so I am glad he wanted to be a part of this. I know God sent Greg to come along side me for this adventure, and for many upcoming future adventures.

Guess what we discovered under the carpet? Oh yes, beautiful original hardwood floors. But remember the dogs, you know, the big dogs? We also discovered there was damage to the wood. And now it became apparent what the root source and cause of the overwhelming odor was.

So now I would need to find a craftsman. I needed someone that could take out the damaged wood and replace it with new wood boards that could preserve the integrity of the floors.

Remember on page two, bringing forth fruit worthy of repentance? No harvest is accomplished single handedly. Jesus Himself expects us to have help removing grave clothes. (John 11:44) Salvation is the work of God Almighty through Jesus Christ. We are saved by grace, the free unmerited gift of God lest anyone should boast. Salvation happens when we believe.

When you become a believer in Jesus Christ, you are delivered out of the kingdom of darkness and translated into His marvelous kingdom of light. As a believer you are no longer children of the dark you are children of the day.

"But ye are a chosen generation, a royal priesthood, a holy nation, a peculiar people; that ye should shew forth the praises of Him who hath called you out of darkness into his marvelous light" (1 Peter 2:9 KJV).

"Who hath delivered us from the power of darkness, and hath translated us into the kingdom of His dear Son: In whom we have redemption through his blood, even the forgiveness of sins" (Colossians 1:13-14 KJV).

When it comes to working the works of repentance, we all require help. Grave clothes are old ways of thinking, what we have learned and how we live and what we don't know. It takes the word (water) of God to soak off dirty grave clothes and bandages that have stuck to our wounds and covered our wrongs and then open us up to healing.

All of us have been injured. Some of us suffered more serious blows and wounds than others. Often the blows in life are beyond our ability to deal with or worse we may be told they aren't that bad. So we just put a band aid on a serious bloody wound, and without proper medical treatment or medication it becomes infected. If this is the case it will take some serious soaking to get it loose, get it? Old bandages that are stuck to wounds cannot just be ripped off. To rip them off would cause more damage to the initial wound and surrounding area but soaking in His word and having the help from others makes this process go as easy as possible. Truth is like surgery; it hurts at first but heals the problem. Lies, like pain pills, may mask the pain of the problem but can be addictive and deadly in the end.

You will require the wisdom and the counsel of other mature experienced godly mentors and leaders, friends and businessmen and women. Chances are good you are not going to be able to go this alone. As believers we are not designed to be islands. We grow and mature and are created as relational beings. Do not hesitate to pray and ask God for wise mentors that can help you grow. Now, let the restoration work to begin.

Prayer:

Dear Heavenly Father, I know it is time to begin the work required, to become fully alive to You. I want to enter Your kingdom, the kingdom that Jesus said is near. I am beginning to understand that repentance is working through some of the rough dirty stuff that got on me in the world. I have covered some really serious wounds with quick fixes and band aids. I wanted to pretend it was in my past and that I didn't have to deal with them anymore. Now I realize that was wishful thinking and not the way You have designed me. I want to do a thorough work of repentance. I want to abide with You forever. I want my heart to be a place You long to dwell in with me. Thank You, Lord Jesus, for sending me godly mentors to help me learn and grow. I want to present my body holy and pleasing to you which is my reasonable service (Romans 12:1-3) Amen

(My prayer is that Holy Spirit will indwell you that your life be Spirit filled and Spirit led.) Amen

Reflection:

What is God showing you that you need to pull up, roll up, and take out of your life? That awful stench has a root cause for the source of the odor that is hidden. You do not have to be afraid to look at this hard stuff now. What old grave clothes do you need help getting off? What has you bound and unable to move freely? You are safe now and are being called into the deep. Deep calleth to deep. God is going to send others to help you, so together with them; you and He will do the repair work, or the restoration of your life.

_____

_____

_____

POETRY: YOU WERE THE REASON WHY

Rolling up His sleeves
    You know those are fighting terms
    He had taken all He would
    Once and for all this lesson must be learned

I turned away when He made a fist
    I just couldn't bear to look
    His arm stretched out then I saw
    It was the nails that He took

What kind of Warrior was He
    I thought He would do it right
    Fisticuffs you know
    Isn't that how real men fight

His arm laid bare to show
    That He had made His plan
    Coming as my Redeemer
    Fully God and fully man

Oh the fight was won I'd say
    The day He laid down His life
    Have you stopped to consider
    It was Jesus who paid the price

But wait there's more I must tell
    About that empty tomb
    The devil believed he had won
    Shocked the people felt doom and gloom

But the fight had just begun
    Because Early on Sunday morn
    Jesus Rose Up out of that grave
    Into the gift of God's Salvation we have torn

The gift God delivered on Christmas
    Well it is opened at the Cross
    Because Jesus showed that ol' devil
    Proving to him exactly who is BOSS

That fight I couldn't bear to watch
    It was bloody and oh so brutal
    He was fighting for you and me
    Jesus won it all, the whole kit and caboodle

I just thought you'd like to know
    The fight has already been won
    When He laid bare His Arm
    Salvation came by way of crucifixion of His Son

The Cross The nails the mocking
    The abject posture of quitting
    It was all part of Gods perfect plan
    Into His tapestry He was knitting

His perfect plan stitch by stitch
    Designed and perfectly orchestrated
    Woven Into the pages Of Christianity
    The fight was won! Now God's people are liberated

He fought and secured at Calvary
    His Resurrection Victory has no end
    Because as long as you have breath
    He'll fight for you and defend

Call upon His Name while He May be found
    Do not let another day slip by
    Because the fight that Jesus won
    You, yes you were the reason why

© 2019 laurette laster

"The LORD hath made bare his holy arm in the eyes of all the nations; and all the ends of the earth shall see the salvation of our God" (Isaiah 52:10 KJV).

"He saw that there was no man--He was amazed that there was no one to intercede; so His own arm brought salvation, and His own righteousness sustained Him" (Isaiah 59:16).

DAY 21

"LIKEWISE, I say to you, there is joy in the presence of angels of God over one sinner who repents" (Luke 15:10 NKJV).

I n this parable Jesus tells about a shepherd leaving 99 sheep to go after one lost sheep. According to Jesus heaven rejoices over one sinner who repents more than 99 righteous who have no need to repent. This verse makes my heart smile and it should make your heart smile also. Jesus was born to save us from our sins and from out of Satan's power. This is why heaven rejoices. We are opening the gift of Gods salvation when we repent and ask for help. Like a stranded sheep we start bleating.

I thought Jesus only wanted the good ones, the ones who made Him look good. With the dung of the world on me, I sure wasn't (clean) good enough. You know the ones from the right families. The wealthy, well balanced, elite, sophisticated, the popular ones with the right clothes. Maybe you have thought this also, but according to this scripture, we are both wrong and aren't we glad? Just because someone looks alright on the outside does not mean what is underneath is healthy or pleasing to our Father. We on the other hand may have suffered and taken a good dousing of dung but it is our heart He sees. Our *do* is not our *who*.

I discovered several cosmetic issues with the house that would add additional time to the repair work. I knew this was God's doing and it was an adventure.

Remember my friend Greg? He and I taught the Bible study together, remember? Well he was there every step of the way with this home. I had never had anyone come along side me like this. When I ask him why, He said, "God told me to help you." Could Greg see that God had placed a big call on my life and I needed help? I made it clear to Greg I wasn't interested in a relationship. He assured me that he liked to hang out with me and he didn't have anything else vying for his time. He said, "God told me to help you and expect nothing in return." Well I thought, we'll see how long this lasts. I've never known anyone who didn't have ulterior motives. Greg later would share with me "God told me to help you, not help myself to you (haha)." And some think God doesn't have a sense of humor.

One Friday evening driving home from work I returned a missed call from Greg. During our conversation I ask him what he had done that day. He said I've been painting. I said where were you painting? He said the East bedroom at the house. I said. "I didn't know you knew how to paint." Now, of course, anyone can slap some paint on the wall but I meant that I didn't realize he had ever painted before. Greg shared with me that he used to work for a man that was a painter and a contractor. The man has even written a book on colors for painting that create atmosphere like creating calm or energy stimulating colors, soothing, etc. It seemed God just kept lining things up.

Greg is a master electrician and a contractor. He is definitely a craftsman in his work. His expertise with his strict discipline to only do quality work and experience from years on jobs from working with other contractors, things just kept lining up.

"As for God, His way is perfect: the word of the LORD is tried: He is a buckler to all those that trust in Him" (Psalms 18:30 KJV).

But even with all this qualified experience there was some tedious work I had to do. Remember the carpet? Carpet is secured with staples, tack board and nails and glue, very large nails and tack boards glued down. Tack board has hundreds of nails that are tilted to grab and secure the carpet. When I began to pull up the tack board it was old and brittle and began to break and split. This made the job even harder, and much more time consuming. There were also several hundred staples that I had to remove.

My tools consisted of a small crowbar, a flat head screwdriver, a claw hammer, needle nose pliers, regular pliers and me. I spent hours on my hands and knees working to remove them. At times I would get tired and sit down and just scoot from area to area. Of course, hoping I didn't encounter a nail or one of those staples along the way.

More than once I wanted to give up with this grueling task. I would think to myself why did I even start this? Was new carpet such a bad idea? Why did I think restoring the hardwood floors was such a good idea? Remember the morning when God asked me if I knew why I was so excited about the house? My excitement was hard to maintain during the very grueling days of pulling staples, removing nails, and tack board, and the work of restoring the house back to what it was when love had it.

During the work on the house I was working a very demanding job as a training general manager for a large casual dining corporate chain, so the restoration work was in addition to my quote, unquote normal everyday work life. Most days I was exhausted when the work began but the excitement would always return, right about the time I would think I couldn't go on, and when I wanted to give up.

This task did get completed and the holes were filled with wood filler. I found a very good craftsman who worked diligently, removing the damaged wood and then replaced new wood boards. That foul stench by this stage of the work was gone. The damage was repaired, and guess what happened next? Greg just happened to be on a job working alongside employees of a very upscale hard wood floor and restoration company.

Greg began telling the owner about my house and my desire to restore the floors. When the owner of this high-end business discovered the home was being readied for my mom, you guessed it; he sent a crew to Gainesville TX. The floors were professionally sanded and stained, toe boards added. This company refinished the hardwood floors throughout the house. The owner even covered the cost of the labor for finishing with several coats of polyurethane for the floor. He told Greg if I covered the cost of the materials to finish the job, he would donate the labor. I didn't have to even look for a floor finisher. I wouldn't have known where to look but this was God's project too and God supplied a superior craftsman for each job. I also believe the company owner received a blessing to his account for these efforts. Each one that helped loved and respected their mothers and helped them in their later years.

But you know God didn't say to me, if you work real hard and do a good job I'll help you. He had the next step lined up but it wouldn't become evident until I had done my part. These exciting events continue to happen and it is all The Lord's doing and it is marvelous in our sight.

"The Lord has done this and it is marvelous in our eyes" (Psalm 118:23 NIV).

Along the way and during repentance we may find the work grueling and somewhat tedious with what we think to be hard boring tasks. Don't quit or give up and look for a short cut. What God requires may at times seem boring or tedious and unimportant to the overall work, but we do well to remember it is the finished project and the smallest details that He sees and we know if we cut any corners.

When we know we are forgiven and accepted in the beloved it is super exciting. Marriage takes work; our covenant with God takes work too. Keep the excitement, fight for it like your life depends on it because it does. If it were easy everyone would do it. The discovery is so exciting but along the way life gets hard and is often demanding. Always remember it is the goodness of God that leads us to repentance, not works lest anyone should boast. The work He gives us is a privilege, considering that we cannot pay the debt we owe.

I have discovered that the only way to truly understand what God is up to is through everyday repetition of simple tasks. He is teaching us so many wonderful things. We will reap if we don't give up. King David asks God to restore to him the joy of His salvation.

"Restore to me the joy of Your salvation and grant me a willing spirit, to sustain me" (Psalm 51:12).

Even a King can become weary during repentance. Have you ever thought to yourself well if I were in charge or rich, or _____ then it would be easy? That is not true according to what we hear in this verse.

King David is known as a master repenter, or Baal Teshuvah, meaning a master returner. In this Psalm, God was dealing with David about sins he had committed and wanted him to confess. David had worked hard to cover up his sin with Bathsheba and God sent Nathan to talk to David.

I know that some may disagree with what I am teaching here and that is okay. Some believe that grace does our part also. I say if you want to remain in the shallow wading pool go ahead. But for those of us that want to experience all The Lord has for us and be part of His team, we are the ones who will go out into the deep and face all of our shortcomings.

It is like deciding to swim out to the middle then deciding it is too hard. You look back and can't see the shore and know you have to keep swimming because you can't touch the bottom any longer. You have advanced to the big pool, leaving the kiddy pool behind. I say to those of you reading: you will reap if you faint not (Galatians 6:9).

This work is kingdom ordained work. You will emerge with an eternal closeness and oneness with God; God The Father, God The Son, and God The Holy Spirit. You will never wonder another day in your life if you are forgiven and if you have purpose. Never again will you doubt or wonder if God has given up on you or ask if it is real. Because each time the enemy comes against you, you will know you completed the work. You will be able to say, oh no you don't Satan, not again. I'm not buying your lies any longer. I am one with Jesus and I've completed all that God requires and He is for me.

This time with The Father isn't because He needs to know what you have done. He already knows everything you or I have ever done. This work, the work of repentance is to shut the enemy up and disarm

Satan of any legal right to your life and your mind. You are bringing everything into the light of God's healing goodness. You can know that you are officially and once and for all kicking Satan and his cohorts out of your life and off of your property. You are not covering up stench you are ripping it out and replacing the damage.

You will know you are bringing forth fruit worthy of repentance. You will know in your heart that every staple, every piece of tack board, every nail and all the holes were filled and it is finished.

Jesus said it is finished and gave up the ghost. He has worked and completed His part but we have a part also. It is foolish for us to think we don't have work to do. We are not adding to Jesus' work, His work is finished. Jesus did a perfect work but now like Peter says to us in 2 Peter 1:5-8 be certain to add to your faith…

Prayer:

Dear Jesus, You prayed and ask for God to remove the cup from You when facing the Cross. In the hard times I can draw from Your words and Your wisdom when You said "nevertheless not My will but Your will be done." God, I pray like King David, grant me a willing spirit and sustain me. Because You know what this finished work will look like and You know what I will look like when I am washed thoroughly with hyssop. You make me new. Thank You Jesus for dying for me, help me to live for You. Amen

What if I had just pulled up the old soiled carpet and had new carpet put down? What if I'd thought to just hurry and get new carpet? We both know what that would have meant. That fowl odor would have seeped up and out, and the pad and carpet would have absorbed it and it would have come to the surface. What I didn't know was that my mom was very ill but not yet diagnosed. This diagnosis would leave her needing oxygen the last months of her life. So the hard wood floors were by God's perfect design. Oxygen can be mobile and the machine is easily moved on hard wood or smooth surfaces. I do not regret one minute of hard work and the joy this house brought to my mom during her last months on this earth. I do wish there had been more time but God was fulfilling prayers for both of us that later became apparent. I am so grateful that God allowed me to be part of this blessing in her life.

It can be much the same way if we do not do the work of repentance from sin and iniquity, according to what God requires. You might hide a dead body but you cannot hide the stench. Remember the dead mouse in my house? Well that is what replacing the carpet would do. It would hide the damage but it wouldn't have masked or contained the putrid odor to God.

They do not say in their heart, Let us now fear and worship the LORD our God [with profound awe and in reverence],

Your wickedness has turned these [blessings] away, and your sins have withheld good from you (Jeremiah 5:24-25 AMP).

Reflection:

Is there an area you are trying to gloss over and take the easy way out, without doing the deep work of facing your sins? You may have never thought or been taught this is necessary or a kingdom requirement. Perhaps you've been told it's in the past don't worry. However, if something isn't working right we owe it to ourselves to stop and examine any unchecked areas in our life. Without confessing the sin you will have to deny or pretend it isn't real. Is there something that you feel like God is asking you to do that you don't see the need or the importance of it? Do not reason, obey quickly and work at it until it is finished. Is there a task that you want to overlook that your next breakthrough might hinge on? Pray and ask God what is holding you back and list three things to work on as God opens the door.

_____

_____

_____

POETRY: AS THE OCEAN KNOWS THE SHORE

Like the ocean knows the shore
　　How I long to know You more
　　As the tides do rise and fall
　　To hear Your voice and know Your call

Sometimes settled and smooth like glass
　　Other times anxious like waves that crash
　　So bold and ferocious the ocean can roar
　　Measured in Your palm I can't ignore

The vast sum of all You will become to me
　　As I continue to sail in Your great sea
　　If I should ever become overwhelmed
　　I'll remember "The Captain" is at the helm

Guiding and showing me distant shores
　　Because, didn't I pray to know You more
　　The kingdom of heaven does suffer violence
　　Together we sail, often in silence

As we sail on together I'll do as You've taught
    I'll speak to the waves and command them to stop
    I shall not fear voyaging with "The Captain" so near
    The "Captain" is You my Lord, what have I to fear

laurette laster © 2017

"Who has measured the waters in the hollow of His hand, measured heaven with a span and calculated the dust of the earth in a measure?" (Isaiah 40:12 NKJV).

"The disciples were amazed. Who is this man?" they asked. Even the winds and waves obey him!" (Matthew 8:27 NLT).

DAY 22

"THEREFORE, let us leave the elementary doctrine of Christ and go on to maturity, not laying again a foundation of repentance from dead works and of faith toward God" (Hebrews 6:1).

I tried for years not to be a leader. With all the emotional dysfunction surrounding my childhood and ongoing into my adult life, I was full of shame and fear and pride. In attempts to fix it I kept going my own way.

We replaced the carpet, so to say, and then would wish for the smell to go away. I was a great codependent. I wanted to be on the backside even though I knew God was equipping me to be a problem solver; I helped and promoted others. I was the one who could see what was inside of them but I was unable to see what God had placed inside of me. I would be amazed later to find out one of my strongest gifts is teaching, and 'problem solving'. No wonder I was always trying to teach them a better way. As I continued to grow in The Lord, I saw this clearly after it was determined through testing. I realized I was trying to earn my way with good works (dead works). I thought I needed to pay God back for my sins first. I am not sure what conditioned me to my Cinderella complex, but I thought that was being a good Christian. I had a good dose of the little peasant girl complex, and I seemed to land myself with those who were happy to let me take care of them while using me or taking advantage of my naïveté. I discovered several people who were happy to allow me to build them up while making me feel I needed to stay in my place so to speak. Insecure people often feel threatened when your gifts begin to show and grow. Secure people will encourage and support you while offering you opportunities to use your gifts. I encourage you, if God is promoting you, do not allow any person to hold you down or cause you to shrink back.

There were many issues that may have contributed to this complex but others who had been through the same struggles didn't become a doormat. I thought my role was a little peasant girl, later allowing this to grow into full blown doormat syndrome. I really just needed to be needed and I would do whatever it took not be rejected. That is a lethal combination, fear of rejection and need to be needed.

I didn't particularly like this about myself, but I thought that was my purpose. I was in the background scrubbing and cleaning and working to get others ready for the ball. My warped sense of belief was that they would appreciate me; they would see and think I had meaning, I would have value, I would be important to them and they wouldn't only need me they would want me, some of you get it. But guess what? God had to call the leader in me out before I could truly start to develop into my calling. To be a leader was extremely frightening to me. What if I messed up? What if I couldn't do it? I knew I wasn't qualified. The truth is fear and responsibility of success was as frightening as the possibility and probability of failure.

I am so thankful to God for leading me to Applebee's and for the door opening with Concord Hospitality. I received the best training and development offered. I learned I was a value adder and have been mentored by the best. I also suffered under some power-hungry individuals but overall I still tell people Concord Hospitality's Applebee's was my defining line.

This in turn equipped me, to lead others, helping them become leaders, or as Jesus said, "go and make disciples." Disciples are disciplined leaders for the kingdom of God. A disciple is a student or a learner.

I was suffering from shame, guilt, insecurity, self-loathing, fear, inadequacy, self-will, pride, and other things, but on the inside, there was a drive to be more. Something kept propelling me. I just thought I had disqualified myself because of my sins so I should be grateful for the opportunity to help others.

I think is was 2005 or 2006, while reading an article by Jack Hayford one afternoon that I finally understood what God was doing. I was already an assistant GM for Applebee's. This position entailed great responsibility; I was in the deep, swimming with all my might, and knew God wanted me to keep going.

In this article, Mr. Hayford asked a question. Are any of you experiencing continued situations where you know God is calling you into leadership and you know you are not qualified? I was like yes, oh yes that's me. His next sentence totally surprised me but sealed the deal for me. The article went something like this. He said, 'then you indeed are called by God to be a leader. God is calling you because He can trust you. You are not power driven and God can trust you, to lead and to do His will. You can lead with His purpose and His passion because you are not driven to manipulate and overpower others while trying to climb to the top, thus destroying them. You will allow God and His ways to take front row and listen to Him. You will do what God wants without promoting yourself. You don't think you have the answers so you will rely on God's Spirit to guide you.'

Then I knew, "Laurette, it is God calling you, are you going to say yes or are you going to continue holding back for fear of your sins?"

I said "Yes" that day. Finally, it all made since. I threw myself all in. I told The Lord, if it's You, I'm in. Now others cannot believe there was ever another side to me. I thought I was being humble, when in reality I was just stupid. Satan had duped me and I bought the lie. On the inside, I knew others were using me and deep inside I was angry about it, but remember I thought this was normal, but not really how the futility of our minds can deceive us.

During this time, all managers were required to take a DISC assessment. I had begun praying and asking God, why am I like this? or like that? I wanted to know why I was like I was and what made me feel certain things. My GM told me I would have an email from the President of the company in my personal email box when I got home and to follow the prompts.

That evening when I got home, I looked and there it was. As I remember it gave me instructions about reading and answering several questions. I remember it was pretty short, maybe 80-100 questions. They were simple questions that at the time didn't seem to have much depth to them to me. When I completed the questionnaire, I was given the choice to have the results printed, so I chose to print the results then hit submit. To my utter astonishment and complete dismay, I received 31 printed pages of why I reacted in certain ways. There were words like; *feels threatened, may become hostile, shuts down, is independent, very disciplined,* and so on. I was utterly devastated to think that all this stuff went straight up the ladder, and into the hands of my superiors and to corporate headquarters.

I thought, "Now they all know how messed up I am." What I found most amazing was it was like an internal mirror looking at many of the things I had been praying about. Several people couldn't handle seeing this stuff about them and I certainly understand. The purpose for the testing was to help us understand each other and be able to work together better. We could read each other's assessment results to learn how to relate better with one other. Every upper management took the assessment. I was so surprised when the AD handed me his results and asked if I wanted to read them. What I realized is we are all results of life and events and we are all individuals who are affected differently. So there is no cookie cutter mold to fit into. I was so glad.

"And He (Jesus) said to them, 'You are those who justify yourselves before men, but God knows your hearts. For what is exalted among men is an abomination in the sight of God" (Luke 16:15).

My sins needed to be repented of, thoroughly repented of, a once and for all work of repentance. I had done the work but I had not appropriated Jesus's finished work to myself and made it personal. I was still learning. I sat down with the results of my assessment and went through it line by line. Praying, asking, seeking, knocking, and repenting of behaviors I wasn't even aware of. The test revealed I tried to lead by influencing others not correcting them. I had very low dominant readings so I knew what I needed to work on. I couldn't hope people would get better or hope things would change, I had to be an active part of the changes I expected. I was also beginning to understand God much better too.

Repentance is the requirement for forgiveness thus setting us free. I needed all the dirty carpet to come up and expose the damaged wood. That is where the all the odor was coming from. I had covered it up with performance in the past, good deeds and so much codependency. I needed help but until I was placed in the right hands of God's love I didn't feel safe enough to be uncovered. All the self-sacrificing to please others had to be acknowledged. I was not a God pleaser but a man pleaser and all the compromising was me punishing myself and my survivor's guilt. I thought if they can't make it neither should I. I didn't realize God was calling me to invoke and challenge others to be more and know they could make it too.

Your sins are not hindering you, if you repent. Your lack of success or fear of success or condemnation is not from God. God not only made a way, He sent The Way, His Name is Jesus Christ, to redeem you back from this destruction. God is not surprised by the damaged wood under the dirty nasty (flesh) carpet. He actually wants you to allow Him in, you see He paid the purchase price and together you can begin the work of restoration. It will be an adventure.

I knew what that house looked like yet I still purchased it. And I was so super excited, why? You know the answer. Because I knew what it looked like when love had it?

Prayer:

Oh my Heavenly Father, help me to feel safe in Your care. Show me how to surrender to the call You have on my life. I give You permission to uncover the old damage and to show me what needs to be replaced. I want to know that I belong to You and that You have good plans for me. Help me to overcome the fear of not being good enough. Amen

Reflection:

What are you most afraid of? What is under the carpet that you hope God isn't seeing or looking at or asking you to admit? It cannot be covered with a new layer of carpet and a little air freshener. PS He already knows and still loves you.

_____

_____

_____

POETRY: HE WHO IS WITHOUT SIN!

He stooped down, began to write
    I couldn't bear to read
    Written in the sand, my plight
    Death by stoning for my deed

I hung my head in shame
    Suffering the guilt and despair
    I dare not look at Him,
    Oh this mocking and the glares.

Others waiting to stone me
    My disgrace on public display
    Then someone ask a question
    What does His writing say

I'm not certain what it read
    Stones dropped, as they all turned
    I braced myself, now He and I
    Shaking, how my heart did burn

He ask me a simple question;
  Woman where are your accusers
  I looked and they were gone
  No stoning today, by angry abusers

He said these words to me
  Now etched inside my heart
  Woman neither do I condemn you
  I've come to give you a new start

When you come face to face
  With your sins and the shame
  I know The Redeemer saves
  All that call upon His Name

For He did not come to condemn
  But to deliver us out of judgment
  To become a child of God
  Partakers of, "life more abundant"

Set free to be led by His Spirit
  Living to do what pleases Him
  Isn't this the least I can do
  Jesus paid the price for my sin!

© laurette laster 2018

"But Jesus stooped down and began writing on the ground with His finger. However, when they persisted in questioning Him, He straightened up and said, "He who is without [any] sin among you, let him be the first to throw a stone at her." Then He stooped down again and started writing on the ground.

Straightening up, Jesus said to her, "Woman, where are they? Did no one condemn you?" She answered, "No one, Lord!" And Jesus said,

"I do not condemn you either. Go. From now on sin no more" (John 8:6-8, 10-11 AMP).

"The thief comes only in order to steal and kill and destroy. I came that they may have and enjoy life, and have it in abundance [to the full, till it overflows]" *(*John 10:10 AMP).

DAY 23

"For the wages of sin is death, but the free gift of God is eternal life in Christ Jesus our Lord" (Romans 6:23).

I knew what that house looked like yet I purchased it anyway and I was really excited. Why? You know the answer. Because I knew what it looked like when love had it? And now God had put this house in my possession and I was going to love it and get it ready for my mom to move in.

Remember earlier I talked about the big holes in the back yard? The previous owner had very large dogs and litters of puppies during the short few years he lived there. So needless to say the yard was a wreck.

The better homes and gardens yard had turned into a dangerous smelly dump. I certainly did not want my mom or anyone for that matter to be walking through the yard and trip and fall, possibly breaking a leg or an arm. I thought I could move a little dirt around and remedy the holes and fix this issue. Was I ever wrong? It takes a whole lot of dirt to fill in what I thought were seemingly small holes, and make the ground smooth and level. I wasn't sure what I was going to do or where I would get good soil.

"If we confess our sins, He is faithful and just and will forgive us our sins and purify us from all unrighteousness" (1John 1:9).

Repentance is not only acknowledging our sins it is also confessing our sin to God and to a safe person. This is so that the enemy cannot hold it over our head. Unconfessed sin is like a yard full of holes and poop. Unconfessed sin has the ability to trip us up. The underlying guilt is like potholes and poop, dangerous and smelly and when you trip and fall, others smell the residue.

Notice the key word in the verse above "IF." So this is contingent upon our willingness to get real. On day one, we talked about being "fessed" up so we cannot be conned. It isn't easy but it is necessary. When we confess we are in essence purging out guilt and the stinky stuff (poop) then it becomes necessary to fill in the holes with spiritual truths. It is very important what we allow into our new ground.

Beware that you don't allow any unwanted weeds.

"The LORD will not abandon His people, because that would dishonor His great name. For it has pleased the LORD to make you His very own people" (1 Samuel 12:22 NLT).

When I first began inquiring about fill dirt for this job, a good friend that is a farmer/rancher said to me, "You'll need to be careful what dirt you get and where it comes from." I had never given much thought to dirt prior to this conversation. So I asked him, "What do you mean?" He said, "You can get all kinds of weeds, Johnson grass, and grass burrs or goat heads, from fill dirt and you don't want that." He was right; I didn't want any of those things.

Jesus talks about this very issue in what we know as the Parable of The Sower. "Some fall among the thorns; but the thorns spring up and stifle it." (Matthew 13:7) this scripture is mentioned in three of the gospels. This scripture is found also in Mark 4:7, Luke 8:7. I choose the Weymouth translation because it makes reference to the thorns stifling us.

Years ago we lived in the country and grass burrs were prolific. To walk through our yard barefoot was not an option. Sometimes unknow-ingly grass burrs would hitch a ride into our house in the hem of our slacks, jeans, or the soles or laces of our shoes. They would catch in the carpet or in the rug. Then some unsuspecting victim, walking bare-foot through the house would step on it, and YIKES! Talk about choking out the thought of even going outside. I have memories of the lawn mower throwing these stickers all over the yard. There is some-thing about this memory that brings the pain to my mind. I didn't want one grass burr or one goat head or one blade of Johnson grass in the yard.

I needed good dirt and I didn't know where to look. I wasn't prepared to pay for a dump truck load of dirt. I began to pray asking God to lead me and help me find *good* dirt. Where was I going to find dirt and how would I get it here? And God answered my prayer, and He supplied the dirt. The dirt He supplied I didn't have to wonder about, I knew it was good dirt. It was dirt from my own yard. The very soil Mr. Crawford had worked. And all I had to do was the hard work of shoveling it into my wheelbarrow and taking it load by load to the back yard. God supplied the dirt but He didn't move it for me. Hauling the dirt from one spot to the desired location was my part.

It just so happened that the underground drainage and sewer pipes in this area of the county were in need of repair. There had been serious flooding in our county. The cause was in part from damaged drainage and sewer pipes that had eroded and collapsed. The lack of drainage and ensuing flooding showed the need for repairs.

The city dug very deep ditches along the roadway in order to install new drainage pipes. Well guess what I had at my disposal when they dug these ditches? Yep, it was dirt—*good* clean dirt and lots of it. So all I had to do was shovel and load my wheel barrow and then push the heavy wheel barrow full of *good* clean soil to the back yard. I must have made at least forty trips with a wheelbarrow full of dirt to the back yard. So much for a little bit of spreading and smoothing, huh?

The Bible tells us, work out our own salvation with fear and trem-bling. "Therefore, my beloved, as you have always obeyed, not as in my presence only, but now much more in my absence, work out your own salvation with fear and trembling" (Philippians 2:12 KJV).

So is this saying we need to fear that we may not gain salvation? No, absolutely not, salvation is our free gift when we believe that Jesus came and paid our sin debt.

But the life you have after salvation will require work. You have to fill in all the holes that are left in your ground.

This is our work to do. God will not do our part. We must work it out with reverence and with integrity, even when no one is looking, when we're not in front of our Bible teachers, preachers, mentors, even in their absence, we look closely and examine the dirt and what we are filling our time and our new life with. Look for what God has provided and what God instructs His people to use. This will put us on level ground, get it? We pray, study our Bible, and choose carefully what we are using to fill our holes. We become doers of His word and the commandments found to walk in love.

You will put something in the empty places of your life. Satan will tempt you with ungodly ideas and sins, you decide and declare no, I don't want any of those deadly weeds in my yard or in my life.

Prayer:

Dear Heavenly Father, thank you for helping me to know what to fill my life with. I want my life to be pleasing to You. I want to be fruitful and discover what You have for me. I believe You are for me and that You will help me to do the necessary work of working out my salvation. Teach me Holy Spirit, You are truth. Amen

Reflection:

What are some things that may not be good for you? Things that could stifle your Christian walk and hinder what The Lord is doing in your life? Is God convicting you of music, television programs, video games, or maybe certain friends? I know it can be difficult to realize and admit at first, but some family members may be toxic. This doesn't mean you will never have anything to do with them but it may require that we distance ourselves until we can get all the holes filled in with what God likes. Who can you go to for help concerning how to hear from God and discern His voice?

POETRY:
#FOLLOWINGHIM@HOLYBIBLE

The greatest blog I have ever followed
> Has endured the test of time
> The greatest read can testify
> Has the power to reprove a mind

The greatest book ever written
> Truth and stories on every page
> The life, the death, and RESURRECTION
> Transforming hearts of every age

This great message is more than alive
> Simply refuses to be quieted
> Now electronically downloaded
> *YouVersion Bible app-how many are delighted

The greatest story ever told
> The one you've heard before
> Will never ever be forgotten
> Written in your heart that is where it is stored

Your mind may attempt to silence
    But that beacon in your heart
    Screams listen up and hear
    In this narrative you take part

The greatest blog I've ever read
    More powerful than a locomotive
    Has the ability to knock down walls
    Are you aware it is the most quoted

Are you looking to follow the in crowd
    Do you desire to be cutting edge
    Just follow His Blog@Holy Bible
    Better than Google or World Wide Web

Eternally written for safe keeping
    Guaranteed to speak to every hearts desire
    It's more than you can think or imagine
    Follow Jesus @Holy Bible if you dare inquire

© laurette laster 2019

"Now to Him who is able to do exceedingly abundantly above all that we ask or think, according to the power that works in us, to Him be glory in the church by Christ Jesus to all generations, forever and ever." Amen (Ephesians 3:20-21 NKJV).

DAY 24

"I CONFESS MY INIQUITY; I am sorry for my sin" (Psalm 38:18).

W hen I think about the house and the filthy carpet over the urine stained saturated floor, I think about our Lord and repentance. Repentance is a thorough work not a quick fix. I wasn't surprised there was damage; the truth is I kind of already knew there was, but I didn't have any idea how severe the damage was. I expected maybe to find plank subfloors or plywood but not the original hardwood floors. The discovery of something wonderful brought a new challenge. How will I repair this? God was well aware of the issues that lay ahead. In His grace and mercy, I discovered them one at a time.

How much more He knows about you and me and the damage caused by conditions we are attempting to cover up, or perhaps they have never been uncovered and we do not realize they even exist.

Acts 22:16 "And now why are you waiting: Arise and be baptized, and wash away your sins, calling on the name of the Lord."

Could the damage be more severe than you are acknowledging? I want to assure you, there is a beautiful original at the bottom of all this.

How can I be so sure? I know because we are created in His image and likeness and God is love.

"I baptize you with water for repentance, but after me will come One more powerful than I, whose sandals I am not worthy to carry. He will baptize you with the Holy Spirit and with fire" (Matthew 3:11).

This was a lot of hard work and I was beginning to see projects completed. Seeing finished work was so refreshing. My mom wanted to move in, she was downsizing from her present house. I was also working hard to get the house complete but cutting corners was not something I wanted to do. Now with the floor repaired and finished and the holes filled in there was still much more work to be done.

Greg was going to add a few light fixtures, remove and replace some old fixtures and add ceiling fans throughout the home.

It was actually fun to plan and modernize the home and we were becoming great friends while doing this. Greg had installed some really neat fans in someone else's home and suggested I buy the same fans for this home. When he showed them to me, I was sold. It was a go.

Greg discovered the house didn't have enough power to add these extras while safely supplying the fixtures and appliances already in place. He said he would need to bring in more power to supply the upgrades. I remember asking what that meant. I would need some help understanding what he was talking about.

I didn't understand. To be honest I was clueless, but I said OKAY. After all this is what he did for a living. He was a master electrician so it was time to trust that he had the expertise to bring in more power. Trust someone. My trust muscle had been damaged and was in the process of healing.

Getting off early from his regular job, Greg, decided it was time to tackle this project of bringing in more power to the house. Greg called and said he would stop by on his way home. When he arrived, I went out to meet him. Greg opened the trunk of his car and grabbed a large case, carrying it over to the side of the house where the breaker box was located. I knew so little about power being brought in, so I just stood and watched.

Greg proceeded to take out and assemble this very large drill and bit. Then after assembling he began to drill directly into the brick. I believe this was the largest drill bit I had ever seen. It was as big around as a half dollar and as long as a baseball bat. I felt this sick queasy feeling in the pit of my stomach. Oh no what have I agreed too?

I began hollering, "Whoa, wait, oh stop. YOU CAN'T DO THIS." I said very loudly, "You're damaging the brick." Dear Lord what was he thinking? You can't drill huge holes into brick.

I was envisioning this huge gaping hole with no way to repair it. I had this image of a patched hole, being a forever eyesore in the brick. Who does this? Greg surely was out of his mind and now I going to be left with a huge hole in the brick. What have I got myself into?

Greg stopped drilling immediately, he was squatted down on his knees, laying this huge monster across his legs he calmly looked up and smiled. He quietly studied my panic ridden face a few seconds before answering. Then saying to me "trust me, I do this all the time." This could not be good. Oh no what have I agreed to? How am I going to fix this? He is surely out of his mind. I felt like throwing up.

I grimaced, saying okay, thinking he is out of his mind but what could I do? Greg drilled the hole, ran conduit, and had to crawl under the house, pull the wire and all the other stuff. I must add he did an excellent job. His work was top notch, very professional and looked perfect. See I knew it was going to be okay, why were y'all so worried?

Wow, trust someone to have my best interest at heart and to know how to help me and believe they really know what they were doing. What a novel idea. Yes we still laugh about this today.

When you are beginning over many people will have advice and good ideas to offer. Some may even want to help you. Beware and be certain you are hearing from God. You must be sure that your motives and their motives are pure, and they know what they are doing. Greg was and still is a licensed master electrician; he is a contractor who does excellent work. Several commercial properties identify him as their electrician. He takes great pride in the work he does and works as unto The Lord. I have never known of Greg to cut corners.

We cannot afford nor should we want to cut corners where repentance is being worked out, especially when it is God's power being delivered.

And whatsoever you do, do it heartily, as unto The Lord, and not unto men; knowing that of the Lord you shall receive the reward (Colossians 3:23-24).

You will need more power brought in to fulfill the call of God in your life. You are receiving a major upgrade with new enlightenment. You are getting a new heart and the laws of God are being written on your mind and warranted by God Himself. It may take some drilling and running new conduit, added breakers, new wiring, and some crawling around under the house. The original is what got you this far but the new is for more light along the way. The path of the just grows brighter and brighter.

As we read our Bible and pray, we begin asking God to open up His word to us. Ask God big questions. Ask God how to do what He wants you to do? He will answer you. I still find it amazing that I find myself in difficult circumstances then realize, oh wait I prayed for this. I find this is how He answers prayers, by giving us hands on training. We are working out our salvation with fear and trembling by faith.

God knows what we are capable of, He desires to grow and stretch us because this is how faith grows and we come alive. I realize now and understand, this is how the information becomes inherent to us, and it isn't only surface stuff, it is embedded and drilled in and hard wired into us for His power to operate in our lives. This isn't some extension cord power; this is hard wired, direct wired to the source. This is the power of God coming straight into us.

Prayer:

Dear Jesus, I know You are bringing power to me and teaching me about safe people. Help me to know how to trust others, give me keen discernment. I want to be sure I am following You and allowing safe people in. Give me the wisdom to test the spirits. I want godly relationships and friendships that please You. Amen

Reflection:

How do you test the spirits? What are three safeguards you can put around your life to keep you safe during this time? What are three healthy godly boundaries you can set to keep you safe? I'll give you one example. You should have mentors and godly counsel around you that you allow to speak openly into your life. If you have to hide to do it, it isn't God.

_____

_____

_____

POETRY: PART OF THE MASTER'S PLAN

I didn't get all I needed
    But it isn't as bad as I thought
    Because I now realize
    Not earthly but the arms of God I sought

I didn't have it easy
    Struggles were part of my days
    Oh but have I mentioned
    It is what drove me along the way

The way of life I decided
    Was hard and part of my lot
    But then the scriptures became real
    And I saw the fight I fought

God was never withholding
    Or keeping me at arm's length
    No! It is Satan mankind's enemy
    Attempting to wear out my strength

So it is with my tomorrows
    And all of my today's
    When I open my Bible and read
    Then in prayer I hear the Master say

This is part of the wilderness journey
    It's part of His Master Plan
    It is His way of leading
    While guiding us with His hand

If we never had a struggle
    If never our hearts did break
    We wouldn't have need of a Savior
    Nor understand the road He did take

For when I discern the brokenness
    Eye Witness of shattered dreams
    It is for me to become compassionate
    Reaching for prayers that silence the screams

For with struggles and the trials
    The brokenness and pain
    I'm reminded of the simple truth
    It is all for His gain

For I have not chosen Ye
    You have chosen me before
    The foundations were even laid
    My days you ordained and more

So as I walk this walk
    And continue on to know
    Teach me Lord what You have for me
    and how I am to go

For I know not the plans You have
Your ways higher and grand
Lead me and guide me now
Walk me into Your perfect plan

Leading me as I go
Heading straight for my assignment
Staying to the way
That keeps me in alignment

Teach me to understand
That pain is helping to unfurl
I am chosen and have been destined
before the foundation of the world

© laurette laster 2018

"And what is the exceeding greatness of His power toward us who believe, according to the work of His mighty power" (Ephesians 1:19 NKJV).

"For this reason I bow my knees to The Father of our Lord Jesus Christ, from whom the whole family in heaven and earth is named, that He may grant you, according to the riches of His glory to be strenthened with might through His Spirit in the inner man" (Ephesians 3:14-16).

DAY 25

"LET us test and examine our ways, and return to the Lord" (Lamentations 3:40).

In one area of the living room, I wanted to add a light in the center of the room. Greg said it could be done with no problem. The room is designed with a side area right off the kitchen, maybe for a dining table or possibly a breakfast nook, to the side of the room. This made determining where the center of the room was the million-dollar question. Should the center be with or without the nook?

We would look, measure, stand back, then look, measure and then I would say I don't know. Greg told me, "When you decide let me know, because until you tell me, I'm not cutting any holes in the ceiling." You think maybe he was a little gun shy seeing how I overreacted to his drilling into the side of the house?

This was new ground for me. I spent much of my life feeling trapped. In the past I allowed unsafe people to talk me into decisions they wanted or agree with their poor choices by guilt tripping me. I was sure glad Greg was making me decide and not in any way pressuring me. This was my second home to remodel since making Jesus

Lord over my life, and not simply hoping He was my savior, but still the decisions were overwhelming at times.

What I had come to learn and love most, was learning to walk by faith. But this project was really stretching me, stretching my faith and my trust, my perseverance and my finances. I truly believed I could ask God anything and He would answer or lead me. This is why I had purchased the house to begin with. Sometimes He pushes, but that is for another day.

By now I believed and knew Jesus was my partner. He was my Partner and I was supposed to discuss all the details with Him; well that is if I wanted His help. I would ask, what, when, where, and even the how on earth can I accomplish this, questions, and by His Spirit He would lead me. I would kneel down beside my bed and pray, "Lord, if I had an earthly father I could call him and he would answer and help me. Then I would recite Jeremiah 33:3 and say I need to know what to do. You may have heard God's number is Jeremiah 33:3. Call on Me and I will tell you great and mighty things to come. Things you know not of.

He actually blew me away by the things He did for me. Sometimes I would become so frustrated that very loudly I would say, will You answer me please? He always answered but not always like I wanted. He led me in ways that taught me to see Him and learn of Him and how to walk by faith.

He would give me dreams, or maybe an assignment that would teach me a truth I was praying about. I wouldn't realize it at the time, it would be looking back or during the storm. He would give me instructions about what to buy, what to wear, giving me ideas that gained me recognition at my job. All of these areas I had to agree to follow. "Obedience is better than sacrifice"(1 Samuel 15:22).

So where does the light fixture need to be? Where is the center of this room? Surely, He can point out the center of the room and where this fixture should go.

After several days of not being certain, one afternoon I looked and knew where the fixture should be. When I told Greg what I thought, he agreed saying, I believe you are right. He said now if I can find a stud to mount the electrical box to we'll be in business.

Greg got the sheetrock saw and began to cut. By now I was learning to trust the process. I no longer freaked out, having major brain cramps when he began to cut into sheetrock, or drill into bricks, or rip fixtures out by their roots. He was a true craftsman and a very qualified contractor. The truth is I had come to enjoy watching him use his skills. But he needn't know this. He is a master in his trade.

I was truly enjoying having a safe friend, one who would help me. I still couldn't believe he was doing all this for me. We were both in a healing season from some pretty big hurts and having made some serious mistakes. We enjoyed talking about Jesus and what He was doing in our lives and we were having good clean fun and continuing to teach the Bible study.

Yes, it is a learning process and a challenge but God was teaching me, as for Greg and I, well we were learning some very invaluable lessons about redemption, repentance, and being on God's team.

When Greg finished cutting the hole, low and behold it was right next to a stud. Wow, it couldn't have been planned any better with the precision God supplied. We both began praising God, but we were amazed at the same time. It was the perfect place, right next to a stud. God is in the smallest details. I am so glad I waited and prayed. I didn't doubt Who provided the answer to this mystery.

Now Greg had to fish the wire over and down the wall so the light could have power. He said put your hand up the wall and feel while I fish this wire over.

I didn't tell Greg but I was kind of leery to put my arm up the wall. My thoughts went to questions like, are there spiders in the wall? What about other dangers? But I was helping him so I followed his lead. I kept my hand in the opening where the light switch had been and then bam, there it was. I could feel the wire. It came straight into my hand and I pulled it the rest of the way down and out of this small opening. Needless to say, all my fears about spiders or unseen dangers vanished the moment I felt the wire. When I touched and held what I was after all the fear left me and was replaced with excitement. When God gives us wisdom, He makes it all work together perfectly and it is exciting. This was a sweat less victory.

Jesus said if you abide in Me, and My words abides in you, you will ask what you desire, and it shall be done for you (John 15:7). Yes I know this is for big things but it is for seemingly simple things also. We usually don't start with mountain moving faith.

I am so glad I didn't think to just hurry through or make decisions without first praying and asking for God's wisdom. We have to live with the results of our decisions and choices, good or bad. Being born again and in covenant with God through Christs redemptive work gives us the ability to be led by God. For those who are led by The Spirit of God are the children of God (Romans 8:14 NIV). The Spirit of God will never lead us in the wrong direction or to the wrong path. I am very glad I was able to say I don't know and then proceed from there. I'm glad I didn't act like a sissy and not reach for the wire. I didn't sense true danger; what I did sense was the old nagging fear of what if. If there had been danger God would have warned me. My advice to you is, do it afraid, God is in the details.

In the past I thought I had to have the answers, I would make decisions or react to the pressure, later regretting the decision I made. My carnal senses led me to follow earthy sensual desires.

Now God was leading me, teaching me to seek Him and to be okay and stand in the authority of saying I don't know and have peace about it. We do not have to have all the answers today and in most cases we do not have to act today. Psalm 46:10 became a life verse for me. I still have a concrete tile hanging beside my front door that says: *be still and know that I Am God.* God leads us He doesn't drive us. Think about this going forward when you feel that pressure that you have to do something or else you'll miss your only opportunity. God leads us, Satan drives us through fear.

This was still new to me. Miles away from the dysfunction of being driven by fear of not being loved was not an issue any longer. I had to learn and reprove my mind that I no longer had to react. Jesus was giving me permission to know it is okay to say I don't know I need time to think about this. When we are starting over and learning new things we may need to slow down and proceed with caution. After we begin our new walk, walking by faith, we gain momentum by trusting Him and the process as we go. These are some of the most precious times, times I will never forget. Learning to trust my Lord and knowing for certain He is with me and He is for me.

He is for you too. Stop right now and say to Him, Thank You for being with me. Jesus I believe You are here with me right now. Close your eyes and breathe in the very real calm He is pouring over you.

He is faithful to answer. In Hebrews 11:6, we are told that "God is a rewarder of those who diligently seek Him."

He has a plan for you and for your future. Don't think to gloss over the damage and take short cuts. It will not profit you. Slow down and trust Jesus. I promise He has your VERY best interest at heart, to give you hope and a future (Jeremiah 29:11).

"Those on the rock are the people who on hearing the Message receive it joyfully; but they have no root: for a time they believe, but when trial comes they fall away. That which fell among the thorns means those who have heard, but as they go on their way, the Message is stifled by the anxieties, wealth, and gaieties of time, and they yield nothing in perfection. But as for that (seed) in the good ground, it means those who having listened to the Message with open minds and in a right spirit, hold it fast, and patiently yield a return" (Luke 8:13-15 WNT).

The International Standard Version (verse 15) says this: "But the ones on the good soil are the people who hear the word but also hold on to it with good and honest hearts, producing a crop through endurance." A good and honest heart is a repentant heart that has changed its mind. A mind opened to the things of God, our good, good Father.

Jesus desires for us to succeed. Read John 10:10, the second part of the verse tells us that Jesus came that we might have life and that life more abundantly. Wow is that a new idea for you? That Jesus wants you to have an abundant life. God requires us to be fruitful. As a matter of fact it is impossible to be unfruitful if we are a child of God. This is how God measures success, by our fruitfulness.

Wouldn't it be senseless if we planted peach trees then got angry or worse, jealous when the tree began to bear fruit? Saying things like how dare you, why do you think you can grow peaches, who do you think you are? You are to be pious and peach less take those peaches off and don't let me see this again; that would be ignorant. Yet often we are taught to believe God doesn't want us to become mature and bear fruit. Christians are to become fruitful? Where is it written that we are not to have nice things, and live in nice houses, and have plenty to eat?

Being needy and eating out of dumpsters is not what God has in mind for His children anymore than we do for our children. God says He will give us houses we didn't build, and vineyards we didn't plant. Does that sound like a stingy father? No. He is our good, good Father. However, this comes with warnings.

He warns us in Deuteronomy chapter 8 saying in verse 7: "For the Lord your God is bringing you into a good land, a land of brooks of water, of fountains and springs that flow out of valleys and hills"; verse 10: "When you have eaten and are full, then you shall bless the Lord your God for the good land He has given you"; verse 11: "Beware that you do not forget the Lord your God." God requires partnership as we become fruitful (Malachi 3:8-10). He requires that we tell others it was by His Hand that we have obtained these good things. He warns us that by forgetting Him we become puffed up and think our own hands got us these things. Watch out for pride it is Satan's scheme against us, and it will destroy us.

When things were not working out as fast as I'd like I would pause and ask God if there was someplace I was not completely surrendered to Him? Lack of surrender or rebellion can hinder our fruit growing. I've discovered that areas I thought I was ready to go deeper I wasn't actually as prepared as I thought. If we are in a holding pattern something is being worked out.

"Beloved, I pray that you may prosper in all things and be in health, just as your soul prospers" (3rd John 2)

Prayer:

Dear Heavenly Father, I believe You exist. I believe You are God and that You have called me to this time. I want to know the plans You have for me. I am going to slow down and seek You. Read Hebrews 11:6 now speak it back to Him. I believe You are a rewarder to those who diligently seek You, not seek only the reward. I want Your goodness and mercy in my everyday life. I determine today to know You and the plans You have for me. I want to be found faithful. In the past I have covered up, bundled up, hurried up, and listened to the wrong people, and I have made a mess of my life. I ask for Your guidance in my life from this day forward.

Jesus I believe You are for me and with me right here right now. Amen

Reflection:

What are some old ways of thinking you need to get rid of? What are some areas of your life you need patience in? What are afraid will happen if you wait on God?

_____

_____

_____

POETRY: FAITH IT UNTIL YOU TAKE IT

To 'Faith It' is not fake
    'Faith It' not a mere game of pretend
    We 'Faith It' because we are commanded
    Called to continue until the end!

To 'Faith It' is a catalyst
    That brings God's will to pass
    To 'Faith It' is the only way
    Jesus, promises will last

We 'Faith It' by love
    Love pure and undefiled
    Faith works only by love
    Leading unto heart's desire

Faith makes manifest, things I cannot see
    'Faith It' is a decree
    Poured out by Holy Spirit
    Because when we believe

Before we see, we are ever so near it
  Now 'Faith Is', make manifest to me
  Now 'Faith Is' is how to truly receive
  By Faith, take hold of what God has given to me

© laurette laster 2018 May

Galatians 5:6 NLT
  "For when we place our faith in Christ Jesus, there is no benefit in being circumcised or being uncircumcised. What is important is faith expressing itself in love."
  Hebrews 11:1 NLT
  "Faith is the confidence that what we hope for will actually happen; it gives us assurance about things we cannot see."

DAY 26

"Pay attention to yourselves! If your brother sins, rebuke him, and if he repents, forgive him" (Luke 17:13).

A s the house was coming together there were other issues that had to be repaired and dealt with. The house has a beautiful covered patio. More than once Mr. Crawford and I had wonderful conversations as he sat on his patio and I stood at my fence.

He had built a small deck leading out of the kitchen patio doors which covered the steps. Under the deck were three concrete steps. The steps were approximately eight to ten inches deep and seven to eight foot wide.

The new owner had an idea; he would enclose the patio area making it into a room, a den (I believe). The owner and several friends decided on a strategy for taking out the steps. It was not a good idea for the removal of the porch and the steps. It was decided they could beat the concrete porch and steps out with sledgehammers and brute force.

"There is a way that seems right unto man but the end thereof is the ways of death" (Proverbs 14:12).

There were two entrances leading out to the patio from the inside

218 | LAURETTE LASTER

of the house. The one I described leading out of the kitchen and another out of the utility room. As you step out of the utility room there is a large concrete porch. This porch is approximately three feet by four feet, with two with steps approximately eight to ten inches deep and about three foot wide. The entrance to the house sets about two-and-a-half-foot above patio level.

Picture this, two, three and sometimes four grown men with very large sledge hammers attempting to beat concrete steps out. Or should I say they were attempting to bust the concrete porch and steps out.

Now I'm left with a mess. The steps half beaten out and a huge mess scattered about. There was busted concrete thrown into the yard and surrounding area. Potholes poop and concrete was the yard prior to God and myself with Greg's help taking the property over. It was more of a disaster than I saw. But the truth is I didn't see all this I saw what it looked like when love had it and that inspired me when the going would get tough.

Greg had an acquaintance that needed work and suggested I hire him to help clean up the concrete and patio. This worked out pretty well because remember, I had a very demanding job that I was working. Drive time and work from home time sometimes topped seventy to eighty hours a week.

I was able to find a local man with a small concrete business that gave me a reasonable bid to restore the porch and steps. I was grateful to hire small business owners and local folks looking to build their businesses during the renovation of the house. I didn't take someone at their word only. There is nothing better than personal references. I didn't need a handy man. I needed someone who would do the job and do it correctly.

Why do I include this you may wonder? It is because of this complete disorder, lack of knowledge, and ignorance that the mess was made to begin with. It was blind youth to think they could beat the porch and steps out and build on top of this. But I've done this in other areas of my life, and I bet you have also. I remember the owners saying proudly, "We are building a room and enclosing the patio."

The new owner didn't possess the knowledge or the ability, or the skills to turn a patio into a finished room. Desire is not enough, vision is not enough, this is where it begins, but we need wisdom and we need ability, or at least the ability to have the wisdom to hire someone who possesses the needed skills. Having want-too alone is not enough. We must acquire skills if we are going to be successful or fruitful. If we don't know how to do something the best lesson I have learned, from many failures, and the best advice I have is 'learn it or leave it'. Leave it to the professionals. Hire a skilled craftsman, one who knows what they are doing.

Jesus Christ is the author and finisher of our faith. So what is faith? Faith is our ability to trust God and His word.

"For by the grace given to me I say to everyone among you not to think of himself more highly than he ought to think, but to think with sober judgment, each according to the measure of faith that God has assigned" (Romans 12:3).

So God has dealt to each one of us a measure of faith to carry out what He desires and to put our flesh under subjection and make it obedient to the word of God.

How do we get or acquire faith? We take our measure and begin to exercise that faith. God gives us the faith we need to carry out His assignments. This is how the just, those justified by the blood of The Lamb, the forgiven, having repented; begin to walk by faith and not by sight. We don't physically see God take away our guilt but by faith we know He has. We feel the burden of guilt as it is lifted from us (Hebrews 10:36-38). We learn about God and His ways by reading His word and following the promptings of His Spirit.

This is where we begin to learn what it looked like when love had it. You learn what God had in mind when He created you. We are all given a measure of faith. But the way we grow our faith is by being stretched and trained, then stepping out into what God has for us. Faith can be compared to a muscle; it will strengthen with work outs, only if and when we put it under or against resistance. This is how we grow. Just as a child grows and develops, so do we as believers. We go from the milk for newborn babes to meat for the mature.

Psalm 119:5-8 tells us a great truth. We cannot do this by ourselves.

There are kingdom truths that follow all through the Bible from Genesis to Revelation.

No matter how awful your sins you haven't destroyed or removed the commandments which God has ordained, which are written in stone, or could we say concrete porches and the steps are not gone. The way back to God is permanent and fixed. The truths are written on our hearts and in our minds.

With our sins we may have blasted at God's commandments, over and over with the sledgehammers of our words or sinful actions but we are not powerful enough to stop the plan of God. We can deny His power and refuse His salvation. **God help us.**

You may have hammered at them with the biggest (sin) sledgehammers you could lift. Your sins may have busted some stuff up. There may a mess all around you due to these sins. But God who is faithful has made a way; God made "The Way" and His name is Jesus Christ.

Pray this prayer and ask God to direct (rebuild) your steps. These are steps He is restoring. This is the porch of protection that He is rebuilding and restoring for your sure success, The Way that leads us back into the safety and protection He provides for us. He is our strong tower and ever-present help in time of trouble, our safe refuge.

Prayer:

Dear Heavenly Father I ask You to direct my ways, all of my ways. Teach me Father to walk by faith.

Lord Jesus, You are my redeemer, redeem my life from this destruction caused by my sinful actions.

Oh, that my ways were directed to keep Your statutes! Then I would not be ashamed, When I look into all Your commandments. I will praise You with uprightness of heart, when I learn Your righteous judgments. I will keep Your statutes; Oh, do not forsake me utterly Psalm 119:5-8. Amen

Reflection:

List three things that you need God to show you. Are there areas that you believe are too beat up to be repaired? These could be relationships with loved ones that have been harmed by your sins. What do you need help cleaning up? Don't sit around hoping, get busy and God will send you help. List them below and pray the scripture above over each of them. Put a date beside each of these so you can have a reminder of when you prayed this prayer of these. You are asking God to come help you. He is our ever-present help in time of need.

_____

_____

_____

POETRY: KEEP ME DESPERATE

Keep me desperate
    For more of You
    In a desperate heart
    Precious promises come true

Eternal grace
    Sealed envelope
    Seeking for You
    With a longing hope

With each desire fulfilled
    Encourage to reach higher
    Never become complacent
    Knocking Your request inquire

Where are You Lord
    What is Your plan
    Not my flagrant
    Blatant foolish sham

You desire truth
    In our inward parts
    Only by Your wisdom
    Holy Spirit impart

Yes keep me desperate
    Not dry and unproductive
    Hungering for more of You
    Your word instructive

Oh Taste and See
    That The Lord is good
    Desperate souls
    Have understood

Ages past
    Kings and saints agree
    The Lord is good
    Oh yes, Taste and See

© laurette laster 2019

"Ask and it will be given to you; seek and you will find; knock and it will be opened to you. For everyone who asks receives, and he who seeks finds, and to him who knocks it will be opened." (Matthew 7:7-8, NKJV).

"Every persistent seeker will discover what he longs for" (Matthew 7:8, TPT).

DAY 27

Acts 17:30

"The times of ignorance God overlooked, but now He commands all people everywhere to repent."

Acts 26:19-20 *"Therefore King Agrippa I was not disobedient to the heavenly vision, but declared first to those in Damascus and in Jerusalem, and throughout all the region of Judea, and then to the Gentiles that they should repent, turn to God, and do works befitting repentance."*

The owner was trying to renovate without the skills, the tools, the knowledge, or the training. He had decided to make a room out of a patio. Have you ever decided to do something your own way? Often good ideas can turn into disaster before we know it, especially without good council or teaching.

To succeed and have the abundant life Jesus died to give us we first must repent, and then we begin to follow instructions laid out in His word, learning what Jesus meant when He said to "seek ye first the kingdom of God and His righteousness and all these things shall be added." (Matthew 6:33)

God's best plan is for us to learn His ways. He desires and requires that we come to know Him through our Savior and redeemer. Jesus told His disciples if you have seen Me you have seen The Father.

When we enter into a relationship with the Lord, He is our Partner, if He shows us a problem, we can know and rest assured there is a solution within us or within our reach. The problem is a prompting, pointing out that we need to seek Him for the solution. The answers are found in Him. Like me finding the man to restore the steps. How could I have begun to look had I denied the problem was serious, refusing to admit the damage? I had to admit I needed help and that I couldn't repair this issue on my own. Then I had to welcome someone in to help me.

The concrete man came and looked at the damage, and after surveying the damage, gave me a bid to restore the porch and steps back to the original design. Try as they may they were not able to destroy the foundation and the base of the steps, so the concrete man had something to work with.

All God needs is your willingness to admit you need help and then to let Him in. Let The Lord assess the damage. He has the wisdom you need to be brought back to right standing.

God see's us right where we are. God is drawing you near through the blood of Jesus Christ that can cleanse your conscience. Only our Savior, Jesus, and His pure blood have the power to cleanse our conscience. You are not without hope. You make the decision to learn God's ways through His Son Jesus Christ, and repent. Change your mind and become willing to learn God's ways. Jesus is the mediator of the new covenant and He is The One and Only, your Redeemer. He chose you, you haven't chosen Him. He will gladly pardon your sins.

"It is not you who chose Me, but it is I who chose you and appointed you that you might go and be fruitful and that your fruit might remain; so that whatever petition you present to the Father in My name He may give you" (John 15:16).

Jesus knows we cannot step out onto the nothingness or the mess of our life without Him. It would be like stepping out of the utility room onto the jagged jarred spikes of broken concrete, falling flat on our face causing bodily harm and further damage. He has called us and patiently waits while we figure this out. Just like stepping out of the house onto broken chiseled heaps of ruin would be extremely dangerous for a toddler; so it is with us at the beginning, we begin as mere babes in Christ. Learning and choosing His ways is how we change direction. Ask Jesus to lead the way. He will. Didn't He say I am the Way? (John 14:6)

Prayer:

Lord Jesus I need Your help and Your guidance. I have made a mess of my life and it is very scary. I don't know what to do. I am asking You to come into my life and teach me about You and Your ways. I am ready to have my steps ordered by You. Amen

PS He already is. This is the Lords doing and it is marvelous in our eyes. Amen

Reflection:

Ask the Lord specifically to show you how He sees the situations in your life. You may not be as aware of the dangers surrounding you as you need to be. Be open to listening to godly mentors and take their advice.

_____

_____

_____

POETRY: HIS OWN WORKMANSHIP

I'm not a song
 But I will sing
 I'm not a bell
 But I will ring

I'm not a clock
 But I tell time
 I'm not the poem
 But I can rhyme

On second thought
 Shall I re-speak
 Called His workmanship
 Poeimo in the Greek

His very own
 Work of art
 It is not who we were
 It's a brand new start

His own workmanship
    Created anew
    Called and chosen
    In Christ a brand new you

You're not the song
    But you can sing
    You're not the bell
    But you can ring

You're not a clock
    But you know the time
    God has set eternity
    In your hearts and minds

You are not the Creator
    So you're not sure
    All He had in mind
    When your life He secured

You are His workmanship
    Created in Christ Jesus
    People that will fulfill the destiny He has given
    You're not useless That is not how He sees us

You are a solution
    For this starving generation
    Look around pay attention
    To where you are stationed

Like that priceless Picasso
    His masterpiece and plan
    His Breath His Pneuma
    The very work of His own hand

"We have become his poetry, a re-created people that will fulfill the destiny he has given each of us, for we are joined to Jesus, the Anointed One. Even before we were born, God planned in advance our destiny and the good works we would do to fulfill it!" (Ephesians 2:10 TPT).

DAY 28

"OR DO you presume on the riches of His kindness and forbearance and patience, not knowing that God's kindness is meant to lead you to repentance" (Romans 2:4).

I've only scratched the surface with what I've shared about the renovation of the house. During the entire renovation of this home, God was so faithful. I continue to be amazed that I was able to purchase the home; Greg and I learned so many spiritual truths during this time. Truths just like I learned with my home next door.

I have discovered when I pray for wisdom; God gives me an assignment or a job and I participate in the answer or outcome. I've come to understand this is how He teaches and trains me, and this is His way of making the answer mine.

When we participate and it costs us something, we become a vested partner, not a spectator. A disciple is a participator not a spectator. Once the truth is in us, it becomes inherent, part of our inner most being and make up; it is ours it is "the truth" that makes us free.

Our spiritual gifts require maturity and development, but God desires that we be witty and skillful and master our physical beings and gifts also. Individuals who are mentally challenged and limited often possess one or more amazing gifts. We call these individuals savants': those who possess or exhibit brilliance and have exceptional skills.

God has given us all things that lead to life and godliness to freely enjoy. If we were not to excel in life, family, jobs, community, and other areas, scripture wouldn't say life and godliness? Because God is the life giver even in the hard times and extreme circumstances, He is with us.

"According as His divine power has given unto us all things that pertain unto life and godliness, through the knowledge of Him who has called us to glory and virtue" (2 Peter 1:3 KJV).

As believers we are to be the hardest working, most dependable, extremely honest, helpful, and skilled people around. We are to represent the Father and His kingdom business while here on earth.

Grace and salvation are free gifts given at the expense of the God Head. Jesus willingly gave His life that we may receive forgiveness for our sins. This is grace. These gifts are grants from God almighty, by His solemn oath and promise. No one can take these gifts from you, ever. However, sanctification and bringing forth fruit cost us something. God gives gifts without repentance but He doesn't always empower us to operate in our gift. The gift is ours, we are accountable for the gift, but if we do not align with our heavenly Father and His ways, the gift can lie dormant not being tapped into.

We must learn how to work with God and His kingdom truths. This is why it is so important to read your Bible. Do not just take someone's word when they tell you something is in the Bible. You need to read your Bible and learn what pleases God. We participate in the process. We are participators not simply spectators.

Pay attention to what is going on around you. Instead of thinking something is too hard; ask yourself this question, is God trying to teach me something? Is God growing and maturing me through this event? You've heard the term growing pains, right? Well sometimes growth and development are painful but it is so worth it.

You might be surprised that the toughest test and the hardest times you go through are exactly what you prayed for. This is how He is developing you spiritually, mentally, and physically, to be able to handle what you prayed for and what He designed you for. Yes, your prayers are being answered and worked out through the test.

Perhaps you have prayed to not be afraid of people, or you prayed and ask God to help you be a God pleaser, not a man pleaser. If these prayers sound familiar you may have to make some hard calls. Practice is how we learn. God may have you in a place right now where you will have to say what you mean, mean what you say, but not say it in a mean way. God does not make us sick or give us diseases to teach us a lesson. That would make God mean and vindictive and He is neither of these. God is love, God is wisdom, and He is apt to teach; didactic.

These are God's didactic lessons. Didactic: definition something designed to teach you by having you do something. It is to convey instruction through moral observations. I'm sure you have heard others refer to this phrase; I learned this in the school of hard knocks. We will either learn through being teachable or through tough situations we may find ourselves in.

Becoming a GM for one of the largest casual family dining corporations in the world grew me and gave me back what the enemy had stolen. It was by far the most difficult, yet the most rewarding adventure and feat of my life.

Accepting this position (responsibility) was my defining moment and line. Had I not applied, supernatural in and of itself, and had I not said yes, I truly shudder to think where I would be today.

After leading me into repentance and restoration, God was developing me, and this was the process for my call and assignment. All of this was very hard work, but the most rewarding work of my life. This grew me, stretched me, and strengthened me; yes, the growing pains were real. Through the pain and the tears, the fears and the doubts, I would do it all again, in a heartbeat.

During the interview, the D.O. ask me if I would go three states away for training for six weeks? I remember *hearing* myself very eagerly say "Yes." It seemed the answer rose up out of me, with a force I wasn't in control of. As I was driving the forty-five miles back home I kept saying who said that? It didn't come from my head it came from Him. I was so scared but I knew that I knew it was Him. so I was excited and I was very scared. This was His assignment for many future alignments. One of many I have had since beginning to do whatever He asks of me.

Perhaps you remember the story of the Potter's House, in Jeremiah chapter 16. God sent Jeremiah to the Potters house. When Jeremiah went to the Potter's House the potter was working at his wheel and God began to explain His sovereignty to Jeremiah, by using the potter at his wheel, molding vessels from clay.

Ephesians 2:13 tells us that it is God who is working both to will and to do in our lives for His good pleasure. If you are working the works of repentance you are pleasing to God. He has a plan. Even in all of the uncertainty, if you are willing and obedient, you will connect the dots as you continue. Keep going. Even if it doesn't make sense and even if you are afraid. Step out into Him, your steps are being led and you are secure. If you make a wrong move He will correct you.

"And you ask (Oh God), what if I fall? Oh but my darling, "What if you fly?" Erin Hanson

Prayer:
Heavenly Father, I know You are doing a deep work inside of me. My heart's desire is to be pleasing to You, in thought and actions. You indeed are the Potter I want to be pliable clay in Your mighty hands. I don't want be dry and of no use. Teach me Your ways oh God and lead me in the way everlasting. I repent of being a people pleaser knowing I was not pleasing You. Amen

Reflection:
What are some tough areas that God may be using to help you learn truth? Not places of making you sick or punishing you, but places where you know He is leading you to be the person He created you to be. Like maybe not going along to get along when it violates your morals. Or maybe not standing up for you, to others in a god-fearing

way. Are there areas you know you should be stronger? Write them down.

_____

_____

_____

POETRY: BEING MADE NEW

What is thunder
    The voice of God
    What is the rain
    That creates blossoms from buds

What is this feeling
    Of gladness and glee
    Where is this from
    Oh this new energy.

Why do I feel as if
    I am filled with gladness
    And what did He say
    Goodbye, so long old sadness

Hard days are over
    Gone are your tears
    I'm being made new
    The Lord has drawn near

That broken heart
    Once familiar to me
    My Lord Jesus
    Calls; "come unto Me."

Those who are weary
    With a heavy yoke
    His promises are true
    This isn't a joke

He gives me beauty for ashes
    The oil of joy for mourning
    The garment of praise
    His love over me, adorning

Spirit of heaviness
    Your days are ended
    I'm planted by The Lord
    Restoration defended

I didn't know His ways
    So pleasant and freeing
    To be His oh this love
    From pureness gleaning

Dressed in His robe
    I'm His, I am home
    Righteousness and peace
    I never fear being alone!

I'm made brand new
    Not mere pretend
    Did you hear what He said
    Face to face, He calls me friend

"You show that you are My intimate friends when you obey all that I command you. I have never called you servants, because a master doesn't confide in his servants, and servants don't always understand what the master is doing. But I call you My most intimate friends, for I reveal to you everything I have heard from My Father. You didn't choose Me but I've chosen and commissioned you to go into the world, to bear fruit" (John 15:14-16, TPT).

DAY 29

"BUT THOSE THINGS which God foretold by the mouth of all His prophets, that the Christ would suffer, He has thus fulfilled. Repent therefore and be converted (or turn again), that your sins may be blotted out, so that times (seasons) of refreshing may come from the presence of The Lord" (Acts 3:18-19).

Repentance is an ongoing process or work available to the born-again believers and children of God. When we ask The Lord Jesus Christ to come into our heart and be our Savior He is our Teacher. He has given us His Holy Spirit to lead and guide us into all truth. We are forgiven and cleansed if we confess our sins and ask for forgiveness. But this is where we begin again. We may have to reset the needle more than once. It takes twenty-one days to establish a new habit. Scripture tells us though the righteous may fall seven times they shall rise up, not so with the wicked, one disaster is enough to overthrow them (Proverbs 24:16). As we work and bring forth fruit worthy of repentance, this shows seasonal work. Peter says so that times or seasons of refreshing may come. So again, this points to seasonal outpourings.

Turn again is from the Greek word meta and noiéō, changing of the mind, to turn having reconsidered the way we were going. The Berean Literal Bible reads turn again, what does Peter mean, again? Is he saying God has opened a new mystery to them that will help them understand this mystery? Does he mean now their eyes were opened? Does he mean, they were following vain traditions previously? I think it would be safe to say yes to all of these. There is a once and for all work, turning away from living ungodly to being renewed unto God. And there are, aha now I get it, light bulb moments that I pray last all my life. I want to always see new truths in His word. This is my prayer and desire for each of us. That you realize you are loved and forgiven if you truly repent. This is my heartfelt desire in sharing this book of reflections. I pray you are being drawn and led as you begin to understand what pleases God and what doesn't please God. Then when we realize we've missed it, we run to Him not hide from Him. Maybe in the past like me you got busy hiding or trying to be good enough, not realizing our only hope is take words and return to Him, like the prodigal (Luke 15:17-19).

In order to be led by The Spirit of God, you have to know Him. I hope you had a loving father and mother. I hope you had both in the same home. The percentage of us that did not sadly is much higher, than those that did.

Picture someone who loved you in your life. I'm sure we all had at least one safe person; that person we knew loved us, we felt safe and secure, and we knew we were loved. Think back on this person now, the one you loved being around and could tell they enjoyed having you around.

When we love someone and respect them we do not want to do something that would repel them, or make them not want to be around us, would we? Of course we wouldn't. Fellowship is broken if this occurs. You are learning how to be a God pleaser, even at the risk and the expense of losing friends and maybe even family. God can and will restore healthy relationships. He is the God of restoration. I've discovered sometimes we must let some go in order to grow.

Years ago, when I moved back in with my mom, I felt The Lord was calling me. Today I can say, I know He was calling and leading me, and I can look back and trace His steps that led me "safely" out. I got on my knees in the early days and prayed asking this question. I said, "Am I psychotic?" I'd like to tell you the heavens parted and I heard the voice of God saying no My child, you are loved and chosen and I am speaking to you and now you know everything there is to know. But that isn't what I heard. But by faith I continued on. Sometimes I know God had to drag me. Have you heard about a poem call butt prints in the sand? It goes on the say these were the times The Lord had to drag us. I'm sure we can all relate.

During this time my extremely loyal, very loving, caring, and intelligent mom said to me; "you need to do _____ and you'll want to do _____ and then you need to do _____. All of the things she was telling me were excellent advice. The problem was most of my life I had followed others advice. I would do what they thought best and then didn't like what was dished out. I would find myself left with what they thought was best, it wasn't that it wasn't good, but today I realize it wasn't God. Most of all I was left with lingering doubt, wondering if I did the right thing. Paralysis of analysis, as I later heard while listening to Joyce Meyers. This is a miserable place to live but I did live this for years. Afraid of doing the wrong thing, or possible punishment, or worse yet that very real fear "rejection" made this my reality. I wanted more than anything to know that I was being led by God and that my choices and my life were pleasing to Him. I was sure sick and tired of doing what I knew was not pleasing to Him.

While she was still taking, I calmly interjected and began answering her. I began by saying; I don't know what I need to do. I don't even know who I need to talk to. But I know you are the smartest person I know and I love and respect you more than any human on this planet, but I know I have to hear from God. I told her, I have to know that the rest of my life is pleasing to God; I have made all the wrong turns and ungodly choices I ever want to make.

I don't know how I knew this. I don't know how I knew any of these things I was saying, these words were just spilling out of my mouth coming from the depth of my soul.

As I was speaking to my mom it was very loving, and with the utmost respect. My mom was by far the smartest woman I have ever known. My mom was intellectually smart and she was street smart. She knew how to not let others take advantage of her, or get the upper hand, so to say. She could see a con a mile away. She was strong and often I mistook this strength as unloving. Today I realize healthy boundaries and accountability is the most loving thing anyone can do for us and others.

When I finished speaking, she looked at me and had a very puzzled look on her face. I knew I meant the words that just came out my mouth. I wasn't sure where the words came from but I had a knowledge that I needed to hear from God. I don't know how I even knew I could hear from God, but I did. I realize today that this was a cry from the deep, and that this cry came from my soul. Those words didn't come out of my mouth or from head knowledge; they came from a deep desire to please God. I wanted to quit being stupid and letting others con and manipulate me or use me for what they wanted and pretend I was loved. I wanted to be good and feel clean and useful. I needed the lies to stop. I was so tired of pleasing others who were only using me thinking this was godly.

As my mom stood there looking at me, a big smile came across her face and she said, "Well, Dorothy is not in Kansas anymore." We had a huge belly laugh, more than once about her analogy. But she was right.

Dorothy or let's just say, Laurette, wasn't in Kansas anymore. Something was happening and I had a boldness rising up. I didn't need to take advice from folks without a brain, or allow cowards to hide behind me, and I certainly didn't need to let anyone without a heart hurt mine. Casting my pearl before swine and allowing my heart to get trampled on had to come to an end. (Matthew 7:6) I realized that the people pleaser, caretaker, codependent behavior wasn't from God and it had to STOP! Often these character flaws mimic Christian values and seem to be part of, be nice, and don't judge mentality. Being abused or used is not biblical nor is it in God's plans. I found the truth when He found me, and He set me free.

That is what repentance does for us. Is this why our Lord Jesus Christ said, "Repent for the kingdom of heaven is at hand?"

Are you ready for the insanity and confusion to end? I believe the answer is a resounding yes. The assignment God has for you to do while you are on earth cannot be accomplished if you are weighted down with sin or guilt or people pleasing. Sin and guilt is a very heavy burden. We are not designed to live in sin or carry the weight of guilt on our shoulders or backs. Jesus carried the Cross on His shoulders that we may take His yoke and not to carry the unbearable weight of sin.

In the Bible, God's chosen people are referred to as sheep. Sheep are not dumb animals as I often heard them described. In fact sheep are forward grazing animals. Sheep don't walk forward and graze then turn back and try to find food where they already had grazed. We are called to go forward without the burden and guilt of sin. Mules are stubborn and they are used as pack animals. We are not stubborn and hard-headed. We become teachable and are led like the sheep of His pasture.

Aren't you glad God has called you to this place? Aren't you seeing repentance in a different light right now? It isn't that God is asking you to grovel over all your sins, dear goodness that would take us our whole life to do, remember we have all fallen short of the glory of God. But God is saying come jump into the living waters and be made new. I know what you did, I saw what has been done to you, I will make you brand new and you will be a beacon of hope to others when they see the work I've done in your life. You can be cleansed from all your sin. The blood of Jesus is what can cleanse our conscience from guilt.

"Therefore brothers and sisters, since we have confidence to enter the Most Holy Place by the blood of Jesus, by a new and living way opened for us through the curtain that is His body, and since we have a great Priest over the house of God, let us draw near to God with a sincere heart, and with the full assurance that faith brings, having our hearts sprinkled to cleanse us from a guilty conscience and having our bodies washed with pure water. Let us hold unswervingly to the hope we profess, for He who promised is faithful" (Hebrews 10:19-23 NIV).

Wow what a promise. God already knows <u>everything</u> you have done. There may not be another human on earth (yet) that knows about that one secret sin, but God knows and He is still calling you to repent and confess that sin to someone and come into covenant with Him. He will provide that one safe person when the time is right. Don't take matters into your own hands, be led.

Prayer:

Heavenly Father, I want to thank You for the gift of forgiveness. What amazing grace, I believe You know everything about me and You still are extending Your hand to me. You love me, because You know what I looked like when You created me. You know what I look liked when Love had me. You see me cleansed even now. Show me how to have a real relationship with You.

Lord Jesus, You desire to have a relationship with me and I want to thank You for becoming my sacrifice. You poured out Your blood that my conscience can be cleansed from all my sin, this is another gift of Your grace extended to me with my salvation. I believe Your blood is cleansing my conscience as I continue to spend time with You in Your word, make it come alive to me. Amen

Reflection:

Are there one (or more) things you are afraid to address? Is there a sin you believe keeping God from wanting a relationship with you? Do you somehow still feel disqualified? Is your conscience still struggling with unresolved issues and guilt? Lift these up to God right now.

Write down what you think it would cost you. What is the worst case scenario that could happen if you come clean about this? I promise you He will send someone safe to you to share this (most safe people I know have also sinned the same sin and know they are forgiven). If you do not feel safe sharing a sin with someone, I recommend reaching out to a pastor or a counselor. They are bound to confidentiality.

(PS Remember, God knows what you looked like when love had

you. He sees you there already. Ask Him for a glimpse of your freedom, spirit, soul, and body.)

_____

_____

_____

"There is now therefore no condemnation to those who are in Christ Jesus, who do not walk according to the flesh, but according to the Spirit" (Roman 8:1 NKJV).

POETRY: I WILL ARRIVE

I arrived at the gate called forgiven
    Finally! This was it
    But as I looked around
    I couldn't locate an exit

Looking around
    What did I find
    Another gate
    One of a different kind

Will I ever arrive
    If all I see are departures
    Then it was as if I heard
    This journey is for My partners

Each time I think I've arrived
    I look around and see
    Another departing gate
    Appearing in front of me

The gate called salvation
    That was only the start
    The One named follow Me
    This is my determined part

I've began to realize
    That each time I think I've arrived
    It is simply a leg in my journey
    This is how I become more alive

My connecting flights
    ordered even before I land
    Departure is the key
    Led by His own right hand

The gate called repentance
    Face to face with all my sins
    The ones I must confess
    Tell and admit them all to Him

I wanted to pass by
    I didn't want to enter
    The corridor marked confession
    Straight ahead-dead center

As hard as it was
    I confessed them all to Him
    I wasn't sure I would be able
    Where and how would I begin

He made it seem so natural
    And the way He looked at me
    Pure love and acceptance
    Forgiveness poured over me

Then ushered to the door
    And behold another gate
    This one called Chosen,
    What was to be my fate

Chosen? This couldn't be mine
    I glanced around confused
    But was guided on ahead
    Overwhelmed by feelings of gratitude

The next gate, how can I explain
    Oh what grandeur, simply amazed
    The gate beyond what I could imagine
    I am made new and completely changed

I thought for sure I had arrived
    When suddenly I heard
    Not ever on this side of time
    Continue in My Word

For now, when you pray
    Seek to know Me even more
    You can freely receive
    From heavens open store

There will be a final departure
    Where I'm eternally alive
    Heaven is my destination
    And I'll know I have arrived

When I meet my Master
    At the Pearl which is 'The Gate'
    I'll hear Jesus say, "you have arrived,
    Welcome home, now we Celebrate."

"Now may the God of hope fill you with all joy and peace in believing that you may abound in hope by the power of the Holy Spirit" (Romans 15:3, NKJV).

DAY 30

"AND PETER SAID TO THEM, "Repent and be baptized every one of you in the name of Jesus Christ for the forgiveness of your sins, and you will receive the gift of the Holy Spirit" (Acts 2:38).

And you will receive THE gift. What gift? I have a gift available to me? So is this like Paul Harvey and the Rest of the Story? Is there more? How can it get better than being forgiven and put in right standing with God and knowing I will be with Jesus forever in heaven when I die? Can there be more than the freeing of the terrible weight of sin when it is lifted off a repentant sinner? Is there something more than this?

I remember when I knew I was forgiven for my sins. I was amazed by God's goodness. I remember realizing He loved me, I saw Him and He saw me, in spite of the awful sins I had committed. And it is still more than enough. But wait can there be more? Yes because this is by His Spirit.

The Love of God is the greatest gift a human heart can receive. This love, His pure Love transforms lives in ways nothing on this earth can come close to. Remember what God told me about my excitement when purchasing the house? I had a vision of what the house could be. I had seen it before the damage and neglect. I saw the house when love had it before it fell into the hands of an owner who didn't and couldn't love it. Before the house fell into the wrong hands it was manicured, loved, and cared for.

Well guess what, God saw you before the damage and neglect, whether of your own making or someone else's. Whether your sins and lawless deeds preceded or followed someone else's actions and abusive ways or you just blew it. Sin is sin, and ALL have sinned and fallen short of the glory of God

Where can I go from Your Spirit? Where can I flee from Your presence? If I go up to the heavens You are there; if I make my bed in hell, You are there. If I rise on the wings of the dawn, if I settle on the far side of the sea even there Your hand will guide me, Your right hand will hold me fast. If I say, surely the darkness will hide me and the light become night around me, even the darkness will not be dark to You; the night will shine like the day for darkness is as light to You.

For You created my inmost being; You knit me together in my mother's womb. I praise You because I am fearfully and wonderfully made; Your works are wonderful, I know that full well. My frame was not hidden from You when I was made in the secret place. When I was woven together in the depths of the earth(in my mother's womb), Your eyes saw my unformed body all the days ordained for me were written in Your book before one of them came to be. How precious are Your thoughts toward me, Oh God! How great is the sum of them! (Psalm 139).

Wow! Just Wow! In the back of the book is a promise that you will sign and date after completing this section.

Remember, He is the Potter you are the clay.

So as you prepare to go forward and make decisions you will need help and encouragement, guidance and wisdom, truth and grace and you will need to hear from God like never before. You need power in order to walk the walk God is calling you too. God is going to sculpt you into the masterpiece He created you to be. You have become a vested partner in this work.

Often people say they are waiting on God to do something, when the truth is they should be doing it. Being transformed into His image takes determination, hard work, along with the "I will not quit" attitude. As we become fruitful and bear fruit worthy of repentance we become active in the work ahead. God does not by divine osmosis, go 'poof' and you have it. If you are serious about becoming all God has designed you to be, and ordained (your days are written in His book) for your life, it is time to get serious because there is work to do. Development is work.

To become good at something you must learn and study and practice. Good athletes practice several hours a day before game day. So your gift or gifts must be developed. This is an ongoing process for the remainder of your born again, after repentance new life. "For we are His workmanship, [poiema] You are a new creation, created in Christ Jesus to do good works that God ordained before you were born" (Ephesians 2:10).

God's desire is to equip every believer with everything we need to be successful. You need the gift of His Holy Spirit to go forward in your walk.

We are sealed with His Holy Spirit on the day we are saved. The day you confessed with your mouth and believed in your heart that you were a sinner and ask Jesus into your heart making Him Lord and Savior, you were sealed with the promise of His Holy Spirit, but there is more. Ephesians 1:13 says you were sealed. This means to stamp for security or preservation; by implication to keep safe for an appointed time. Well now I think God is about to equip you so that you are no longer a secret.

When we receive the baptism of Holy Spirit we are baptized with the infilling of His Spirit and given the gift of Holy Spirit. Now we are plugged into and fully connected with His Power. Holy Spirit is an empowering Living Spirit that equips us to do the will of God. Think of it like an expensive lamp. Even with a new bulb the lamp cannot be used and fulfill the purpose it was created for, to shine and put forth light, without being plugged into a power source, and as believers neither can we.

Read Acts 1:5-8. Jesus explains that to be baptized with the Holy Spirit means they will have the power to be witnesses. A witness helps others be able to see something through their eyes. The whole purpose of repenting is to denounce self and the selfish desire to sin. Then having changed your mind you are ready to make a bold proclamation to live for Jesus. If it were easy everyone would do it. Being a bold Christian takes a dogged determination and faith, these come only through and by His power from the Gift of The Person of Holy Spirit.

We are imperfect people but we no longer live in sin, our desire is to be pleasing to God. We didn't become perfect we are redeemed. But now we are not agreeing with the enemy of our souls to retain the free will to sin. Having had a real heart change we have repented of our sins and sinful ways, and we are willing to be vessels fit for the King and His use. Being a new creation and having received the gift of eternal salvation, we have a new life; our life is now hidden in Christ becoming part of Gods family. As heirs, we are learning the family business and are appointed with our assignment. Having been given an assignment comes with protection and assistance for fulfilling our call. We now have an advocate working for us 24/7.

As a born-again believer, you cannot be comfortable and choose sin over doing the will of God, but you will not have the power to be perfect. God is not looking for perfection He requires faith and is looking for obedience. Faith and Obedience to His word is His perfection at work in our human frailty. In other words, you won't sin on purpose but when you do, you will have an advocate interceding for you in the courts of heaven. Often wealthy people and business owners keep a high-profile attorney on a retainer fee. They have access to the best defense and the only way to insure this is to pay a retainer fee. They pay them a fee to be certain they have legal aid if the need were to arise. They do not wait until there is a need for this counsel, it is set in place before hand, for the company's security and protection. So to put it in legal terms, in the court of heaven, The Holy Spirit and Jesus are your guarantee from this day forward. And His blood paid it all. If we are doing the will of The Father, His mercy and goodness follow us all the days of our life according to King David in Psalm 23. Grace is covenant talk and we are covered and surrounded by His grace.

The Holy Spirit is at work on the earth while Jesus is interceding for you and I, day and night in the great court room of heaven. A top-notch qualified attorney will not come hunt you down when you are in trouble. Attorneys that do that are called ambulance chasers, and they are not of good report. Satan will offer quick fixes, lies and schemes beware that you don't buy his lies. He is craftier than all the other animals, he is cunning and attempts throughout our life to deceive us. He is a snake.

Top notch attorneys make a name for themselves based on their successes and word of mouth of their clients. This is how others know about them. Their successes are what make others aware of their services, but you must go to them. It is the same with Holy Spirit. You ask Jesus to send you THE gift of HIS Holy Spirit. If you do not ask and pursue Him, He cannot come. He wants to help you, He is here to help you, but He must be retained by you (invited, hired with purity of heart, put in charge) and asked by you and you must be in the family to qualify for this heavenly protection.

In the kingdom of God there are kingdom laws that God Himself will not violate. He will not come without your consent. He will not violate or side-step your free will.

We must put down the rights to self and align with His will for our life. We are now heirs to the wealthiest family estate ever known in all of creation. Our finite minds cannot even comprehend all this entails.

God told Cain in Genesis 4:17, " if you do well will you not be accepted?" God was saying to Cain if you give it all you've got to please and obey Me, that is more than enough. God will never ask you for more than you have, but He will ask you for all that you have that you are not even aware of (Mark 12:30-31).

The problem is you really don't know what you have until God begins to call it out of you. You don't work to gain God's acceptance your (heart) work comes because you are accepted in the Beloved. You could never work enough to gain His acceptance and repay His goodness. But now that you realize the price He paid you have a deep desire to do only what pleases Him.

Prayer:

Heavenly Father I desire THE gift of the baptism of Holy Spirit and Fire. I need help and I need the power that can only come from You. Your word says if I ask You will send me THE gift of Your Holy Spirit. I desire to do Your will. I am so thankful for Your forgiveness. I know You have brought me here to this place, now for this time. I have wasted so much time and I need Your help. King David said he thirsted for Your presence as a deer pants for water, oh God fill me with Your Holy Spirit and with Living Water. Oh Deep calls unto Deep in the roar of Your waterfalls; all Your waves and breakers have swept over me.

Lord Jesus, You told the woman at the well if she knew the Gift of God and who was asking her, she would ask You for a drink and You would give her living water, water that would become a spring of water, welling up to eternal life. That is what I am thirsting for, I thirst for living water. Give me to drink of this living water so that I never thirst again. I don't want any more watered down worldly lukewarm water. I ask for "The Gift" the gift of Holy Spirit to fill me. Amen and amen. (*See Promise on page 350*).

When Jesus began to tell the woman at the well all she had done, she didn't run away from Him. She was honest and didn't hide anything. This is the first place in the Bible Jesus tells anyone He is the Messiah. He told her after she had confessed to Him what He already knew. He told this woman He was the Messiah before He told any others. We can guess by the time of her coming to draw water, she probably was an outcast. The others came earlier in the day; she however came around the noon hour or in the heat of the day. The Bible says it was about noon. Her encounter with Jesus led her to go tell others (the men) and then her entire town was saved. What an assignment.

Reflection:

Tell Jesus what you need.

_____

_____

_____

POETRY: COULD THIS BE MESSIAH

At that very moment
    I dropped my empty water pot
    My heart had been completely filled
    What I imagined not what I thought

When He first began to speak
    I could not make sense of His talk
    Speaking and asking of me a drink
    A Samaritan woman out of wedlock

He continued to teach and explain
    He told me all the things I had done
    The sins the pain the rejection
    While naming them all one by one

Others had simply shunned
    Naming and shaming my condition
    Maybe He is a prophet
    Something about Him seems so different

If you knew gift of God He said
 You'd ask of Me a Drink
 He didn't even have a dipper
 Strange comment what was I to think

How can You give me this water
 Sir so that I never thirst again
 Oh tell me now I beg
 While we talked He began

Asking again personal questions
 But I answered honestly never the less
 For I perceived this man a prophet
 He knew so I didn't have to guess

I told Him Messiah was coming
 And He could explain everything to us
 It seemed we didn't understand
 And I didn't come to fuss

He opened His mouth declared I Am He
 At that moment they began to gush
 Eternal Springs of Living Water
 Oh to tell the others, yes I must

He told me first, a woman
 Before His trial, Exclaiming I Am He
 The eternal well of Salvation has come
 To my town through a Samaritan, and a woman, me

When we shall worship in the Spirit and truth
 A time is coming and now has, He said
 Worshipping the Father in The Spirit and truth
 Bringing back to life what was once thought dead

"The woman then left her water pot, went her way into the city, and said to the men, 'Come, see a Man who told me all things that I ever did. Could this be the Christ?' Then they went out of the city and came to Him" (John 4:28-30 NKJV).

DAY 31

"But the [a]Helper (Comforter, Advocate, Intercessor—Counselor, Strengthener, Standby), the Holy Spirit, whom the Father will send in My name [in My place, to represent Me and act on My behalf], He will teach you all things. And He will help you remember everything that I have told you" John 14:26 Amplified Bible (AMP).

Notice in the above scripture, the amplified translation lists a seven-fold office for Holy Spirit. Holy Spirit is the third person of the Trinity. He is a He, not an It, not a feeling or goose bumps. He is THE very real living Speaking Spirit that guides us into all truth. When we encounter God's Holy Spirit we will feel Him and yes we may get goose bumps or like I say I glow in the dark after an encounter with Him, I still do with every encounter. One friend of mine says I felt His Holy Spirit and now my allergies are making my eyes water. No it isn't allergies those are cleansing waters in the form of healing tears.

The Helper

He is our Helper. Yesterday we talked about wealthy business owners hiring and retaining high profile attorneys for their businesses.

The law office is hired by the business owner to represent them and help protect their interests and protect their property. The law office services are available to the business owner at all times, willing to immediately go to work at the drop of a hat.

Do you think God would have something as valuable as heirs to His kingdom and not protect His interests? God's most valuable possessions are His people. Everything apart from miracles that God is doing in the earth is done through His people and their obedience to His leading.

When we do the work of repentance, we acknowledge that we have sinned against God and His ways. Making the sincere earnest vow from our heart to follow God, Satan puts us on a hit list and marks us for destruction. Once we repent we are an extremely valuable asset to the kingdom of God, and God knows Satan will launch an attack on us. He launched an attack enticing us to sin but now we are not ignorant of his devices (2 Corinthians 2:11). Satan's desire is to make it so hard we give up or give in, and God uses these attacks to strengthen us and build our character, God equips us with everything we need for a life of godliness.

God is ALL powerful and we are protected, but there is a fight that ensues. This is why The Lord wants us to be endued with power from on high. Jesus came to earth and walked as a man but never sinned, to show us how, by the word of God, we can destroy the works of the enemy in our life. Jesus was manifest to destroy the works of Satan once and for all. Jesus came and did this fully man with the Power of The Spirit of God to show us how it is done. All of heaven supports and helps us when our battle is raging.

There is a power deep within us that drives and propels us forward during and after repentance. Remember it is the grace of God that is leading us or bringing us into repentance? We can think it is us, but it is not. It is Holy Spirit empowering us to continue. If we had the ability we would have done this much sooner and not waited until we created so much damage to ourselves and others. Hardness of heart that leads us to hate, is sin, just as much as murder according to Jesus.

As we repent, we are growing in the grace and goodness of our heavenly Father and His only begotten Son, Jesus Christ. The Godhead, Father, Son, and Holy Spirit, have a Very real Vested interest in all born again believers and those who are heirs of salvation. He has angels working for us even before we are born again. "Are they not all ministering spirits sent forth to minister for those who will inherit salvation?" (Hebrews 1:14).

Satan doesn't want us becoming stronger and learning how to fight the good fight of faith, for the kingdom of God. He does everything he can to stop us with discouragement, doubt, disappointment, often trying to make us think it is God who is working against us. We now know better. God is for us and if God be for us who can be against us? And we know nothing can separate is from His love, *nothing*.

Do not ever let Satan deceive you and make you think that you are alone. Jesus tells us in John 15 that it is expedient that He leave the earth so that the Helper who He will send, His Holy Spirit can come. The Helper is our help while we are on earth.

Jesus also promises, "I will not leave you orphans." Wow what a promise. I was a fatherless girl, so this and the many scriptures about the fatherless and the orphans ministered to me in an amazing way. One or both of your parents may have had issues that caused you to be an orphan or motherless or fatherless, maybe you have had an orphan spirit too, but hallelujah those days are over. I promise being a born again child of God is a game changer, a major game changer. You will never be the same. Our Father is the creator and the God of the entire universe. That is a GAME CHANGER. Read Psalms 27 over and over.

When Father God became my Father, you can just imagine what a game changer that was. I have never been the same. I am an heir to the kingdom of God and to all of His promises and I want more than anything to make Him proud. All those years of wishing and wanting a good dad do not compare the enormity of God becoming my Father. If having an earthly father with me would have diminished the closeness and desire I had for God, well I'm sure glad he wasn't there.

The Greek word for Helper is *parakletos* this is where we get the English word *paramedic* from.

Strong's Concordance #3875 *paráklētos* (from 3844 */pará*, *"from* clos /*kaléō*, "make a call") – properly, a *legal advocate* who makes the right judgment-*call*, *close* enough to the situation. 3875 /*paráklētos* ("advocate, advisor-helper") is the regular term in NT times of an *attorney* (lawyer) – i.e. someone *giving evidence that stands up in court*.

Properly, summoned, called to one's side, especially called to one's aid; hence,

1. "one who pleads another's cause before a judge, a pleader, counsel for defense, legal assistant; an advocate".

2. universally, one who pleads another's cause with one, an intercessor: so of Christ, in his exaltation at God's right hand, pleading with God the Father for the pardon of our sins (in the same sense, of the divine Logos.

3. in the widest sense, a helper, succorer, aider, assistant; so of the Holy Spirit destined to take the place of Christ with the apostles (after His ascension to the Father), to lead them to a deeper knowledge of gospel truth, and to give them the divine strength needed to enable them to undergo trials and persecutions on behalf of the divine kingdom: John 14-16, John 15:26; Mark 13:11; Luke 12:11; God in creating the world had no need of an adviser, counsellor, helper.

Read the above passage again, He is a legal advocate. He is your legal advocate, (guarantee) on retainer at all times. Remember yesterday we talked about wealthy business owners retaining the best lawyer's money can buy, well guess what? You now have the best-known counsel in heaven and on earth.

God Himself is your father. The Godhead is representing you and leading you daily. And now there is another step to take. You must do what He tells you (Isaiah 1:18-19).

A friend of mine told me a story; years ago, he was in serious legal trouble. His father hired a top notch attorney; the best Dallas TX had to offer. The attorney told my friend, not to say anything unless he was told to. The attorney said, "let me do the talking, I will defend you." My friend did just what his attorney told him to do and the attorney was able to keep him from serving time in prison. My friend was guilty and caught red-handed. My friend said he never wanted to risk being in that kind of trouble ever again and how he was so glad to have had good legal counsel.

That is how we should be also. When we realize Jesus paid, in full, our sin debt and the price of redemption and has sent us The Helper, we should never risk offending or not obey what He says.

"And do not bring sorrow to God's Holy Spirit by the way you live. Remember, He has identified you as His own, **guaranteeing** that you will be saved on the day of redemption" (Ephesians 4:30 NLT). I love this translation. Do not bring sorrow to God's Holy Spirit...

I'm sure all of us at one time or another has been guilty of hurting someone we love. You know that feeling you get deep in your gut? You know the nagging feeling that does not go away. It may over time intensify or get worse. That my friend is known as conviction. This is completely different from feeling guilty. Feeling guilty is caused by knowing you did wrong. Conviction shows and teaches us what God likes and dislikes. Conviction of the Holy Spirit is how we as believers are led by His Spirit. Holy Spirit's job is to convince us to live a life pleasing to God. He DOES NOT condemn us.

"For if you live according to the flesh, you will die; but if by the Spirit you put to death the deeds of the body, you will live. All who are led by the Spirit of God are sons of God. For you did not receive a spirit of slavery that returns you to fear, but you received the Spirit of sonship, by whom we cry, "Abba! Father!" (Romans 8:13-15).

Holy Spirit will not scream or holler or threaten, He has spoken very boldly and very loudly to me before. He has complete authority and He has authority and a voice to match. And believe me He isn't afraid to use it when needed. He has only been abrupt when I was in danger of not obeying or ignorantly in harm's way. As we are being led, He simply prompts and pricks our hearts and our conscience. When you know you did or said something callous and uncaring He will keep that tug on your heart until you apologize (repent) from a sincere heart. Our first apology is to Holy Spirit, second is to the person or persons we hurt. You cannot just repent and not make it right with the other person. This is what is meant by not grieving His Sprit. Now we have the tools and the learning to immediately repent and let

Holy Spirit know we are sorry. If we do not go to the other person, that would be prideful and we do not want to grieve Holy Spirit and have Him leave due to our insensitivity or insincerity. It is better to swallow our pride and know we are right with Holy Spirit. This is how we keep our hearing ears open and our airways unclogged.

You cannot afford to be dull of hearing. That actually means mule headed. You are finished with all known disobedience.

You have The Helper if you ask Him to come be with you. Do you want Him to come and lead you? I believe the answer is yes.

Prayer:

Heavenly Father, You said if we then, being evil, know how to give good gifts unto our children: how much more shall *Your* heavenly Father give the Holy Spirit to them that ask Him? Luke 11:13. I am asking for the gift of Holy Spirit. I want to receive the gift, Your gift of Holy Spirit. I am asking You now for this precious gift. I want to be filled with Your Spirit. I am a child of God. I need Your help at all times. I want to be led by Your Spirit. I want to be included in the family protection plan.

Reflection:

Write down any confirmations you receive over the next few minutes, hours, and days that you know God heard your prayer.

_____

_____

_____

POETRY: WHISPERS

When I don't know what to do
    I hear You whisper, just be still
    In that whisper I understand Your voice
    I answer, "I know You will"

When my heart is scared
    And again I sense that dread
    I am so grateful for Your whisper
    Shhh in You Father my fear falls dead

Your whisper causes me to lean
    Enter into Your personal space
    You however have invited me here
    For an intimate encounter, face to face

Your word is Your bond
    My safe tower and protective hedge
    Never fear just continue
    Summons me onward onto the edge

Whisper again Father
    As I ignore the wind and rain
    For in Your very being
    I find the peace to just refrain

Refrain from fear and doubt
    Reminding myself You are God
    And what You have began
    Will not return unto You void

It shall accomplish what You please
    And prosper in what You have purposed
    As long as I stay close to You
    Reminded of what You purchased

So gentle like the early rains
    Soft like summers breeze
    When I hear Your whisper
    Just relax and rest and breathe

For when the time is right
    Until then just press on and prepare
    For eye has not seen You whisper to me
    All that I have for you there

© laurette laster 2019

Psalm 46:10 *Be still and know that I am God.*

1 Corinthians 2:9 (this is one of my life verses).
    "But as it is written: "Eye has not seen, ear has not heard, neither has entered into the heart of man the things God has prepared for those who love Him.""

DAY 32

"REPENT AND BE BAPTIZED every one of you in the name of Jesus Christ for the forgiveness of your sins and you will receive the gift of the Holy Spirit" (Acts 2:38).

"But the [a]Helper (**Comforter**, Advocate, Intercessor—Counselor, Strengthener, Standby), the Holy Spirit, whom the Father will send in My name [in My place, to represent Me and act on My behalf], He will teach you all things. And He will help you remember everything that I have told you" (John 14:26 (AMP).

Numerous times in the Bible, God's goodness is seen again and again. In Psalm 34:8 we are told to taste and see that the Lord is good. What a savoring thought. Have you ever smelled the aroma of a cake or pastry, or maybe homemade yeast bread baking in the oven? And what about a homespun milkshake, have you had your mouth water thinking about something? This is what the psalmist is describing here.

We talked previously and used David's very own words when he had personally experienced God's goodness and forgiveness. I find it so comforting to read the words of those who have blown it and have experienced firsthand the grace of the Almighty. When they describe His goodness, His grace, and yes, His comfort for His people we understand His great love toward us. This makes me hunger and thirst for more of God and His goodness.

The next descriptive office we see of Holy Spirit is as 'The Comforter'. He is referred to as The Comforter in several scriptures. What do you picture when you think of a comforter? Do you picture a large soft down filled covering? Do you picture a large lap with secure arms to hold you tightly? Do you think of soothing words, saying, *it's okay,* or *I know*, or words like, *we'll get through this*? Or do you imagine a cup of hot chocolate with warm cinnamon toast with warm butter oozing all over it, like my husband Greg? We each have comfort foods, clothes, blankets, and more.

All of these can be a source of comfort but what is Jesus describing to us? Jesus understands repentance better than anyone. He was tempted but never sinned. Accordingly, He is familiar with our struggles and He is touched with the feelings of our infirmities. Hebrews 4:15

He is the second person of the Trinity. He is the Son, the Lamb of God, our Savior, and our Redeemer. John the Baptist said when seeing Jesus coming, behold The Lamb of God who comes to take away the sin of the world. (John 1:29) John explaining to the people who he was and who Jesus was said I indeed baptize you with water unto repentance, but He who is coming after me is mightier than I, whose sandals I am not worthy to carry. "He will baptize you with The Holy Spirit and fire" (Matthew 3:11).

Only God can understand the depravity of the human soul. He knows the temptations of Satan. He knows we cannot repent and face our sins without be comforted by His comfort. Thank God for His comfort as we face our sins and go through this hard work.

Years ago, as I read the amplified version it became evident to me, we need and require every office described when the grace and goodness of God draws us to repent. To take an honest look at ourselves and realize we have blown it is overwhelming.

If like me, you've been trying to do the right thing, and continued doing the wrong thing but thought somehow you could fix it you're not the first to do this. I kept thinking I know better why I am always messing up. My sins were great and I had this uncanny feeling I owed God and I should pay Him back somehow. You know what I mean, get cleaned up before going to Him. How foolish. I later came to the realization that I was self-punishing. I knew my sins were great and I should be punished. I had very little knowledge of God's mercy and love for me. I only saw Him as a harsh Judge with a gavel. I was running for my life, but it was my own guilt driving me. Jesus leads us. He says come to Me all you who are weary, take My yoke upon you for my yoke is easy and my burden is light. Follow Me is a decision and a choice not an order. Jesus will not violate our free will.

As I felt this tender drawing from The Lord, I really wanted to go, but I kept thinking about how to get myself cleaned up. How do we prepare our self to meet Jesus? I knew I needed Him and I began to seek Him with all I had. If He were pursuing me then...

At just the right moment, The Comforter appeared, His voice telling me, "it's going to be okay. I've come to help you. I knew all you had done when I came for you." I was invited into His lap; His arms of love surrounded me as I wept bitterly. These were tears of sadness, tears of joy, and tears of relief, tears of regret, but more they were cleansing my soul and my conscience, I cried and I cried. Captured by His safe, sure love, I didn't have to run anymore. I was being comforted to face my past and embrace my future. His covering is amazing and His comfort is indescribable.

Years ago, a terrible hateful argument broke out between my sons on Christmas night. One was defending me, the other defending a lie told by someone else. It was Christmas, dear Jesus, it is Christmas and now this. At 11:15 PM, I knelt down beside my bed and said I don't know how this is going to work out; things are getting much worse not better. I had to be up by 4:15 AM for work so I had to have some rest.

I had gone through a divorce, leaving behind a very dysfunctional ungodly life. I was being pursued by God but things continued to fall apart. I saw firsthand why God hated divorce and grieved deeply for this truth. I also saw and experienced the hatred of those who were determined to make me suffer no matter what.

Around 2:00 AM I woke up, wide awake and heard these words. "It's okay Laurette, it is okay."

I said out loud, "it doesn't look okay to me," I heard again, "it's okay Laurette" and went back to sleep.

The next morning when I woke up, I had the very real feeling that it was okay and this comforted me. Nothing had changed but I had been comforted in my tribulation.

No matter what your sin or sins, He knows. He has been sent to help you during this time and in the days, weeks, and years ahead. He has come to stay forever. One of the hardest truths is facing all our wrongs and accepting that we are guilty and have brought much of the heart ache on ourselves. But it is also hard to resist the temptation to give up. That is why Holy Spirit has the offices He has. We need and require a Helper 24/7.

Prayer:

Heavenly Father, I long for Your comfort. I want to be wrapped in Your loving embrace as I heal from what I have done and from what has been done to me. Cover me under Your feathers, hide me under the shadow of Your Almighty wings, comfort me with Your great comfort, (Psalms 91). Amen

Comforter, the God of all comfort will comfort you so that you may comfort others. Isn't that just like our Father, at our lowest He offers and brings us a Gift. Repent and be baptized in the Name of The Lord Jesus Christ, for the forgiveness of your sins and you will receive the gift of The Holy Spirit. What comfort.

Reflection:

What is the thing that brings you comfort? Fix yourself and Holy Spirit a place and invite Him to join you. I have coffee with The Lord every morning, because Jesus loves coffee and aren't we glad?

_____

_____

_____

POETRY: I HAVE TASTED GRACE

I have tasted grace
    That cannot be explained
    I am now washed clean
    Never to be the same

I have tasted love
    One so pure and undefiled
    As it washes through me
    It cleanses my insides

Not more doubt or unbelief
    Not more guilt and shame
    Only knowing I was different
    And called a brand new name

The name He called on that day
    I had never before heard
    Never once did I expect
    To me it would be inferred

Looking straight at me
    And speaking to my face
    Saying "REDEEMED!"
    The past now completely erased

Only then did I know the depth
    Of a love so strong and pure
    That no matter what my past
    My future is secure

He said repent and change your mind
    For the kingdom of God is at hand
    And you can hear this also
    Heard only on the 'willing band'

To confess all of my wrongs
    Seemed so dirty and so strange
    But it is the only entrance
    Into His great exchange

He paid for all my debt
    With a love I'd never known
    Now free I get a brand-new start
    This is not an installment loan

No this payment ensures forever
    It is paid for with His blood
    Repentance is the key
    That unlocked all His love

So if today you're hurt
    Feeling rejected and alone
    Just know there is One
    Who will love you as His own

Do not place this death on Him
 Jesus came only to give us life
 So repent and be baptized
 Become part of the bride of Christ
 © laurette laster

"Therefore laying aside all malice, all deceit, hypocrisy, envy and all evil speaking, as newborn babes, desire the pure milk of the word that you may grow thereby, if indeed you have tasted that the Lord is gracious" (1 Peter 2:1-3 NKJV).

DAY 33

"REPENT AND BE BAPTIZED every one of you in the name of Jesus Christ for the forgiveness of your sins and you will receive the gift of the Holy Spirit (Acts 2:38).

"But the [a]Helper (Comforter, **Advocate**, Intercessor—Counselor, Strengthener, Standby), the Holy Spirit, whom the Father will send in My name [in My place, to represent Me and act on My behalf], He will teach you all things. And He will help you remember everything that I have told you" (John 14:26 (AMP).

The Advocate

The first role of The Holy Spirit is to help us gain our freedom. He ushers us into freedom by convicting us of sin and guides us into all truth. He plays a major role in the application of our salvation and our sanctification. When we begin to walk out the will of God in our life there is a powerful foe that comes against us, in an attempt to stop us. I use the word attempt because God is ALL powerful and if we agree with The Father and The Son and His Spirit we will win. We with, and on God's side are the majority.

You may believe this isn't necessary if you are saved. We have an accuser; his name is Satan. He will constantly bring up your past before the throne of God. However, once you repent and turn your life over to the will and care of God you have an attorney representing you at all times. And after we repent the charges are cancelled.

In a court of law before a judicial court, before giving your testimony or being allowed to testify there is an oath you must take. You are asked these questions. Will you tell the truth, the whole truth and nothing but the truth, so help you God? How many of us could do this before becoming a Christian? How about now? I bet like me, you failed also. Knowing that a half truth is a whole lie, how do you score?

What is the role of the Advocate? The Webster definition is:

(n) a person who publicly supports or recommends a particular cause, or policy.

(v) Publicly recommend or support or defend.

So our Helper and Advocate is a Person with an action to perform. The Holy Spirit is going to represent us and help us get back on track quickly when we mess up. He is the person who publicly recommends or supports a particular policy. What policy or policies do you think these would be?

If you said the things pertaining to God's kingdom you would be correct. The Advocate STRONGLY advises us pertaining to the kingdom of God. He is the third person of the Trinity. He is not going to speak of anything apart from God and His kingdom. He will not speak of Himself or bring glory to Himself. He will speak of and glorify Jesus Christ only. (John 16:13, John 14:17, John 15:26)

We are reminded that we have been redeemed by The Lord, for Him and His purposes, we must think and act differently. So we have The Person and The Action. Here we have the noun and the verb, The Actor (Author) and The Action. He will lead and guide us until we are complete in Christ! So that we become complete or mature, pleasing to The Father.

He will plead our case. This is so deep that I certainly cannot do this subject justice. I am not an expert and this is not an attempt to be exhaustive. I am however a recipient of His great leading and His help. I want to remind you there is so much going on in the spiritual realm we are unaware of. If our eyes were open to all that was going on, our human minds couldn't contain it. It is so advanced that we couldn't for one moment comprehend or grasp all that is happening and it is all happening at one time, but over the course of eternity in time. Stop and think about that for a moment.

There are so many great books on Holy Spirit. I strongly recommend you read some of these books. One I recommend is *The Helper* written by Catherine Marshall. I received this book as a gift when being introduced to The Living Power of God and have read it three times. The first reading I absorbed this book in one day.

You are here now, but according to psalmist (Psalm 139) your part is already written. So when we repent and are forgiven God redeems the time. He puts us back into our rightful place and we have work to do.

This is a supernatural mystery for sure, but He does it beautifully and perfectly every time. As we are praying some things seem to happen instantly. Other times it may take years to come to completion. I believe all the while Holy Spirit is leading, guiding, and orchestrating all things. Remember, we are His Symphony and His Spirit is working all this together into a beautiful tapestry or rhyme.

"And we know that all things work together for good to them that love God, to them who are the called according to his purpose" (Romans 5:28 KJV).

So, now that we have repented and are saved, everything changes. Isn't this amazing? Even the bad will now be used for good. In Genesis, Joseph after being reunited, told his brothers, what the enemy meant for evil God intended for good. We may have thought the enemy was orchestrating the chaos, but God has been with us all the time. Remember the God of all comfort, The Comforter, will comfort you so that you may comfort others. God saves us, restores us, equips us, calls us, and then sends us to others to help them.

We are called with a Holy Calling, we are given a ministry. I hear you saying, what? I can't be a minister. I say to you, oh yes you can and you already are. You are given the ministry of reconciliation. We become living epistles after receiving salvation through repentance.

For all of this we need The Helper, The Comforter, and we need The Advocate pleading our case. We cannot do anything perfectly simply because we have repented and have received salvation. Heaven is God's Holy habitation; we need representation and guidance, we cannot become perfect. So we become partakers of His divine nature being called a holy priesthood.

Prayer:

Dear Lord Jesus, I am amazed to be called one of Your ministers. I am a witness and I am in the witness protection plan. I am a valuable part of Your kingdom. You have made me a partaker of Your divine nature and I am receiving a new gift, Your Holy Spirit to come and live inside of me. I have a ministry to help others see Your truth and then experience Your love. Jesus I want to tell the world about You. I need help for all of this. According to Your word I am a living epistle. I am Your story to others. The story of Your great love and redemption. Help me to walk in my new calling and to tell others of what You have done. Thank you for sending me The Advocate to represent me and to lead and guide me into all truth. Thank You Holy Spirit for showing me who I am to become as I seek Him, the One You Glorify. Amen

Reflection:

Take some time in prayer and ask God what truth He longs to show you. Write down and date and what He shows you. Read John 16:13-14

_____

_____

_____

POETRY: TIME TO GET SERIOUS FOR HEAVEN'S SAKE

I'm not worthy to wash Your feet
    Yet beside You I am assigned a seat
    Also unworthy to unlatch Your sandals
    A place beside You in spite of the scandals

Can this be real my heart is screaming
    Is this for real or am I dreaming
    You loved me before I ere did know You
    Yes I agree all my love is due too

To You, My King, and Kinsman Redeemer
    This is perfect; I am Your forever dreamer
    Taking Your hand I'll run this race
    Until in Your arms and face to face

I want to bring many along on this journey
    Show me how to get off this gurney
    No more dead works or idle displays
    Time to get serious for heaven's sake

laurette laster © 2018

"Therefore come out from among them and be separate says the Lord. Do not touch what is unclean, and I will receive you. I will be a Father to you, and you shall be my sons and daughters, Says the Lord Almighty" (2 Corinthians 6:17-18, NKJV).

DAY 34

"REPENT AND BE BAPTIZED every one of you in the name of Jesus Christ for the forgiveness of your sins and you will receive the gift of the Holy Spirit" (Acts 2:38)

"But the [a]Helper (Comforter, Advocate, **Intercessor**—Counselor, Strengthener, Standby), the Holy Spirit, whom the Father will send in My name [in My place, to represent Me and act on My behalf], He will teach you all things. And He will help you remember everything that I have told you" (John 14:26 (AMP).

The Intercessor

Webster defines Intercessor as a person who intervenes on behalf of another, especially by prayer.

What would you think if I told you your deepest sighs and inward groaning are audible, intelligible prayers and requests to Our Intercessor and go before the throne of our Mighty God. Our Helper and Intercessor understand those deep sighs; He captures our tears and places them in a bottle. He understands our heart and our spirit and even hears our thoughts. Yes, you heard me right. He hears our thoughts.

One night years ago, I was driving home, from an extremely long and tedious day. My job as a general manger was very demanding and a typical "day" consisted of a lot of multitasking and problem solving. Putting out numerous fires, fixing immediate problems and planning the shift through following up with others. Encouraging the staff and greeting the guest. Following up with truck orders, uniforms, health dept., check lists, and numerous other details and activities all in a day's work. As I drove down the moonlit interstate I was thinking to myself, no I was actually reminiscing how I loved to wake up before my eyes opened. Do you know what I am talking about? Those of you who know understand this sweet place. The place between consciousness and wide awake, aware that it is morning but not having opened our eyes. I still love to be able to do this, but at that time it wasn't a luxury I had.

Taking the job with Applebee's changed many things, there were some long late nights and some extremely hurried mornings, rising long before dawn. And both of these within my week, we can certainly surmise this made for some challenging days that left me feeling drained. Some nights it would be after 2:00 AM when I crawled into my bed, dog tired and praying for rest. I needed rest not sleep.

Many mornings I had to wake up by 4:00 AM to insure I had my quiet time with The Lord and Bible reading before arriving at work by 6:00 or 7:00. Some days I felt like I was meeting myself coming and going.

Back to the story, I was driving home on this night remembering how I loved to wake up without an alarm. I was reminiscing how refreshing it felt. I didn't ask The Lord to do this for me nor was I complaining I was simply remembering to myself.

The next day I didn't have to be at work until 9:00 AM. I was so grateful to not have to set an alarm. When I awoke, I heard His tender voice, He said, "Like this?" I immediately knew what He was asking. He had been eavesdropping, listening in on my thoughts. I said, yes! I felt His love; His love poured over me and was a covering as much as the comforter on my bed was a covering. I was loved; He heard my thoughts and gave me a desire of my heart, just to let me know He cared and He was aware. So I said again, YES just like this.

This still amazes today as I am writing this. He was listening to my thoughts and desires. My job had more to do with learning about His call and getting me back to 'the me' He had created me to be than it did about making a living. Don't misunderstand I was making a nice salary with bonuses too. But my job was His will for my life during those years. I never doubted after hearing His voice during a... let's say prayer, (resignation) I lifted up to Him.

Just as sweet as that sounds there is a flip side. There are times of extreme drama, turmoil, uncertainty, anger, confusion, heartache, and other emotions that have no words. The feelings of I cannot keep on going are real.

And He, Our Intercessor, takes our deepest groaning, from the battlefield of our minds, deciphers them and reassures our heart, according to what He has heard from Heaven. His assignment is to assure us that it is going to be OKAY, He intercedes on our behalf. That deep sigh may seem to us an unintelligible groaning, but from heaven our all-knowing Savior has sent His Holy Spirit to be our Helper. He interprets our needs and our prayers, showing us all things that pertain to life and godliness.

In the early days of my recovery, from years of dysfunction, I was mentally and emotionally exhausted. I remember one of my employees asking me, "Are you okay?" I looked up from the pile of paperwork I was attempting to complete before closing and said, "I am so tired." I was bone weary and mentally and emotionally drained. I was flooded with the thought of not being able to take anymore. I wasn't suicidal, but thought this is much too hard I can't do it.

After I uttered those words to her, I laid my head down on my folded arms on the desk. I didn't pray I caved!! "Oh God I am so tired." I didn't have my head down more than a few minutes before lifting my head back up. The extreme emotional tiredness had left me. No it had been lifted off of me by The One who interceded for me. My groaning became a prayer; the answer was delivered and I was completely unaware.

I remember thinking later, "how did that happen?" It happened because The Intercessor had intervened on my struggle. I didn't realize by confessing I was sending out a SOS or HELP telling my coworker I was so tired. Later I realized saying I was tired was actually confessing a cry for help. Now I am not suggesting your life has to be this hard before He will come to your aide. What I am saying is I had made a vow to God to do my part and to fight the good fight of faith. I wasn't wimping out, I was in a fight and He intervened for me on my behalf.

Likewise, The Spirit also helps our infirmity for we know not what we should pray for as we ought; but The Spirit Himself makes intercession for us with groaning which cannot be uttered. And He who searches the hearts knows what is in the mind of the Spirit, because He makes intercession for the saints according to the will of God (Romans 8:26-27).

He comes to assist us so that we may fulfill the call of God or fulfill the will of God in our lives. If we do not engage in this fight, He isn't needed nor will He come to us. He is our Helper, the One who comes along side us. If we are fulfilling the life of the flesh we should not expect to be comforted. We will be convicted by Holy Spirit if we are fulfilling the life of the flesh. He will convince us we are out of sync with The Father and The Son. Conviction makes us aware that our actions are not glorifying God.

Condemnation fills us with hopelessness; and is not from God, but from the enemy. Nothing you or I have done is unforgivable, if we confess. The scripture tells us that if we confess our sin He is faithful and just and will forgive us our sin *and*… yes there is more, He will cleanse us from all unrighteousness. He will cleanse us. Confession is simply stating and agreeing God's ways are right and we have missed the mark, then deciding we are going to align with His ways.

Prayer:

Dear Jesus, thank you for sending me the Helper. Thank You that You have not left me an orphan without guidance. You have sent Your Holy Spirit to lead and guide me into all truth. I am comforted knowing You will untangle my groaning and deep sighs. When I don't know how to pray as I ought Your Spirit is searching my thoughts and helping me clear the path to right thinking. Amen

Reflection:

What do you need help with? What is something that you could ask Holy Spirit to teach you? Do you need to set healthy boundaries? Do you need to break off a relationship? Do you need a job? Do you desire to understand the word of God more? Ask Him, The Helper, right now to help you. List what you would like Him to help you with.

_____

_____

_____

POETRY: WHAT IF I TOLD YOU, YOU COULD SAY ANYTHING

What if I told you, you could say anything
    And it would never be repeated
    What if you were aware of the lies
    Realize God will not allow you to be defeated

What if today you decided
    To throw those filthy rags on the ground
    And run into His safe same arms
    And you could feel His love surround

What if others who have hurt you
    Were used by the enemies as ploys
    To keep you from actually knowing
    His pure love and security enjoy

What if I told you
    He is waiting to meet you here
    Then you would have a picture
    Of His love becoming clear

Don't shut yourself off any longer
 Don't you dare allow that enemy the win
 Because those lies he told you
 Have a deadline and need to come to an end

You are loved and valued and treasured
 You are the work of His hands
 Hidden beneath that anger and shame
 An original work of art, His plan

Run if you will and dance in the rain
 Just refuse to remain trapped
 The lies, when opened, loose all that pain
 Now God's goodness can be unwrapped

What if I told you could say anything
 And it would never be repeated
 What if you became aware of the lies
 Realize God would not let you be defeated

© laurette laster 2019

"Who gave Himself for us to purchase our freedom from all iniquity, and purify for Himself a people who should be specially His own, zealous for doing good works" (Titus 2:14, WNT).

DAY 35

"Repent and be baptized every one of you in the name of Jesus Christ for the forgiveness of your sins and you will receive the gift of the Holy Spirit" (Acts 2:38).

"But the [a]Helper (Comforter, Advocate, Intercessor—**Counselor**, Strengthener, Standby), the Holy Spirit, whom the Father will send in My name [in My place, to represent Me and act on My behalf], He will teach you all things. And He will help you remember everything that I have told you" (John 14:26 (AMP).

The Counselor

Have you ever thought to yourself *I need a counselor*? Or have you thought you knew the answers to all of life's problems only to find yourself repeating a pattern? Wouldn't it be wonderful if we had a 24-7 go to person to help us? That is what our Helper is. He is living on the inside of us and speaking to us and hearing from heaven. We have unction's and promptings and we just know stuff. How many times have you heard someone say, something just told me I should do this? Or something told me I should go there? How often has it happened to you? Something's other name is God or

Holy Spirit. Even before we commit our life to Him He is speaking to us through our inner being or our conscience.

The reason we need to repent or metanoia- meaning to change our minds is because, if we can be gut honest, we are and have been incredibly stupid going our own way. How many times have you said I knew better, or I just knew I shouldn't have? I know that is not a good feeling or an easy thing to admit but if you are one that hasn't made mistakes you wouldn't have a book like this in your hands. So we admit we have been stupid and ignored warning signs but thank You Jesus, we do not have to remain ignorant. We have our Helper and Counselor now.

Jesus said He didn't come to call the righteous, but sinners to repent. He came for us. Thank You, Jesus. I remember being so comforted when I would read this scripture. Realizing that the work He did on the Cross was for those of us that couldn't repay our sin debt. When I would be really down on myself He would remind me through The Counselor I came for you, you are forgiven.

We are told to ask God for wisdom according to James 1:5. But, we are also told we must believe that God's desire is to help us gain wisdom. God will not open up our heads and pour wisdom in. But oh boy wouldn't that be nice? How nice it would be to place an order for wisdom, then supersize it or like going to a service station, fill the tank up and wash the windshield while we're at it? Sure it would but that isn't how it works in God's kingdom. We have work to do now that we have become children of God and heirs to the kingdom. We are inheriting a kingdom assignment being part of the family business. We are told to put on, take off, put to death, repent, forgive, add too, believe, and pray just to name a few things. How can we do all this and in what order are we doing all this?

Jesus compared the kingdom of God in the parable of the Sower to seed. Jesus gives us an analogy or an allegory about fields and harvests. Field work is very hard demanding and rewarding work. It is plowing, planting, cultivating, and watering before gathering in the harvest. All of the above steps take time and hard work, determination and yes wisdom. Gardening or working in a field is hard physical work.

We have to learn and become aware of growing seasons, planting seasons and we have to have the right tools and equipment for this work. That is why The Helper comes alongside us. God knows we do not come into His kingdom equipped. We realize we need help and guidance and we become eager to learn. You notice I didn't say we become patient. We come to realize much of what we have had a knack or desire to do aligns with what He has called and equipped us for.

Jesus says the kingdom of God is like a man who scattered seed on the ground. Night and day while he slept it sprouts and grows though he does not know how, here we see seedtime and harvest. This means we plant the word in our hearts and in our minds, and water the seeds with His word and prayer, by reading our Bible and praying, and God supernaturally promises and gives the increase. I would often get impatient wanting it to grow faster or wishing I didn't have to wait so long to see the change. I understand today the change is occurring even when we cannot see it. While we sleep our spirit is awake.

Parakletos –Strong's Concordance #3875 One who comes along side, one who pleads another's cause before a judge, a legal assistant, we are backed by an intercessor, a defender who is working for our pardon. Remember we were ignorant, once walking in darkness but now we are children of light.

When we become part of the family, we are protected by the court system of heaven. While we commit to working to gain wisdom from His word in order to fulfill the will of God we have the best legal defense known to heaven. He is The Spirit of God, come to work on the earth. Jesus ascended to heaven and to The Fathers right hand and God sent the Helper, Comforter, Advocate, Intercessor, and Counselor …

Each of these has a role to fill when the Counselor is at work. We have all of His offices at work in us simultaneously or all at the same time. He is inside us dwelling in our born-again spirit and comes along side us. It is not what we may picture of going to a counselor's office.

The counsel of Holy Spirit doesn't allow us ramble on and on about our problems. His purpose is to guide us into <u>all truth</u>. He will warn us of impending danger, convict us of what is not pleasing to The Father and The Son. He will teach us to be others minded in a healthy way. He will direct our paths in the will of The Father. We are at peace knowing we do not have to panic or believe we must figure it out? We are being led.

Several years ago before we were married, Greg was going through an extremely hard time emotionally. He later told me he felt frozen in fear and didn't know what he was going to do. He said during his (prayer) time he would say, "I don't know what to do, I don't know what I'm going to do." He said this over and over for several days. Greg said he clearly heard the words, **"Stop saying that."** Greg said he realized later it was like having your car in reverse with your foot on the accelerator while wanting to go forward. It will not happen. The Spirit of God said stop saying that. His counsel wasn't to go anywhere it was to get Greg to stop what he was saying.

Greg realized when he was saying I don't know what to do; he was blocking the legal counsel of God in his life. Our words have power. In order for Holy Spirit to counsel us we must read the Bible. When we are changing directions we are changing our minds (metanoia) and we need instructions. We are going in a new and different direction. It isn't enough to just stop doing the wrong thing. We need to know the correct thing or action to take. God's plan from the beginning has been to usher us back into His kingdom and His call.

From the time of the fall in the garden, The God head, has been working to help us see the plan of God. We need to learn our kingdom rights about The Father's great love for us and His immeasurable love poured out for our redemption. We need to study to know Him and who He is.

Until we stop doing and saying, the wrong thing we cannot go forward. It is impossible to move forward while going backward.

The most important thing our Counselor may say to us some days is STOP DOING THAT or STOP SAYING THAT. That is great legal counsel I suggest we pay close attention.

When my heart is overwhelmed

The Psalmist tells us in Psalm 61: 2-4, "From the ends of the earth I call out to You whenever my heart is faint. Lead me to the rock that is higher than I. For You have been my refuge, a tower of strength against the enemy. Let me dwell in Your tent forever and take refuge in the shelter of Your wings. " Selah…

Prayer:

Lord Jesus You are The Rock of my salvation, my Redeemer, and my Savior. Thank you for Your Holy Spirit who helps me to change my mind giving me sound counsel in Your word. When my flesh is screaming my spirit is learning to follow You. I want to please You and learn about my kingdom rights and I want to study about The Father's great love. The Love that Led You to go to the Cross that I may be forgiven and justified. I am freely pardoned by Your sacrifice. What amazing grace. And I am amazed. May I never lose this amazement? I pray to see deeper into the grace that has been extended to me from this day forward. May I never lose this amazement? Amen

Reflection:

Have you felt 'Something' tell you to do a certain thing? Or to go a certain place, Or not do something? Write down a few promptings you have had. Pay attention and begin to ask The Lord to teach you to recognize His promptings and unction's. Something's other name is God. I feel it is important to remind you that Satan attempts to mimic God and try to deceive us, the Helper is at work showing us The Truth, Jesus. The Holy Spirit only glorifies Jesus.

_____

_____

_____

"Whosoever cometh to Me, and heareth My sayings, and doeth them, I will shew you to whom he is like: He is like a man which built an house, and digged deep, and laid the foundation on a rock: and when the flood arose, the stream beat vehemently upon that house, and could not shake it: for it was founded upon a rock" (Luke 6:47-48).

POETRY: THE LATTER AND
FORMER RAIN

There is way that seems right to man
    But in the end destruction
    For when we seek to go our way
    Ends in ideology and destruction

There is way that is proven
    To be right and even desirous
    This is The Way our Lord advised
    To advance His kingdom, Jesus required us

For when we seek to go our own
    We thwart God's power and toss
    Having no one to blame we're deceived
    And become an enemy of the Cross

But if we continue on to know
    Pursue knowledge, let us come and grow
    We have so many securities
    So many proofs He longs to show

For as the evening and the morning
    The darkness turns into light
    The Former and the latter
    Becomes a continuous passage right

Let us pursue the knowledge
    Of The Lord as we continue on to know
    His going forth is established
    As the morning, He has spoken and He shows

He will come to us and heal us
    Where we are torn He longs to heal
    When we pursue with all our heart
    Continue on to know His will

Harvest rains in spring and autumn
    Our Lord sends rain in season
    Lord water our hearts and show
    Your going forth and reason

Come and let us return to The Lord
    Our wounds He hath bound
    Call upon His Name
    While He is near and can be found

laurette laster © 2018

"Come, and let us return to the LORD; for He hath torn, and He will heal us; He hath smitten, and He will bind us up. Then shall we know, if we follow on to know the LORD, His going forth is prepared as the morning; and He shall come unto us as the rain, as the latter and the former rain unto the earth" (Hosea 6:1,3, KJV).

DAY 36

'Repent and be baptized every one of you in the name of Jesus Christ for the forgiveness of your sins and you will receive the gift of the Holy Spirit" (Acts 2:38).

"But the [a]Helper (Comforter, Advocate, Intercessor—Counselor, **Strengthener**, Standby), the Holy Spirit, whom the Father will send in My name [in My place, to represent Me and act on My behalf], He will teach you all things. And He will help you remember everything that I have told you" (John 14:26 (AMP).

The Strengthener

Transitive verb: to make stronger. A transitive verb must have an object. The object in this definition is believers in Christ, you, me, and all the others. We are the object that our Strengthener is going to make stronger. Stronger in what, you may be asking. Well the answer is in everything pertaining to life and godliness, in the kingdom of God, that's what He is going to strengthen us in.

Without faith, it is impossible to please God (Hebrews 11:6). So we will need to spend time working out our own salvation with fear and trembling. You may be saying, "hang on a minute; I thought this was a gift. If it is a gift why do I need to work out anything?" That sounds like a fair question but the answer isn't as simple as you might think.

Salvation is a gift, but so is a car. If someone wanted to gift you a new car and you had never owned a car nor been taught to drive a car, this gift will come with opportunities that require additional training and teaching. The highway is a dangerous place full of rules and responsibilities. As powerful as a car is this is nothing compared to the Holy Spirit and the Power of God. So we have received a gift, the car title is free and clear and our name is written on the title deed. Now it is time to learn how to operate, maintain, and maneuver this gift. Wouldn't we be foolish to think we could just get in and drive not understanding the rules or the gauges or the maintenance required to maintain the gift? Even though we take drivers education this is only the basic knowledge that allows us the legal right to drive. The ability to handle the vehicle in inclement weather comes by driving in inclement weather. Road hazards are common and are marked with roadblocks or cones that must be heeded.

I am sure there are still options available in my car that I don't know about and haven't used, yet. But when a problem comes up I know that the owner's manual is in the glove box and I can pull it out and begin to locate and solve the problem. But the information in the owner's manual is separate from learning to drive. The owner's manual is about the car's maintenance but it is my responsibility to learn how to drive and operate the car.

So it is with the kingdom of God. What The Lord is gifting us requires education, training, discipline and care. This gift comes with great responsibility.

This gift attracts an enemy. His name is El Satan, and he launches an all out attack on us and will do everything in his power to cause us to fail or crash. Like he did with Adam and Eve in the garden so he will try to deceive us, again. He does not have new tricks, he uses the same strategies that were evident in the garden, the lust of the flesh, the lust of the eye and the pride of life. (Genesis 3:6) The attack is on God and Satan is against God. So in order to hurt God who he knows he cannot touch, he attacks us God's chosen people and kingdom ambassadors to hinder the plan of God.

Strengthen is also an Intransitive verb: to become stronger. The result of the action is to become stronger because He is strengthening us for kingdom work.

So again we come back to teamwork. The Helper's work in us and our working (retraining) at becoming what God had in mind all along. (Ephesians 2:10)

If I go to the gym and lift weights the bar bell without weights does not make me stronger. By making the effort to go to the gym and lift weights added to the bar bell, by repetition and weightlifting we will become stronger. By learning how to operate in the free gift of His Holy Spirit and walk in our salvation as an heir of God we are becoming stronger.

We and God (Father, Son and Holy Spirit) are a team. Wow, just wow. Heaven is on our side. We have the best defense team known in eternity and it is gifted to us, to believers in Christ. Reflect on this and never take it for granted.

No matter where you are right now, God is there with you. You may be recovering from an overdose, you may be in a psychiatric hospital, you may sitting in your car about to go in to court to finalize your divorce, or you may be about to graduate from college, you may be watching your child suffer from addiction, no matter what age you are, He is with you in the details of every part of your life. It doesn't matter what season you find yourself in, He is there.

Prayer:

Heavenly Father, thank You that You are in the details and with me in every season of my life. Thank you for loving me and not giving up on me. Thank You for this reminder. Show me and teach me how to drive and operate in this new life You have given me. Teach me Holy Spirit and strengthen me to do what is pleasing to God. I know I cannot earn this gift, but I receive and wholeheartedly accept this gift from You. I will keep both hands on the wheel. I love You, Amen

Reflection:

In what areas do you lack control? List three areas you need to tighten your grip or learn control in. Lift these up as prayers to The Lord. He is your Strengthener. I feel I must warn you to prepare to be tested in these areas. The test isn't to cause you to fail; the test is your gym workout. When you have struggles, say to yourself, Thank You Lord for helping me become strong.

_____

_____

_____

POETRY: THE THRILL OF VICTORY

It is not easy to grow in The Lord
    It does not come natural at first
    But just like the thrill of the hunt
    It's the catch that creates the thirst

Oh but once we taste success
    And finally pass a test
    It is then we begin to grow
    The fight becomes the quest

Sweet savor and thrill of victory
    Taste of His glory indeed
    When we come to realize
    The Company that we keep

Armies of angels go with us
    The Host of Heaven is beaming down
    When at last we realize
    Our triumph is all to Him a crown

I shall not go up empty handed
    On the day of the great feast
    For I want to bring him beauty
    Ornate crowns to lay at His feet

Oh how sweet the thrill of victory
    Does conquer the sorrow of defeat
    As long as we stay in the fight
    Don't relinquish or take a backseat

For our Lord is calling forth warriors
    Step up and take your place at the front
    If you truly believe He is Commander
    Take His Word be bold and blunt

Oh church it is time to conquer
    And fight with the sword of His word
    For God is not a man that can lie
    And we are not beat down or conquered

No church we are the victors
    And I hear our Masters heart
    We will taste the thrill of victory
    As long as we do not tuck tail or fall apart

The battle is not to the fierce
    But only to those who believe
    Our Commander and Chief
    Is none other than the Host of Heavens Armies

He would not send us out
    If we should be defeated
    No it is for success and victory only
    That is why in heavenly places we are seated

So listen for the bugle call
    The trumpet of Voice will blow
    He is calling forth His warriors
    Church rise up it is time to show!!

We are the church of the Firstborn
    In Zion, part of The Master's plan
    Church we cannot be overtaken
    If we take Him at His command

© laurette laster 2019

Read Hebrews 12:18-29

"So be made strong even in your weakness by lifting up your tired hands in prayer and worship. And strengthen your weak knees, for as you keep walking forward on God's paths all your stumbling ways will be divinely healed!" (Hebrews 12:12-13 TPT).

"So now wrap your heart tightly around the hope that lives within us, knowing that God always keeps His promises!" (Hebrews 10:23 TPT).

DAY 37

"REPENT AND BE BAPTIZED every one of you in the name of Jesus Christ for the forgiveness of your sins and you will receive the gift of the Holy Spirit" (Acts 2:38).

"But the [a]Helper (Comforter, Advocate, Intercessor—Counselor, Strengthener, **Standby**), the Holy Spirit, whom the Father will send in My name [in My place, to represent Me and act on My behalf], He will teach you all things. And He will help you remember everything that I have told you" (John 14:26 (AMP).

Standby
Webster's dictionary defines standby as: One to be relied on especially in emergencies. One that is held in reserve ready for use

A synonym for standby in the Greek language is an anchor or pillar.

In Hebrews 6:17-20, we are told that we have an anchor for our soul, which is hope. We have fled to take hold of hope. Hope becomes our windshield. We are leaving behind anything that hinders our walk with God and that is not pleasing to God.

We repented changing our mind and turning toward the will of God. Now our entire view and outlook has changed. The view that used to be in our windshield is now only visible through our rearview mirror or back window. We have turned around, repented, changed our direction; we are going the right direction now. We are looking forward to our new life that is hidden in Christ. The further we go with God the smaller the past becomes. The more distance we go in the right direction, the further away from wrong thinking we get. And the images in the rearview mirror become smaller. They are becoming a distant memory.

Now our new life has the needed attributes, hope, trust, courage, and faith, with these a desire deep within our soul has been awakened. The things we dreamed about now have emerged. What do you see in the rearview mirror? You should see fear, doubt, unworthiness, unloved, not good enough, sinner, forsaken, forgotten, failure, unwanted, shame, guilt, no good, drug addict, alcoholic and all the other lies of the devil. These are leaving; no you are leaving, and you are leaving them behind as you go forward in your new life. These things are no longer in focus.

When you first begin to go in a new direction you aren't very far away from where you were. It is the same with your new life. Life changes are a process. Be patient. This is a marathon not a sprint. This is from now on. This is a long road trip all the way into eternity. All the scenery isn't going to be pretty. Your entire trip won't be on sunny warm glorious days. Some trips will be through the mountains during the early spring and all will be right with the world. Some of the trip will be through torrential down pours, check your wind shield wipers you are going to need them. Some of your driving will be in the dark, make sure your head lamps are burning brightly. You won't always enjoy the company of every passenger as you travel, but you can't toss them out because they are family. Some of the trip may be a little hazardous as you drive on icy roads. Just remember you are only the copilot. You are being led into new ways of thinking and when there is a problem pull out your trusty friend Mr. Bible, the owner's manual.

All the needed directions for correction are in there for this new gift and the terrain.

An anchor holds a ship or a seaworthy vessel steady and in place. We drop anchor to ensure that we are not allowing the boat or ship to drift aimlessly.

"So Christ Himself gave the apostles, the prophets, the evangelists, the pastors and teachers, to equip His people for works of service, so that the body of Christ may be built up until we all reach unity in the faith and in the knowledge of the Son of God and become mature, attaining to the whole measure of the fullness of Christ. Then we will no longer be infants, tossed back and forth by the waves, and blown here and there by every wind of teaching and by the cunning and craftiness of people in their deceitful scheming" (Ephesians 4:11-14).

You are learning to steer your vessel. It is time for you to drive; you are no longer a passenger in the chaos of life tossed about. You are manning the vessel taking control. You are receiving messages from the tower.

You are sailing the boat, you are driving the car, you are choosing the route, and you are well able to make healthy decisions. Involved with every detail of your life you are becoming His own workmanship. But you are doing all of this with The Helper at your side. He is The One who comes alongside to help you. The Helper, your very own parakletos, your own paramedic or immediate 911 number at your fingertips. The Comforter, your very own encourager during the hard times. He is your very own defense team all at the same time, The Advocate the one representing you, pleader, spokesman, apologist. You have your very own intercessor, The Intercessor that is intervening for you in heaven, before the throne of God, day and night the mediator with a view to reconcile.

You have a 24/7 counselor, The Counselor you can immediately get advice from by lifting up simple prayers, the consultant, advisor, director. Only advising according to the plan of God for your life. You have The Strengthener right there with you giving you courage to do the right thing. He is there to reinforce, invigorate, and amplify. Helping you as together you work out your salvation with fear and trembling. And you have <u>The Standby</u> as an anchor for your soul.

You are no longer tossed to and fro; you will be led and are being led. The Standby is there to help, to prove, to secure. You are choosing safe godly people to speak into your life. You are serving The One True Lord; you are reading and studying your Bible. You are being built up by The Helper. You are learning to trust yourself. You are not wishing; you have hope. Hope has a name—Jesus. And He is your Redeemer.

You have God's very best, His only begotten full of mercy and grace, You have The Father, who is long-suffering not wanting any to perish but all to come to repentance. You have The Helper who will guide you into all truth. You have heaven backing you, you cannot fail if you go forward in faith.

Prayer:

Holy Spirit, thank You for being all of these things to me and for me and working in me to do Your will. Help me believe in You in me, as I go forward. I ask You to show me anything I need to repent of. I want to walk forward and bring forth fruit worthy of repentance. Thank You that You are leading and guiding me into all truth. Help me to look forward and not backward. Open my eyes to the love God has for me. Open my heart to receive Your truth. I want truth, and I desire to go forward. I want to grow and become strong in You Lord and the power of Your might. I'm tired of pretending and failing. I am determined more than ever to follow You. Lead me in the way everlasting. Amen.

Reflection:

Think about and list three areas of self-reliance that you divert back to in times of struggle. Like telling yourself I don't need them, I can do this on my own. Or who cares what they think and building a wall against good caring individuals. What is a reaction you revert to in tough times? Now list three healthy ways to cope. Find three scriptures that talk about patience, gentleness, kindness, tender hearted, etc. Whatever you mentioned find a scripture that is the way Jesus would have you act or respond.

POETRY: I HAVE THE KEY

I have the key
    To Jesus heart
    It's at the beginning
    A Precious part

The start of my day
    Continues until noon
    Then onward I go
    By evening swoon

A one of a kind
    Integral part
    It is a precious key
    This key to His heart

It Cannot be purchased
    Not available for franchise
    It is poured and molded
    Not for the ignorant only the wise

It is a special key
    That you must embrace
    Cannot be copied or ignored
    Each one kept on display

What is this key
    And where do I apply
    It is fashioned from purity
    Pours out of your eyes

It is tears and sobs
    When you see His face
    When you come to realize
    He took your place

When out of pure desire
    You behold Your King
    It's golden and glorious
    Awe invoking inspiring

When praises like rivers
    Out of your belly flow
    Bowing before Him
    This is how to grow

Willing to be molded
    Into a work of art
    That is the key
    The key to His heart

For we each are a masterpiece
    From The Potters design
    Created in Christ Jesus
    Not a counterfeit but one of a kind

It is a praise in the morning
  With prayers and rejoicing
  Giving Him entrance
  Agreeing while endorsing

The key is our praise
  Acknowledging all He has done
  So don't wait any longer
  To His Throne we must run

You're His own workmanship
  Created to show His glory
  You're are a special key
  to unlock His story

That others may share
  In His kingdom inheritance
  Don't wait another day
  Use your key open the entrance.

It is a song and a prayer
  Given new wings
  Rising from the ashes
  Until my soul does sing

Praise Him in the morning
  And when it seems dark
  Because praise is the key
  The Key to His heart!

laurette laster © 2018
  "What He opens no one can close; and what He closes, no one can open" (Revelation 3:7, NLT).

DAY 38

"THOSE WHOM I LOVE, I reprove and discipline, so be zealous and repent" (Revelation 3:19).

We may be tempted to believe that our closeness and walk with Jesus will keep us from failing. We may feel like the Bible describes, painting the picture for us, saying as white as the freshly fallen snow. I know I did and still do after a time of soaking in His word and His presence.

I admit that when I have a struggle, my thoughts have to be reeled back in. I'm not always proud of my thoughts but I do realize it is part of my carnal nature. It is not a sin to be tempted. The sin is the giving into the temptation. So I do not act on my thoughts but nevertheless I have them. But the truth is these are not my thoughts they belong to the enemy who is attacking my mind. I know the words of my Savior and I hear His voice, therefore I obey. You notice I didn't say I enjoy, or I know what I will do; no I obey the commands and the wisdom of God through His word. I have come to love Him and His ways but when I was reproving and renewing my mind it wasn't always easy.

This is how we become trained, by being doers of His word not hearers only (James 1:21-22). Just like a good athlete, repetition builds strength and stamina.

Becoming a doer of the word is work, and sometimes is a work-out. You know like working out your salvation with fear and trembling. Scriptures like bless those who so spitefully use and abuse you and if your enemy is hungry give him or her food, takes practice, right?

God is disciplining us to get over ourselves, and not allow the person or situation to have rule in our thoughts. If we are dead to sin, well, a dead person has no feeling when someone is poking or prodding him. A dead man isn't given to sin and temptation. If you don't believe it go to the funeral home and try to tempt a corpse. I think it is safe to say you'll get no response.

We are renewing our mind and training our body to become doers of the word and not hearers only. We are crucifying our flesh and carnal desires. Our born again spirit desires to do the will of God. Please do not confuse carnal desires with Godly desires. God has given us good things to enjoy. Some religious thinking can try to make you ashamed for very natural God given desires. You cannot give into them outside of God's ordained will and covenant, but you do not need to be ashamed for having these desires, it is part of our human experience. We manage our desires and keep them orderly. Actually, it is proof you are alive unto God. But we wait to have these desires fulfilled according to what is pleasing to God.

When we have done the work of repentance break through comes. We realize these are spiritual growing pains. We begin to understand God and His ways. We come to understand we are not as smart as we thought we were. We thought we were so smart and could have it our way and not get caught. Perhaps you thought you could quit (whatever), before the consequences caught up with you. We find The God of our Salvation calling us to repent or admit and acknowledge our ignorance. I used to beat myself up unmercifully. I would tell myself. You knew better, you knew better. Then I would get up and get back in the game. I would find myself repeating the pattern, until one day I decided to seek Him with my whole heart. He was calling me and I had to surrender or risk missing my day of visitation. I am so grateful I surrendered. I have no regrets.

Prayer:

Dear Heavenly Father, thank You for Your constant perusal of me. I do not have to fear Your discipline. I believe You want and desire for my life to be pleasing to You and bear the image of Your only Begotten Son Jesus. Jesus I want to be a doer of the word not a hearer only. Make Your word come alive in my heart as I read and study Your word. I want to have the wisdom of God working in my life. I desire Your word to produce a harvest in my life. Amen

Reflection:

In what areas do you sense The Lord's discipline? In what areas do you know you require discipline? Is there an area you tend to be lazy or complacent in? Do you have wishbone or backbone when it comes to be a doer of the word? Lift these up and ask The Helper to come alongside and give you strength.

_____

_____

_____

POETRY: I HAVE A HOPE INSIDE MY HEART

I have a hope inside my heart
    One that won't let go
    That God is calling us forth
    To discover and to know

That He alone is God
    Creator and King of All
    Whatever you need Him to be
    Open your mouth and make the call

Do you need a Savior
    Do you need a friend
    Do you need a healer
    There is so much more to Him

Do you need some hope
    Do you need a touch
    Never hesitate to ask
    His love covers all and much

He knows the plans He has for us
    To never be alone
    So today If you find yourself in need
    Bow your head and just call home

© laurette laster

"The Lord is my Shepherd I shall not want, He makes me lie down in green pastures; He leads me beside still waters. He restores my soul; He leads me in the path of righteousness for His name sake. Yea, though I walk through the valley of the shadow of death, I will fear no evil; for Your rod and Your staff, they comfort me. You prepare a table before me in the presence of my enemies; You anoint my head with oil; My cup runs over. Surely goodness and mercy shall follow me all the days of my life; and I will dwell in the house of the Lord forever" (Psalm 23 1-6 NKJV).

DAY 39

"FOR I HAVE no pleasure in the death of anyone, declares The Lord God, so turn and live" (Ezekiel 18:32).

Turn: Hebrew Strong's #7725 shub, meaning repent, turn back, return, answer, come back, bring back, repeat, replace, restored, and go The Way of Jesus. When we think of God telling His people to *turn* it is for a purpose.

As our Lord continues to draw and woo us, we begin to realize God is for us. If God wanted to destroy us, He could have done this a long time ago. I remember when I didn't understand God's grace through the Cross of our Savior Jesus Christ. I remember thinking oh no I have to be really good to make up for my bad, as if this were possible. To be carnally minded is enmity with God. So how is it that in our ignorance we can be enemies of God? Well just like the scriptures says, by being carnally minded. The flesh is the wrapper or the covering, it is our earth suit. We have to have the flesh to operate in the earth realm. But just like our car doesn't tell us where we are going, neither should our flesh dictate to us what to do. God is after our heart or inward parts. God wants all of us especially the inside that has eternal value. When we are born again our spirit rules and governs the flesh. We do not continue to allow our flesh to rule over our feelings and actions.

Romans 8:5-7 says this:

"Those who live according to the flesh set their minds on the things of the flesh; but those who live according to the Spirit set their minds on the things of the Spirit. The mind of the flesh is death, but the mind of the Spirit is life and peace, because the mind of the flesh is hostile to God: It does not submit to God's law, nor can it do so...."

Before we were born again from above and asked Jesus to come into our heart and Holy Spirit to come into our lives we were fleshly bodies trying to have a spiritual experience? Our flesh is our earth suit that allows us access on earth. We cannot operate legally without a body. Our five senses are where Satan attacks us. Even after being born again we are told to be transformed by the renewing of our mind. Why would you renew something if it was correct or in date?

Renewal is a term often used when speaking of bonds, stocks, and contracts. It is also a term for changing out an old for something new. Renewal is a legal description that requires in writing some form of action which marks that the new is in effect. Some synonyms are rebirth, regeneration, resurrection, resuscitation, revival. Do the words in that list sound familiar? Yes they do. Remember day 1 and revival?

If you then are in Christ you must be renewed, the old way of living will not fit your new self.

2 Corinthians 5:17, "Therefore if any man be in Christ, he is a new creature: old things are passed away; behold all things are become new."

In Romans chapter 12:1-2 the apostle Paul is telling us to be transformed by the renewal of our mind, and to not be conformed to the things of the world any longer. When we didn't know God we may not have known that He had a specific way of doing things. But now that we know Him we have a desire to know what pleases Him.

"I beseech you therefore, brethren, by the mercies of God, that ye present your bodies a living sacrifice, holy, acceptable unto God, which is your reasonable service. And be not conformed to this world: but be ye transformed by the renewing of your mind, that ye may prove what is that good, and acceptable, and perfect, will of God" (Romans 12:1-2 KJV).

Most today are familiar with the movie and figures, The Transformers. Transformers have a dual character they become. Often the purpose is to fight off an enemy or advance a cause. My sons had these toys when they were little. I remember one had a human form but could transform into a race car.

Paul is describing such an event in these scriptures. He is describing to us a transformation we are to undergo becoming our true spiritual being. Strong's Concordance #3339 metamorphoo: to change into another form, to transform, to transfigure. It is like the caterpillar emerging from the cocoon as a butterfly. Just as our physical beings had to be fed and nourished to grow so must our new spiritual beings.

When we are alive to God our spirit rules our flesh. Our spirit is indwelled with Holy Spirit and they are communing all during the day and night. The more we exercise and put our flesh under subjection the more room we are making for The Spirit to indwell us. Our spirit never sleeps so we are being taught and empowered during our sleep through dreams and impartations. When we read our Bible and listen to godly ministers we are feeding and supplying our spirit. Pay close attention that the messages you are hearing are Christ centered messages and not sugar coated. If the message or the messenger is not talking about sin being enmity with God you are hearing a watered down gospel.

Now that you belong to Christ, Holy Spirit has work to do. He is going to convict, convince, speak, nudge, prompt, implore, encourage, and even push you, all for the call of God.

Ephesians 2:13 tells us that He is working both to will and to do according to God's good pleasure. He needs and requires a willing vessel to work in.

I had to legally purchase the property before I could get the keys to enter the dwelling. I was not allowed to begin any work or repairs to the property before legally purchasing the property. The transaction had to be completed according to the laws legally governing our system.

When I purchased the property all the official and legal paperwork was signed and the deed was transferred and renewed. The deed now states this property is under new ownership. I own all rights to this property. And if you have surrendered your flesh to God, He owns all rights and the legal description has been renewed and recorded. You are now property of the kingdom of His dear Son and it is signed in His blood. It is official, legal, and binding and it is recorded in heaven.

Prayer:

Heavenly Father, You have signed the property deed to my life. I have received forgiveness for all my sins by the blood of Jesus and His work on the Cross by confessing my sins and my need for a savior. I am a new creation under new ownership. Take my life and make it Yours. I grant You access and all rights, both now and in the future to speak into my life and order my steps according to Your design. Holy Spirit, help me crucify any selfish carnal desires daily that are not pleasing to You. I want to be fully pleasing to You Lord, teach me, lead me, and guide me into my future that is secure in You.

Reflection:

Now that you are under new Ownership what will you need to renew? If you said your mind you are correct. Property that is redeemed shows improvements immediately. We also show changes and improvement as we follow God and His word.

List three things you are asking Holy Spirit to show you. You may realize He already has been showing you these things and teaching you.

_____

_____

_____

POETRY: SEARCHING FOR MORE OF YOU

As I draw near, my heart begins to ponder
    How can I have more of You, oh Lord, I wonder
    How I can I grow to know You more
    Like the ocean knows the shore

Sure as sand that does not harden
    Or like flowers multiply in a garden
    To watch our relationship grow and flourish
    Your word like water, my soul doth nourish

By Your Spirit seasoned with grace
    As I draw nearer to seek Your face
    How I long for more of Your presence
    It is for You oh Lord in all Your excellence

I will seek and I will knock
    Dig deep, secured upon "The Rock"
    I will ask and I will find
    With all of my heart and all of my mind

"I wait [patiently] for the LORD, my soul [expectantly] waits, And in His word do I hope. My soul waits for the Lord More than the watchmen for the morning; More than the watchmen for the morning" (Psalm 130:5-6, AMP).

"Then you will call on Me and you will come and pray to Me, and I will hear [your voice] and I will listen to you. ~'Then [with a deep longing] you will seek Me and require Me [as a vital necessity] and [you will] find Me when you search for Me with all your heart. ~'I will be found by you,' says the LORD" (Jeremiah 29:12-14, AMP).

DAY 40

"THEREFORE SAY TO THEM, Thus declares The Lord of hosts: Return to Me says The LORD of hosts, and I will return to you, says the LORD of hosts" (Zechariah 1:3).

Returning to The LORD may not be easy, or comfortable, when we have fallen short (hard) on our end. But remember God already knows every dirty deed we have done and He still pursues us and loves us. The flesh is an enemy to God and unable to please Him. But now we have repented and changed our mind, we are making our new declaration to live for Jesus and show the world all the great things He has done for us.

Being made new creations and renewed is exciting, and fun, and scary, and hard, and rewarding and frightening, and wonderful, and the list goes on and on...

When I took possession of the property, Greg and I began ripping out, tearing out, stripping off, cleaning up, and just plain cleansing from top to bottom. Little by little it began to take shape. Before it looked better it actually looked much worse, before the vision began to come together. After we removed and replaced the damaged wood the foul stench was no longer lingering in the air. It had been removed by removing the damaged areas and so it is with you and me.

We no longer smell like sin to God. We are now a pleasing aroma to God, the aroma of burning flesh on the altar. When men cook on the grill, you know that smell, the smell of wood and charcoal and meat on the grill and how good it smells.

The Lord revealed to me years ago that He is the original grill master. He called for the sacrifice to be on the altar over the wood. The sacrifice The Lord longs for is our flesh on the altar being burned up.

Little did we know that God is more practical and in our everyday life events that we could think or imagine. So as we crucify our flesh it is a pleasing aroma being lifted up to God. As we do the work of repentance we are crucifying the part of us that is at war with God. This is the damaged part with the putrid smell of sin. We now are working out our salvation by bringing our lives into subjection to the will of God no matter how long it takes or how bad it feels. We desire to live for God.

He is renovating His property. Say to the Lord right now; make me whatever You want me to be. Remember when God instructed Jeremiah to go to the potter's house?

Jeremiah 18:1-2, "The word which came to Jeremiah from the Lord, saying: 'Arise and go down to the potter's house and there I will cause you to hear My words."

God caused Jeremiah to hear His words by allowing Jeremiah to see the potter working at the wheel. The clay is subject to the potter. God was causing Jeremiah to hear and learn of His sovereignty by seeing something practical. Pay attention to what God is saying to you.

You are in the hands of The Potter and He doesn't make junk or have a reject pile of discarded unwanted vessels. Trust Him. Allow Him to remold and remake you. Your life was always designed to be beautiful and have purpose and now you are ready. You are ready and cleansed. You have begun the restoration part of your journey. He has the keys to your heart. He can unlock all this hidden beauty that has been waiting for the right buyer to come and redeem the property. This part of the journey is ushering you into the most exciting, the hardest, the most grueling and the most exhilarating time of your life. It is absolutely the most rewarding, and you are entering into a supernatural life with God. Only His children are allowed to swim in this water. It is living water where all the bad is washed off.

From this point Jesus will lead you, and take you back into the places and help you, He will help you recapture the original, the way it was when love had you. There is so much more Jesus has for you. He paid the ultimate price for your redemption. Because He knows what you looked like when LOVE had you. Ask Jesus to show you what that is. It is a truth on the inside of you that no one can take away from you.

You are God's masterpiece; you are His poem, His song, His symphony, His chorus, His painting, His canvas, His sculpture, His work of love. He is proud of you and He loves you with an everlasting love. *(See the vow and pledge on page 349 & 350)*.

Repentance is beautiful to God and as we visit this scene you will understand more fully.

Prayer:

Dear Heavenly Father, like the song says I surrender all, Jesus, all to You my blessed Savior I surrender all. Make me over. As I renew my mind in Your word, Lord make it come alive in my heart. Your word is powerful and I want only Your will for my life. I repent of my ignorance. I repent of my rebellion. I repent of my stubborn self willed pride. I repent for my _____ and my _____. Forgive me and make me brand new. I surrender to the wheel at the hand of You the Potter; I want to be Your own workmanship created in Christ Jesus for good works. I want to be all You have created me to be. I want to make You proud, I want to tell the world, one person at a time of the marvelous things You have done for me. Amen

Reflection:

What is God doing in your life that makes you know this is Him and not you? What are three things you can tell other's God is doing in your life right now? List them below and lift them up to Him as a thank you and bless Him for all He is doing in your life and go tell the world. Bless His Holy Name.

_____

_____

_____

POETRY: THE GREATEST GIFT HE GAVE TO ME

The greatest gift He gave to me
    He bore my sin on Calvary!
    Fully forgiven of all my sins
    Set free to worship and adore Him

The second greatest gift to me
    The freedom to just be
    All that He had in mind
    When by creation and design

Free to speak and free to feel
    Learning that Jesus Christ is real
    Knowing that His wisdom calls
    Breaking down life's hardened walls

Knowing He cares about every matter
    Even if to you it's nonsense and chatter
    My mind is sharp and when in doubt
    I silence confusion, no speaking out

Hearing Him say, "touch and see,
  My side, My hands, and My feet."
  Broken and wounded placed on display
  Eyewitness accounts to point the way

The greatest gift I have to bring,
  Is telling about Jesus our Savior and King
  The greatest gift I have to give
  Is measured by the life I live

Free to explore while spending time
  In His word, His loving kindness I find
  Into His courts and presence to explore
  A Fathers love, pleasures for ever more

The greatest gift He gave to me
  The curse He placed on that tree
  In fellowship of His sufferings to share
  His resurrection power, what can compare

The greatest call He called to me,
  Placed on me-a carrier to be
  I pray that you have eyes that see
  Our risen Savior, Christ The King

© laurette laster 2018 April

"Because of that experience, we have even greater confidence in the message proclaimed by the prophets. You must pay close attention to what they wrote, for their words are like a lamp shining in a dark place--until the Day dawns, and Christ the Morning Star shines in your hearts" (2 Peter 1:19, NLT).

"Not as though I had already attained, either were already perfect: but I follow after, if that I may apprehend that for which also I am apprehended of Christ Jesus" (Philippians 3:12 KJV).

AFTERWORD

Fall is my favorite time of the year. I really love all of the seasons but the season of fall has always called to me. I feel blessed I was chosen to live in North Texas where I actually get to see the beauty of the changing seasons as they come and go. But there is something about the fall that calls to me. For years I had this lonely feeling at the beginning of the fall season. I would feel like I needed something but what? I didn't have a clue? It was a yearning from deep within and I didn't understand or know what this feeling was. It was a lonely deep sadness that I couldn't understand. I really didn't even know how to describe it at the time. That is until the fall of 2009. God brought me revelation and finally it all made sense. I understood what that feeling had been all those years ago. And I know and understand why repentance is so beautiful to God.

Please keep in mind in a few paragraphs I'm going to describe to you what He has shown me over ten years of seeking Him concerning this subject. In 2001, I turned back renewing my vows to Jesus and ran into the comfort of His arms and I have never left. I found myself in the Lap of The Comforter weeping bitterly and pouring out my heart and my sorrow for my sins. That feeling didn't seem so strong after this and I now I know why.

In the fall the trees know that winter is very close. Winter is root season. All work above ground ceases for the work that is going to take place in the heart or root of the trees. A deciduous tree cuts off supply to the leaves, no longer sustaining them with nourishment. The tree takes the nourishment from the leaves to store in the roots in order to maintain the tree during the cold winter months.

When the tree stops nourishing the leaves, the leaves begin their end of season duty and begin to die. The dying process is actually beautiful. Leaves turn gold, red, yellow, amber and the trees burst with color. Some of the most spectacular foliage is during the fall season.

One fall afternoon in 2011 as I was on my commute home from work, I was marveling at the beautiful fall foliage and telling The Lord how beautiful it was. I was praising Him for allowing me this sight when He interrupted my thoughts and said to me; in my spirit He spoke these words,

"Laurette, They Are Dead!"

Wow, talk about a wakeup call. That jarred me into a reality I didn't fully understand then but have more revelation as He continues to speak to me. I remember thinking to myself, how can something dead be so beautiful?

In the fall of 2009, Sarah asked me about the meaning of Rosh Hashanah. I knew I should know what it was, but I didn't. I was honest in telling her I didn't know but I would find out and get back with her.

After calling my mom and asking her, she didn't know either but said she would check. A couple of hours later she called me back and said Oh Laurette, "You are going to love this." She let me know she had sent me a couple of emails about what she found. I was so excited to get home and learn about Rosh Hashanah. She said it is the Jewish New Year.

Rosh is head, and HaShanah is year in Hebrew. Rosh Hashanah is the head of the Year or beginning of the year in Israel. Israel has a civil and an agricultural calendar.

Now long story short; in the fall of 2009 I wanted to teach on this at our Bible study. I talked to Greg and he was in agreement. I began to study about the fall feast of The Lord (Leviticus 23).

I was working about seventy hours a week, including drive time and responsible for all the upkeep on my house. I had learned about repentance, Teshuvah in Hebrew. A Jewish Holiday before The Day of Atonement. A new term for me, Teshuvah (repentance/return) the 10 days of Awe and I was more confused than ever. Rosh Hashanah is also known as the Feast of Trumpets or Trumpets or Yom Teruah, the day of the great trumpet blast. Feast of Trumpets is the beginning of the Ten Days of Awe that lead up to the Day of Atonement (Leviticus 23). At the last trump those who believe in the rapture are called to meet the Lord in the air. I encourage you to read and study this subject. This is from our deep Jewish roots and heritage. The rains and the harvest are cyclical just like our lives.

Monday afternoon before the Bible study I had gone out to mow. I was hurrying because I needed to be ready for Bible study. I would need to shower after mowing and have time to try to study more about the fall feast' and Rosh Hashanah. What did all this mean? How could I teach what I didn't fully understand? God was drawing me deeper into this subject but I had only scratched the surface.

As I was mowing I hit a huge patch of leaves and scattered the debris all over the back yard. I thought, oh no, I don't have time to rake. I finished the mowing drove the mower to the shed in the back lot, grabbed the rake and went to work on the scattered leaves. I was praying, no I was begging. I said oh Lord Help me I need to hurry. I need to shower and I need more time to study. As I was spilling out my plea to The Lord, He spoke to me in an **audible** loud clear voice. The heavens opened and He said,

"Laurette, The tree is in Rosh Hashanah."

WOW! I got it, I truly understood. The leaves are for a season. Their work was done. The leaves represent our seasonal work, good or bad, and the lessons we have learned, good and bad. The lessons after being learned, the dead works, the mistakes, the good ideas, the bad ideas, the look what I've done, look what I can do, all of this is but for a season. Even the God things will need a root season to be nourished and grow deeper roots and become taller next year. But they also represent the life God gives us and the ability to grow and mature.

A tree has to go through season after season to grow and mature. It looks the same year after year but in reality the tree is growing stronger and taller each season. As the root season produces deeper roots the tree can grow taller and become more fruitful.

Welcome to Teshuvah (repentance) my favorite time of the year. Teshuvah begins on Elul 1 on the Hebrew Calendar and goes through the ten days of Awe to Day of Atonement on the tenth day Tishrei each year. This coincides with the Gregorian calendars in the months of August and September.

No matter what it is you have done it is over. It is dead. If you repent then it is cut off from your life. Just like the leaves from the tree. You no longer nourish the things that are over. We learn from the lessons of this season and store the needed truths in our inner man or in our roots.

Sin is for a season but the end is death. So we put to death sin.

When we repent of our sins it is beautiful to God. It is a full, big and bold panoramic view of fall to heaven and it is pleasing to God. No matter what you have done God will forgive you if you repent and turn away from that life and the sin. Hebrews 12 tells us to lay down the sin and the weight that so easily besets or entangles us. God knows it is a struggle, but we are not without a High Priest who like us was tempted on all counts, but Jesus didn't sin. His temptation was very real. He knows the schemes of the devil and He longs to help us when we are tempted.

No matter what you have done, remember repentance is beautiful to God. He will forgive you and He will justify you, making you just as if you never sinned. You can start over right now, today. And we can repent again tomorrow and again next week, until we overcome the temptations and come out of the world. We never want to take for granted the grace of God and we do not want to trample underfoot the blood of Jesus. We certainly do not want to grieve Holy Spirit by which we are sealed until the day of redemption of all things.

We are in the world but we are not of the world. We are His new creation, His masterpiece, the redeemed. We wear designer clothes; our robes are white.

"Come let us reason together and talk this over. Though your sins be as scarlet I will make them white as snow." (Jeremiah 1:18-19)

There are seven feasts or moedim's in total. The first four have been fulfilled in Christ. He is our Passover Lamb. His sacrificial sinless life represents unleavened bread, first fruits, His resurrection and Shavuot is Pentecost the outpouring of His Spirit on the day of Pentecost, The outpouring of the Holy Spirit marks the birth of the church.

The fall is the time of Feast of Trumpets, Rosh Hashanah and The Day of Atonement followed by The Feast of Tabernacles. God is calling and wooing His people. He wants us to repent, pull away from and out of the world and the business of even ministry and come away with Him. This is a time to replenish, to refresh, to repent, and also prepare for the deeper things of God. It is our root season so that we may become mighty oaks of righteousness.

If you want to learn more about Teshuvah, look for my upcoming book The Days of Teshuvah, as we cry out, I need more of You Lord.

Romans 6:16 "Do you not know that when you offer yourselves as obedient slaves, you are slaves to the one you obey, whether you are slaves to sin leading to death, or to obedience leading to righteousness?"

Romans 6:21 "What fruit did you reap at that time from the things of which you are now ashamed? The outcome of those things is death."

Romans 8:27 "And He who searches our hearts knows the mind of the Spirit, because the Spirit intercedes for the saints according to the will of God."

Romans 8:7, 13 "because the carnal mind *is* enmity against God: for it is not subject to the law of God, neither indeed can be..."

God has one desire for your life and it is for your good. Not your comfort so much but for your training and your good and His Good Pleasure. God's one and only desire is that you bear the image of His only Begotten and that you become all He created you to be. Say to yourself God loves me (insert your name here_____). God desires that I train and discipline my flesh like an athlete who is competing for the championship of his or her lifetime.

Isn't it comforting to know that when our Lord disciplines us it is because He loves us? Perhaps as I mentioned earlier you have been in the hands of a harsh disciplinarian. If so it is time right now to forgive them completely. Not because what they did was acceptable, it was not. Nor is it biblical.

Let us return to the Lord and He will have mercy on us: and to our God for He will abundantly pardon. God's ways are higher than our ways and His thoughts are higher than our thoughts Isaiah 55:7-8. Thank God for leading you safely out and getting you ready to breathe and live again.

God will change us, not shame us. We may have picked up a sense of shame from peers or from our nuclear family unit. If a member of our family has a problem or problems such as, addiction to drugs, gambling, alcohol, lying, or overall poor choices we may take on that identity and lose sight of Gods design. Through the work of repentance and with discipline we can be changed and train or reprove our mind. As we begin to change through His training we are being strengthened.

"Awake to righteousness, and sin not; for some have not the knowledge of God: I speak *this* to your shame" (1 Corinthians 15:34).

Will we fail? Yes, we will. Of course we will. If you have had trouble with worry about what others think of you, or with perfectionism you need to stop right now and repent of those issues. Renounce perfectionism and replace this with the desire to be pleasing and acceptable to God. Your value from this time on, will be what God thinks. God expects you to grow and mature. We grow in many different ways and in every season. Just like a tree. Because the tree begins to grow, it doesn't reach maximum growth the first season and neither will you. Fruit trees do not produce fruit the first season.

When a toddler is learning to walk do they fall? Yes they do. But I have never seen a time or a fall that stopped them from trying again. A hard fall can send the toddler crying for comfort, but the tears dry, the pain subsides and they are off again. And so it goes with us as believers because we have The Helper, Comforter, Advocate, Intercessor, Counselor, Strengthener, and Standby, The Spirit of Truth compelling us into all truth. He is with us forever.

"For a just man falleth seven times, and riseth up again: but the wicked shall fall into mischief" (Proverbs 26).

It is less about the fall and all about how quick you get back up.

So for now I leave you with one final poem and this word: Wait patiently for the LORD. Be brave and courageous. Yes, wait patiently for the LORD.

God bless you and keep you along The Way.

Forever, Laurette

POETRY: IN THE WINTERTIME BY THE TREE

It's utterly hopeless
    What should I do

Trust In God
    He'll see you through

Such nice words
    But you don't know
    It's dead and lifeless
    There is nowhere to go

If you have a minute
    Come sit with me
    "In the wintertime
    by the tree"

I believe you are wrong
    Speak life and believe
    You're sure to be amazed

When your words receive

Don't hinder your faith
    God's working this out
    Don't become discouraged
    There's no time for doubt

Oh You don't get it
    Can't you even see
    It's dead and lifeless
    Exactly like this tree!

Keep the faith
    It's not as it appears
    This tree is dormant
    It has no fear

It has a knowledge
    Deep within
    That as it rests
    The renewing begins

What are you saying
    What do you mean
    There's life in this tree
    Even though it's not seen

You seem so sure
    But how can I trust
    Just because you say
    My thinking should adjust

It's hopeless, It's over
    This is the end

There is no glimmer of hope
Been nice talking with you my friend

I want to believe
    And walk like you say
    I haven't the time
    This just isn't your day

Can we meet again
    Another time
    You'll understand then
    Maybe you won't be so blind

Just one more thing
    If you can spare
    Tell me about
    This tree we share

You've seen it before
    And you'll see it again
    It's a lesson in hope
    And there is no end

To all that The Lord
    Will do and say,
    If you'll be patient
    And walk in His ways

For just at the right time
    When you least expect it
    You will see new blooms
    This tree is expectant

See you in March

And bring your pen
We have so much to learn
My sweet, sweet friend.

Glad you're back
What do you see

The hope and the promise;
there is life in this tree

The blooms, the fragrance
Bursting with life
I do think you're right
About my plight

I'm beginning to see
And I do have hope
I won't give up
Not only no, but nope

I'll speak the promises
And believe His word,
And know He'll answer,
Because He heard.

Thanks for the lesson
And thanks for caring
This tree taught me a lot
These truths I'll be sharing

With any who'll listen
And come sit with me,
"In the wintertime
by the tree."

Psalm 27: 13-14 NLT

"Yet I am confident I will see the LORD's goodness while I am here in the land of the living. Wait patiently for the LORD. Be brave and courageous. Yes, wait patiently for the LORD."

PLEDGES, PROMISES AND VOWS.

Salvation:

Lord Jesus, today I receive Your gift of salvation. I vow to follow Your ways. I make You my Savior by acknowledging I am a sinner. I accept Your work on the Cross, Your death and Your resurrection, and believe I am now forgiven and I am a new creation.

Signature_____

Date_____

Specific Forgiveness or struggles:

Lord I have trouble believing I am forgiven for my sin(s). Today I confess and receive Your complete forgiveness. I choose to believe You have forgiven me and I choose to forgive myself. I reach out and receive Your grace. Help me to release this struggle to You.

Signature _____

Date _____

Your Masterpiece:

I choose today to believe that I am created in Your image and likeness. You do not see me as useless and without value. You call me

Your own and I am Your workmanship created in Christ Jesus, for good works.

Signature _____

Date _____

Believing with You, I Can:

Lord Jesus, I believe I am called to be a kingdom participator. Show me how to fulfill this dream of _____ and how to use my gift to glorify Your Name.

Signature _____

Date _____

Gift of The Holy Spirit:

Lord Jesus, You said if I ask God He will give me the gift of Holy Spirit. I desire to be a witness of Your goodness and to live the life You are calling me to. I ask today to receive the gift Your Holy Spirit. Lead and guide me into 'all' truth. I reach out and lift my hands fill me with Your Spirit of love and truth. Amen

Signature _____

Date _____

Covenant for Prayer:

Lord I have not been faithful to make a set time to meet with You every day. I want to meet with You every day and hear from You. I make this promise to pray each day and seek Your face. I am setting aside a set time to meet with You.

Signature _____

Date _____

ABOUT THE AUTHOR

Laurette Laster is a new and emerging author. Her passion and desire is to help any who have lost their way restore the intimate relationship with The Lord who loves them. Her writing contains Christian poetry and blogs. She invites and challenges you to plunge deep into genuine biblical repentance as you explore your calling and destiny. Her desire is to ignite or reignite passion from the believer toward The God of the Bible and His forgiveness. This is Laurette's first book.

facebook.com/Laurettebasslaster

twitter.com/laurettelaster

instagram.com/Laurettelaster